CO-TEACHING IN HIGHER EDUCATION

From Theory to Co-Practice

Co-Teaching in Higher Education

From Theory to Co-Practice

EDITED BY
DANIEL H. JARVIS AND MUMBI KARIUKI

UNIVERSITY OF TORONTO PRESS
Toronto Buffalo London

Toronto Buffalo London
www.utppublishing.com

ISBN 978-1-4875-0192-1

Library and Archives Canada Cataloguing in Publication

Co-teaching in higher education : from theory to co-practice / edited by Daniel H. Jarvis and Mumbi Kariuki.

Includes bibliographical references and index.

ISBN 978-1-4875-0192-1 (cloth)

1. Teaching teams. 2. Education, Higher. I. Jarvis, Daniel, editor II. Kariuki, Mumbi, 1961–, editor

LB1029.T4C68 2017 371.14′8 C2017-903067-1

University of Toronto Press acknowledges the financial assistance to its publishing program of the Canada Council for the Arts and the Ontario Arts Council, an agency of the Government of Ontario.

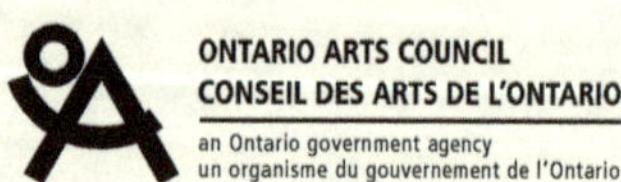

Funded by the Government of Canada
Financé par le gouvernement du Canada
Canada

Contents

Figures and Tables

Figures

Tables

Contributors

Elizabeth Ashworth is an associate professor of art education within the Schulich School of Education, Nipissing University, North Bay, Ontario, Canada. She taught at the elementary and secondary levels in Manitoba and Ontario for sixteen years before moving to Nipissing University in 2003. She holds an EdD from the University of Glasgow, an MEd from Nipissing University, and a BA and BEd from Queen's University. Her research interests include confidence issues among generalist teacher candidates regarding visual arts, visual inquiry methods for understanding social issues, cross-curricular connections between art and other subjects, and environmental considerations in art studios.

Jacqueline Ferguson holds an EdD from Texas A&M University (Commerce campus) and is currently a principal within the Department of Defense Dependent Schools in Japan. Dr Ferguson's educational background consists of a BS in interdisciplinary studies and an MEd in educational administration. Her doctorate is in curriculum, supervision, and instruction. She has worked at all levels of education K-12, including teaching for DoDEA and in Texas, as well as serving as an assistant professor at Texas A&M University–San Antonio. Dr Ferguson has presented at many national and international conferences. Her current research interests include collaborative teaching and educational leadership.

Ann Game is a professor emeritus in the School of Social Sciences at the University of New South Wales, Sydney, Australia. She is the author of the book *Undoing the Social: Towards a Deconstructive Sociology* (Open

University Press & University of Toronto Press, 1991) and co-author, with Rosemary Pringle, of *Gender at Work* (Allen & Unwin, 1983), which was voted, in 2003, one of the Top Ten Most Influential Books in Australian Sociology. Her six books since then have been jointly written with Andrew Metcalfe. Their first book, *Passionate Sociology* (Sage, 1996), was nominated in 1997 for the Amalfi Prize for the best social science book published in Europe, and was, in part, a sociology of the teaching of sociology. With Demelza Marlin, Ann and Andrew wrote *On Bondi Beach* (Australian Scholarly Publishing, 2013), which addresses questions of belonging, hospitality, community, and ecology. For more than twenty years she taught with Andrew Metcalfe, during which time they won various prestigious teaching awards. She continues to explore her research interest in the nature of relationship, with a particular focus on interspecies relations.

Rob Graham holds a PhD from Lancaster University, United Kingdom, in the field of e-research and technology-enhanced learning, and a BA, BEd, and MEd from Nipissing University. His doctoral research resulted in the publication of the book *Techno-Resiliency in Education: A New Approach for Understanding Technology in Education* (Springer, 2015). He has designed and taught pre-service teacher education courses, including technology-enriched teaching and learning (TETL), classroom management, imagination creativity education (ICE), and classroom methods. His diverse portfolio also includes teaching appointments in Japan, Hawaii, a penal institution, an intermediate public school, and adult education at a community college.

Blaine E. Hatt is an associate professor in the Schulich School of Education at Nipissing University, North Bay, Ontario, Canada. He holds a PhD from the University of Alberta and an MEd, BA (Honours), and BT from the University of New Brunswick. His doctoral research resulted in the publication of the book *Heart in Teaching: Attending the Pathic* (Lambert, 2008). As a strong proponent of collaboration and co-construction, his articles, book chapters, and conference presentations have often been co-authored with colleagues, former graduate and undergraduate students, and/or in-service teachers. He has, for many years, been the leader of the imagination creativity education (ICE) team at Nipissing University. This group has been responsible for introducing an option (now an elective) course for pre-service teachers titled Imagination Creativity Education in the 21st Century Classroom, as well as for sponsoring several annual ICE conferences. His research interests include ICE, transactional curriculum, pedagogical relationality, principles and practices of educational leadership, and pathic principles of pedagogy.

Daniel H. Jarvis is a professor of graduate and mathematics education in the Schulich School of Education at Nipissing University, North Bay, Ontario, Canada. He holds a PhD in education studies from Western University, an MEd and BEd from Nipissing University, and a BA from the University of Waterloo. His background is in the areas of mathematics and visual arts, having taught both topics at the secondary and post-secondary levels. Previous works include the co-authored book (with Naested) *Exploring the Math and Art Connection: Teaching and Learning between the Lines* (Brush, 2012) and the co-edited book (with Elliott-Johns) *Perspectives on Transitions in Schooling and Instructional Practice* (UTP, 2013). His research interests include instructional technology, integrated curricula, and mathematics for the workplace.

Mumbi Kariuki is an associate professor of education in the Schulich School of Education at Nipissing University, North Bay, Ontario, Canada. She holds a PhD in education and an MA in international affairs, both from Ohio University, as well as BEd and MEd degrees from Kenyatta University, Kenya. She has a strong background in the use of technology in education. Her area of specialization is curriculum and instructional technology, with a special focus on the application of technology by pre-service teachers; she has authored several articles in this area. Other related areas of research interest include cyberbullying and the use of assistive technology among pre-service teachers.

Roberta La Haye is an associate professor of mathematics within the Faculty of Science at Mount Royal University, Calgary, Alberta, Canada. She holds a PhD in mathematics from the University of Alberta. Her interest in the ties between mathematics and the arts has manifested itself in community outreach activities, research, and course development and co-teaching.

Ilana Levenberg is a senior lecturer, head of the Mathematics Department and M. Teach Program in the Gordon College of Education, Haifa, Israel. She holds a PhD in mathematical education, and her post-doctoral research was done at the Technion Institute, Haifa, Israel. She has published two co-authored geometry books (with D. Patkin). Her research interests include mathematics teaching (particularly geometry), matriculation exams, teacher professional learning, and teaching gifted students.

Andrew Metcalfe teaches in the School of Social Sciences at the University of New South Wales, Sydney, Australia. His PhD dissertation, a historical ethnography of a coal-mining town, won a prize as the best sociology thesis in Australia/New Zealand (1985–86), and was later published as a book, *For Freedom and Dignity* (Allen & Unwin, 1986). He has further co-authored (with Ann Game) six books, including *The First Year Experience* (Federation Press, 2003), focusing on the experience of first-year university students; *Teachers Who Change Lives* (Melbourne University Press, 2008); and their most recent book, *What Is a Social Relation?* (Australian Scholarly Publishing, 2015). Until recently, most of his teaching has also been done with Ann Game, and they have won various prizes for their innovative approaches, including a national prize for team teaching. His research has been concerned with the nature of relationship and meeting, dialogue, gift relations, pedagogical relations, relations of belonging, and creative relations.

Irene Naested is a professor emerita, formerly chair of the Department of Education in the Faculty of Teaching and Learning at Mount Royal University, Calgary, Alberta, Canada. She is an educator, author, and artist. Among other things, she served as a teacher, department head, and curriculum leader for the Calgary Board of Education for twenty years (K–12); and as an instructor, area coordinator, assistant chair, professor, and chair at MRU for twenty years.

Dorit Patkin is an associate professor in the Kibbutzim College of Education, Tel-Aviv, Israel, where she serves as head of the MEd program in mathematics education. She holds a PhD and an MA in mathematics education, and a BA in mathematics and educational counselling from Tel-Aviv University, Israel. Her background is in high school mathematics teaching; she also served as a mathematics education academic coordinator and as a scientific consultant for Israeli Educational Television. Her previous works include eight mathematics textbooks; a co-authored article (with Y. Wolffensperger) titled *Self-Assessment of Self-Assessment in a Process of Co-Teaching* (2013); and three co-edited books, including *The Narrative of Elementary School Mathematics Teachers: Features of Education, Knowledge, Teaching and Personality* (co-edited with A. Gazit; MOFET, 2014). Her current research interests include pre-service mathematics teacher education, particularly in geometry, and the professional development of in-service mathematics teachers.

Sal Renshaw is an associate professor in the Department of Gender Equality and Social Justice and the Department of Religions and Cultures at Nipissing University, North Bay, Ontario, Canada. She holds a PhD in philosophy from the University of New South Wales, Australia, and is the author of *The Subject of Love: Hélène Cixous and the Feminine Divine* (Manchester University Press, 2009). Her current research on the ethics of interdisciplinary scholarship and collaborative pedagogy draws especially on her experience as chair of the gender equality and social justice program for the past ten years.

Susan Srigley is professor of religions and cultures in the Faculty of Arts and Science at Nipissing University, North Bay, Ontario, Canada. She holds a PhD in religious studies from McMaster University. Her background is in the area of religious ethics and literature. She is the author of *Flannery O'Connor's Sacramental Art* (University of Notre Dame Press, 2004) and editor of *Dark Faith: New Essays on Flannery O'Connor's "The Violent Bear It Away"* (University of Notre Dame Press, 2012). Her teaching includes courses on spiritual journeys, death and dying, and world religions.

Astrid Steele is an associate professor of science and environmental education in the Schulich School of Education, Nipissing University, North Bay, Ontario, Canada. She holds a PhD in education and an MEd degree from the University of Toronto, and a BEd, BPHE, and BA from Queen's University. She has a strong background in outdoor environmental education and secondary science education. Her current research interests are in teacher development in science and environmental education, and her research focuses on teacher development in the overlapping areas of STSE (science, technology, society, and environment) and STEM (science, technology, engineering, and mathematics) education. She is involved in various collaborative projects with colleagues in art and science education.

Renée Valiquette is a lecturer in the gender equality and social justice and interdisciplinary liberal arts programs at Nipissing University,

Ontario, Canada. She is currently completing her PhD in social and political thought at York University, Toronto, Ontario. Her research is focused in two areas: the first draws on French philosophy to better understand the structural elements of environmental crises, while the second considers the practical and wider social applications of interdisciplinary education.

Jennifer C. Wilson is an associate professor in the College of Education and Human Development at Texas A&M University, San Antonio, Texas, United States. She holds a PhD from the University of Texas at Austin in language and literacy studies with a concentration in cognition and instruction. Dr Wilson teaches undergraduate and graduate courses in literacy and focuses on college connections to public schools. Her research interests include socially embedded literacy practices, remediation of reading difficulty, experiential learning for teachers, and co-teaching.

Sarah Fiona Winters is an associate professor in the Department of English Studies at Nipissing University, North Bay, Ontario, Canada, where she teaches children's literature. She holds a PhD in English literature from the University of Toronto. She works on the representation of evil in British post-war children's fantasy and has published on C.S. Lewis, J.K. Rowling, Philip Pullman, and the New Zealand author Margaret Mahy, as well as in the field of fandom studies. She also teaches and researches in fandom studies and has published two articles on fanvids, one of which makes a pedagogical argument about using fanvids in the school and university classroom.

CO-TEACHING IN HIGHER EDUCATION

From Theory to Co-Practice

Introduction

DANIEL H. JARVIS AND MUMBI KARIUKI

Teaching is undeniably a complex endeavour, whether one is involved with young learners (pedagogy) or adult students (andragogy), as each of these two groups bear their own specific challenges and opportunities. Teaching with excellence has often been associated with an outstanding individual educator: one who possesses a remarkable giftedness in creatively imparting knowledge; maximizes learning potential through the facilitation of stimulating learning experiences within safe learning environments; and provides ongoing, varied, and meaningful assessment for learning.

As inscribed on Albert Einstein's plaque of dedication for the new observatory at Pasadena City College in 1931, "It is the supreme art of the teacher to awaken joy in creative expression and knowledge" (English translation of the German inscription, Calaprice, 2013, pp. 100–1). This popular image of the *individual* instructor "awakening joy" is so deeply embedded in Western literature, film, and personal experience that it is perhaps difficult to reimagine a context for learning wherein two or more gifted educators regularly collaborate in their planning, teaching, and assessment practices.

In recent years we have had the wonderful (and humbling) opportunity to co-teach, together, three graduate level courses within the Schulich School of Education at Nipissing University in North Bay, Ontario: once at the master's level (Survey of Research Methods, in fall term 2012) and twice at the doctoral level (Critical Conversations in Educational Research, during two summer residencies in 2012 and 2013). In so doing, we discovered that while co-teaching did not reduce the amount of work associated with any given co-taught course, it did offer certain undeniable and powerful benefits for teaching and learning, a finding based both on our own observations and on the feedback from our learners. We had inadvertently witnessed something of what El Kadri and Roth (2013) described in their co-teaching summary statement: "The point of co-teaching is to maximize teaching and learning in the here and now of actual, transformative and therefore revolutionary teaching praxis" (p. 93). These experiences had proved to be so profoundly educational and fascinating for us that we decided to conduct some follow-up research with the doctoral students and fellow co-instructors, as well as to co-author some form of publication to share our observations and findings.

As we surveyed the literature, we noted that while substantial formal and anecdotal research has been reported by teachers at the elementary and secondary school levels, far less material exists at the post-secondary and graduate study levels. Several such studies from undergraduate and teacher preparation programs were encountered, and we briefly highlight those papers here.

Chanmugam and Gerlach (2013) reported on their undergraduate sociology co-teaching experience as doctoral students, noting both perceived strengths and challenges of this teaching arrangement. For example, they shared that while the "ongoing exchange of ideas with one another and the opportunity to act on them [was] intellectually stimulating," they also found that the "level of collaboration [that they] sought to model and truly enact required [their] full energies and attention more than may have been the case with an independently taught course" (p. 116). They also claimed that research regarding the effects of co-teaching in higher education on students and faculty is sorely lacking: "Our experience and the scarce literature on co-teaching indicate that further exploration is needed of whether and how co-teaching influences student learning, to guide instructors and programs in implementing this approach" (p. 116).

Bacharach, Washut Heck, and Dahlberg (2008) conducted an analysis of sixteen co-taught university-level courses in teacher education programs and concluded their study as follows:

> According to the data collected, co-teaching not only benefited co-teaching candidates but also had positive impacts on the co-teaching faculty. Faculty unanimously report having had an enriching experience in which they learned new material and instructional strategies. The experience of sharing the planning and teaching with a colleague allowed them to utilize different teaching strategies along with expanding their knowledge

> base about the subject ... The co-teaching experience provided an energizing opportunity for faculty to renew their passion for their profession ... The use of co-teaching in teacher preparation is a promising practice for fostering collaborative skills, increasing student participation, and improving classroom instruction and professional growth for all participants. (pp. 15–16)

Several participatory action research studies that involved co-teaching initiatives in teacher preparation programs at the post-secondary level have also been reported (Kluth & Straut, 2003; Weiss, Pellegrino, Regan, & Mann, 2015). The Kluth and Straut (2003) study involved one college course, Academic Curricular Adaptations, and another titled Elementary Social Studies Methods and Curriculum. The Weiss et al. study (2015), drawing upon symbolic interactionism, focused on the creation and implementation of a new course that focused specifically on collaboration for general and special education teachers. In both of these qualitative studies, key issues such as the collaborative process, co-teaching models, the impact on faculty ideas and teaching practices, integrated curriculum and assessment, and the negotiation of logistics were discussed.

The literature review revealed that there are a number of similar but different terms used to describe the situation in which two or more teachers are involved in jointly planning, implementing, and assessing a course or learning experience. These terms include "co-teaching," "collaborative teaching," "cooperative teaching," "team teaching," "parallel teaching," "co-instruction," and "co-education." For the purpose of consistency, we have used the term "co-teaching" throughout our co-written chapters.

Selection Process and Co-Author Teams

This book collection was born from a shared desire to more thoroughly investigate the practice of co-teaching in higher education and to document some of the very creative co-teaching practices that we knew were happening here in Canada and internationally. Following a review of the existing literature regarding co-teaching in higher education, invitations were sent via email to approximately twenty scholars who were known to have experimented with, and reported on, co-teaching experiences at the post-secondary level. Sixteen of these professors (along with the two of us), representing four countries (Australia, Canada,

Israel, United States) and a wide variety of expertise (for example, undergraduate areas such as English literature, religious studies, social justice, and sociology; teacher education discipline-based areas such as mathematics, language arts/literacy, science, technology, and visual art education; graduate education areas such as research methods and educational theory), ultimately agreed to take part in this book project.

Of the nine main chapters in the text, five represent co-teaching teams from Nipissing University. It should be noted here that these particular chapters are all quite different in terms of type of course/program (undergraduate, pre-service teacher education, graduate education), teaching team structure (partners, small/large instructor group), and classroom implementation (alternating, shared). These chapters, and the various co-teaching initiatives described within them, also represent professors from across three different faculties within the institution (Faculty of Applied and Professional Studies, Faculty of Arts and Science, Schulich School of Education). In other words, the Nipissing chapters are not five examples of the same type of co-teaching initiative, but rather represent a diverse set of rich experiences, thus warranting separate treatment within the text as they serve to demonstrate the kind of instructional leadership and risk-taking that a relatively small, primarily undergraduate institution like Nipissing University has been able to achieve.

Guiding Research Questions

When asked to consider submitting a chapter to this project, authors were directed to include observations and/or research results pertaining to three broad categories: (1) *co-planning* and the co-creation/development of co-teaching curriculum and experiences; (2) *co-facilitation*, or implementation, of the learning experiences; and (3) *co-assessment* considerations and practices for co-teaching. In the interest of encouraging creativity and personal voice, no further restrictions were put on contributing author teams when it came to style of writing. As a result we have ended up with an intriguing combination of co-teaching narratives, which we believe makes for an interesting and informative read.

This unique collection features topics ranging from undergraduate projects/courses to graduate level co-teaching experiences at the master's and doctoral levels; from co-teaching pairs to group co-teaching endeavours, some also involving an extended network of guest lecturers; from pre-service teacher education to in-service teacher training;

and from co-taught single-subject courses to innovative cross-curricular, "dialogue course," and interdisciplinary experiments.

Structure of the Collection

The book is purposefully organized according to three main principles. First, the chapters exist in *order of the level of post-secondary schooling*. Chapters one (Game and Metcalfe), two (Renshaw and Valiquette), and three (Srigley and Winters) focus on undergraduate university courses in which co-teaching practices were implemented. Chapters four through seven (Hatt and Graham; Steele and Ashworth; La Haye and Naested; Wilson and Ferguson) deal with pre-service teacher education contexts. Chapter eight (Patkin and Levenberg) describes an in-service teacher professional development initiative. Finally, chapter nine (Kariuki and Jarvis) recounts a series of graduate level (MEd, PhD) co-teaching experiences.

The second organizing principle is one of *experiential connection*, insofar as several sets of chapters relate directly to one another by virtue of overlapping academic or professional experiences. For example, Renshaw (chapter two) had been a graduate student of Game (chapter one) in Australia years previously and thus directly builds upon the theoretical underpinnings and logistical co-teaching structure and ideas of her mentor's work within the interdisciplinary courses described in her own chapter. Srigley and Winters (chapter three) both partook in the large group of co-teaching instructors who were involved in one or more of the interdisciplinary course offerings described by Renshaw and Valiquette (chapter two). Likewise, Steele (chapter five) was one of the original five founding members of the imagination and creativity education (ICE) course described by Hatt and Graham (chapter four). The vision that had characterized the cross-disciplinary development of the ICE courses would later inspire Steele and Ashworth (chapter five) to launch their own unique interdisciplinary experiment. Finally, the interdisciplinary mathematics and visual arts course described by La Haye and Naested (chapter six) grew directly out of a book project that was co-written by Jarvis and Naested several years previously (*Exploring the Math and Art Connection: Teaching and Learning Between the Lines*, Brush Education, 2012).

The third and final organizational principle of the text is that of *theoretical development*. While all nine main chapters deal with the notion of interdisciplinary co-teaching to some extent, there exist certain predominant emphases within groups of chapters. For example, in the first chapter, co-authors Game and Metcalfe provide an approach that prompts the reader to reflect on the philosophical underpinnings of co-teaching as they situate their presentation within the concept of "dialogue." Chapter two, by Renshaw and Valiquette, flows naturally from the first as it builds philosophically upon the work of Game and Metcalfe, and expands upon the foundational theme of "dialogic pedagogy." Taken together, the first two chapters are thus positioned primarily for the purpose of providing a wider theoretical and foundational framework for the text. The third chapter, by Srigley and Winters, further extends the dialogue theme, exploring the introduction of a debate format within their "dialogue" course. These co-authors also present the powerful benefits of interdisciplinary planning and implementation in terms of achieving student learning outcomes and more fully engaging the co-instructors themselves. Chapters four to six focus heavily on the cross-disciplinary nature of their ICE, science/visual art, and mathematics/visual art initiatives, respectively. Chapters seven to nine, all three of which involve formal research studies (journals, surveys), each possess a strong theoretical emphasis as these co-author teams share findings from the existing literature and from their undergraduate and graduate co-teaching experiences.

Overview of the Chapters

In chapter one, "Dialogue and Team Teaching," co-authors Game and Metcalfe, who have co-taught large undergraduate sociology courses together for several decades and have previously published in this area, provide insights into their effective team teaching methods. They describe how a co-teaching context developed by learning how to create and maintain a truly dialogic learning experience and regularly modelling this approach for their students helps to create an educational environment in which "everyone involved in the class is working at their creative edge." They maintain that their classes have been radically transformed through the use of reflective journals, which they refer to as "student workbooks," and a variety of co-teaching techniques and structures, as they cultivate a relationship that "allows them to support each other, to relax their fears, desires and defences, to be open to the possibilities emerging in the classroom."

Chapter two, "Complex Collaborations: Co-Creating Deep Interdisciplinarity for Undergraduates," co-written by Renshaw and Valiquette, builds both literally and philosophically upon the work of Game and Metcalfe (Renshaw being a former co-taught undergraduate student of these two scholars in Australia in the mid-90s). In this chapter, the authors not only exemplify how a dialogic learning space can be effectively supported, but also extend the idea of crossing boundaries in search of "deep interdisciplinarity" experiences for their students. By inviting colleagues from different domains of expertise to address specific, single-word themes (for example, DIRT, SLOTH, WATER, SECRETS, GENIUS), which form the essence of each interdisciplinary analysis course, Renshaw and Valiquette, who have worked together for over fifteen years, have pioneered a new and creative way of conceiving undergraduate education. In their own words, they have challenged themselves "to create curricula that draw on the best of a deeply interdisciplinary, exploratory liberal arts education in order to strengthen disciplinary and professional training, and to reimagine the relationship between liberal arts and sciences and vocational application."

Chapter three, "Undisciplined Debate: Coursing through Dialogue," co-authored by Srigley and Winters, relates the planning and delivery of a special "dialogue course" focusing on the Bible as a cultural text. In this particular case, the two co-teaching colleagues from different disciplines (religious studies, English literature) actually became acquainted through the creation and implementation of this new course (as opposed to having a long-standing prior relationship). In retrospect, the authors highlight a number of advantages of co-teaching, both for the students and for themselves as educators, including the use of a lively, non-scripted debate format; learning from each other's areas of expertise; and enriched assessment for students. Challenges experienced with institutional support are also recounted.

In chapter four, "Forming ICE in Pre-Service Teacher Education," Hatt and Graham describe the coming together of an interdisciplinary co-taught ICE course for pre-service teachers. A team of five educators (Aquino, Ashworth, Graham, Hatt, and Mantas) from across the disciplines co-created, co-taught, and co-assessed this course with the main goal of helping pre-service teachers to develop awareness of the interconnectivity of the arts, special education, creative writing, technology, literacy, and numeracy. The incorporation of multiple class venues, both at the university and within the local community, as well as the inclusion of student choice in assignment structure and focus, promoted a shared sense of excitement and ownership among students and faculty members alike. The chapter also points out the significant challenges inherent in creative workload scheduling at the post-secondary level, as well as highlighting co-teacher feedback regarding the logistics of planning, implementation, and assessment strategies that were developed and shared by the original core group of five participating co-teachers.

In chapter five, "From Shafts to Drifts: Collaborating to Strengthen Integrated Teaching and Learning," Steele and Ashworth use a metaphor of a series of mine shafts and mine drifts to contextualize their discussion of a collaborative teaching and learning experience in preservice teacher education. Unlike typical co-teaching experiences where the co-instructors share the same group of students in the same course, often in the same meeting space and time, the collaboration described in this chapter represents a context in which two courses from different disciplines (visual arts education and science education) were taught in a requested parallel structure by the two instructors and featured the overlapping completion of a shared integrated major project that drew upon expectations from both disciplines' curricula. These stimulating visual arts/science projects allowed room for student choice and creativity, and were co-assessed by both instructors. Using a conversational approach to shared reflections and focusing on the distinction between *multidisciplinary*, *interdisciplinary*, and *transdisciplinary* methods, the authors recount the realities of co-planning, co-implementing, and co-assessing the integrated project, as well as the perceived positive effects on their students and on their own professional growth and relationship as collaborating peers.

Chapter six by La Haye and Naested, "Visual Art and Mathematics Integration: An Interdisciplinary Co-Teaching Experience," represents another rich example of an interdisciplinary co-teaching model within teacher education. Driven by a desire to demonstrate to their teacher candidates the balanced integration of disciplines at the elementary school level, La Haye and Naested co-planned, co-taught, and co-assessed a fully integrated visual arts and mathematics education course. The chapter highlights the need for co-teachers to draw upon each other's strengths and past experiences in order to create a rich learning environment characterized by trust and mutual respect. The co-authors emphasize that in order for successful co-teaching to happen there is also a need for institutional support without which "teaching innovations fail to flourish, and face the danger of becoming mere educational fads."

It is said that co-teaching has the potential to change praxis at all levels of education. According to Wilson and Ferguson, this statement was especially true of their higher education classroom as described in chapter seven, "Co-Teaching in Undergraduate Education: Capacity Building for Multiple Stakeholders." Wilson and Ferguson recount the co-teaching of an undergraduate reading methods course in which they modelled teacher collaboration for their pre-service teachers as an important way of preparing them for the profession. The authors highlight observed co-taught classroom dynamics, as well as discuss other key issues that "may be universal in a collaborative setting," such as co-planning strategies, power dynamics, and workload implications of co-teaching within a university context.

In chapter eight, "Co-Teaching and Co-Assessment in a Geometry Course for In-Service Teachers," Patkin and Levenberg describe a co-teaching experience in mathematics education within an in-service (that is, for certified, working teachers) teacher training program in Israel. The chapter highlights the benefits of involving students in certain aspects of planning and assessment with the goal of improving overall student engagement within a subject such as geometry, in which teaching and learning can be particularly challenging. Through discussion, teacher participants agreed that they would keep ongoing diaries and engage in a self-assessment process as part of the overall assessment in the program. This self-assessment helped to empower the participants as learners and teachers; the option of regularly accessing the learning diaries also greatly assisted the co-authors in terms of planning the course activities and adapting the teaching pace.

In chapter nine, "Co-Teaching in Graduate Education," Kariuki and Jarvis similarly discuss significant lessons learned from three co-teaching experiences, the main difference from those discussed in chapters one to eight being that all of their courses were taught at the graduate level. In addition, the co-authors also report on a survey study in which graduate students involved in the same doctoral program reflect on their summer residency learning experiences, providing rich student insights into perceived strengths and weaknesses of the co-taught courses. Based on their three similar, yet notably different, graduate co-teaching experiences, Kariuki and Jarvis also discuss related issues such as co-planning strategies, participation logistics, co-assessment responsibilities and options, and evolving workload dynamics.

The book ends with a summary tenth chapter, "Coda: From Theory to Co-Practice in Higher Education," in which co-editors Jarvis and Kariuki analyse the book project's content and comment on the nature and purpose of co-teaching; on the overarching themes of co-planning, co-facilitation, and co-assessment; and on some observable conclusions regarding co-teaching practices at the post-secondary level. Overall, we are not making the case that co-teaching should replace all individual instruction at the post-secondary level; however, we remain convinced that the power and promise of co-teaching at all levels of education, including university undergraduate and graduate education, deserves further exploration and research, regardless of the impediments that appear inherent to these pursuits.

REFERENCES

Bacharach, N., Washut Heck, T., & Dahlberg, K. (2008). Co-teaching in higher education. *Journal of College Teaching and Learning*, *5*(3), 9–16.

Calaprice, A. (Ed.). (2013). *The ultimate quotable Einstein*. Princeton, NJ: Princeton University Press.

Chanmugam, A., & Gerlach, B. (2013). A co-teaching model for developing future educators' teaching effectiveness. *International Journal on Teaching and Learning in Higher Education*, *25*(1), 110–17.

El Kadri, M.S., & Roth, W.M. (2013). "I Am a Pibidiana": Societal relations as the locus of sustained development in a teacher education program in Brazil. *Australian Journal of Teacher Education*, *38*(5), 89–114. http://dx.doi.org/10.14221/ajte.2013v38n5.7

Jarvis, D.H., & Naested, I. (2012). *Exploring the math and art connection: Teaching and learning between the lines*. Edmonton, AB: Brush Education.

Kluth, P., & Straut, D. (2003). Do as we say *and* as we do: Teaching and modeling collaborative practice in the university classroom. *Journal of Teacher Education*, *54*(3), 228–40. http://dx.doi.org/10.1177/0022487103054003005

Weiss, M.P., Pellegrino, A., Regan, K., & Mann, L. (2015). Beyond the blind date: Collaborative course development and co-teaching by teacher educators. *Teacher Education and Special Education*, *38*(2), 88–104. http://dx.doi.org/10.1177/0888406414548599

1 Dialogue and Team Teaching

ANN GAME AND ANDREW METCALFE

Introduction

Dialogic pedagogy begins with the paradox that teaching is an impossible project. No matter how determined or knowledgeable they are, teachers can, as independent agents, teach students little or nothing. The role of teachers is only carried to fruition when students act, grow, and learn. Rather than an action that one person performs for or on another, teaching is what a teacher and student do together. By the same logic, learning is also a collaborative exercise, and, moreover, a necessary element of teaching. Real learning, like real teaching, occurs in the dialogue that constitutes the meeting of teacher and student (see Felman, 1982).

People often assume that the "di-" in dialogue refers to two parties, in contrast to the one party of a monologue. The corollary of this conventional view of dialogue is that it is based on a variety of exchanges between two prior and identifiable positions – that is, it arises from interaction, competition, opposition, and the reconciliation of positions. In fact, however, the "dia-" of dialogue indicates "through." As Bohm (1985) puts it, dialogue implies "a new kind of mind" that carries and is carried by the participants: the dialogue moves through them and they through it. Dialogue is not located in any or even in all of the individual participants, but rather in a whole that is incommensurable with the sum of the finite parts. Thus, Merleau-Ponty (1974) argues that dialogue is a relation arising between participants, controlled by no one:

> Speaking to others (or to myself), I do not speak of my thoughts; I speak them … [n]ot [as] a mind to a mind, but [as] a being who has body and

> language to a being who has body and language, each drawing the other by means of invisible threads like those who hold the marionettes – making the other speak, think, and become what he is but never would have been by himself. Thus things are said and thought by a Speech and a Thought which we do not have but which has us. (p. 19)

In this chapter we will show that the pedagogic potential of team teaching only becomes apparent when its dialogic possibilities are recognized. While the term refers to a diverse range of practices (see Goetz, 2000; Smith, 1994), team teaching is often thought to involve no more than the summative logic of sharing loads and adding perspectives in order to maintain the exchange model of dialogue. In fact, team teaching can more radically transform the learning–teaching relation. By creating a holding space and holding time that transform the classroom, team teaching can produce a dialogic community among all participants in the classroom. When there are no longer individual sources of energy and knowledge, the dialogue involves everyone as learner and everyone as teacher.

This chapter draws on our own practice of team teaching. Although we have designed and coordinated our courses together since 1990, in the late 1990s we began experimenting with joint rather than sequential lectures, developing techniques that allowed us to introduce an increasing variety of dialogic components to the lecture. In 2000, when our faculty cut costs by shifting from one- to two-hour lectures and from two- to one-hour tutorials, we took the opportunity to creatively reconsider the role of lectures and tutorials. Lectures became fully interactive large classes, leaving tutorials free to focus on collegial academic skills development. While it is difficult for a solo lecturer to depart from a monologue, a teaching team can focus large classes (up to 300 students in our case) around dialogic activities that have been traditionally associated with tutorials or seminars (Game & Metcalfe, 2007). By having more than one teacher present in front of the class, the position of the knowing teacher is diffused. If students can see teachers engaged in dialogue, working out difficult questions between them, they come to trust teachers, seeing them not as people with a complete knowledge but as people devoted to learning and thinking. Team teaching opens opportunities for students to join the team as teachers and learners. Although students and teachers have different responsibilities, we are all learning through our collective dialogue.

Dialogue

Classroom relations constantly shift between different social logics. One form is based on exchanges between self-conscious individuals motivated by subjective purpose. The other is based on the relaxation of identity and subjectivity that comes with a dialogic relation. While these different states imply each other, each arising in relation to the other, they involve fundamentally different senses of being, space, and time; of who, where, and when we are. Bohm (1985) made this point in a description of a weekend dialogue in which he participated:

> In the beginning, people were expressing fixed positions, which they were tending to defend, but later it became clear that to maintain the feeling of friendship in the group was much more important than to hold any position. Such friendship has an impersonal quality in the sense that its establishment does not depend on a close personal relationship between participants. A new kind of mind thus begins to come into being which is based on the development of a common meaning that is constantly transforming in the process of dialogue. People are no longer primarily in opposition, nor can they be said to be interacting, rather they are participating in this pool of common meaning which is capable of constant development and change. In this development the group has no pre-established purpose, though at each moment a purpose that is free to change may reveal itself. The group thus begins to engage in a new dynamic relationship in which no speaker is excluded, and in which no particular content is excluded. (p. 175)

Dialogue arose on this weekend when there was a shift from the negativity of identity logic to the openness of dialogue. At first, people were defending positions and identities. But there was a change, Bohm says, when people realized that what they were doing together was more important than the protection of the self.

The significance of this dialogic shift for educational theory is that participants change their cognitive capacities when they are no longer self-conscious individuals. People who identify with knowledge take it personally, seeing the world and others only for what these say about themselves, as a mirror of themselves. People in dialogue, however, are able to hear the differences offered by others because they are not personally affronted. They can imagine the experience of others, and therefore understand how different perspectives can coexist. Through the play of differences, they are making something that they share with others but which is no one's personal property. "Same" and "different" are no longer qualities attributed to discrete individuals: each participant makes a unique contribution, but no one can say who contributes what. All participants are connected to this "common pool of meaning," but connected in their unique ways; they all learn from the different possibilities in the common pool, but they learn in a way that makes particular sense to each one of them.

Education is this drawing out of potential. The meeting of what is common and what is different is the primal encounter referred to by such pedagogic concepts as interest, inspiration, engagement, wonder, fascination, curiosity, and relevance. Through meeting the differences of others, we meet the difference in ourselves. We change by becoming who we are: what we know of the world reveals unexpected potential when recontextualized through dialogue. It follows that dialogue is always a learning experience, and that there is no learning without this dialogic meeting with difference. Moreover, if there is no learning, no sense that one experience significantly differs from another, there is no sense of aliveness.

Deep learning only occurs through this engagement. Using their own bodies and lives as learning tools, participants in dialogue live ideas. In holding an idea, playing with it, they feel its inner form from within their own. It is therefore not simply metaphorical to say that dialogue transforms us, opens new worlds, and expands minds. It is our difference as beings that allows us to see the world differently: no longer confined to subjectivity, we discover unexpected potential through being in embodied relation with the world. These ontological shifts are everyday aspects of classroom life. To learn more about the world, we must learn how to live in it differently, and we do this through dialogue (see Brookfield & Preskill, 1999; Metcalfe & Game, 2006).

The Teacher's Responsibility

If teachers do not control the classroom dialogue, what do they do? The teacher's primary responsibility is to facilitate informed dialogue among and between teachers and students, retaining an awareness of the learning process itself. This task requires the creation of a safe learning space where participants are neither self-conscious nor self-protective, and where, therefore, they can make the ontological shift required if they are to get into dialogue.

These pre-conditions for dialogue can be understood in terms of Winnicott's (1991) concept of "potential space" or "holding space," terms that describe the state where the once isolated individual feels carried by the enlivened environment. In this space, people experience a wholeness that cannot be described in terms of a dichotomy between inside and outside; it is a space that involves a sense of organic rather than chronological time, where the future is experienced as the unfolding of present potential (see Metcalfe & Game, 2002). Based on the relational logic of both – and rather than the individualist logic of either/or – potential space is the environment that allows mother and baby, therapist and patient, teacher and student to carry each other. In all these learning situations, the holding, or potential space allows possibilities to be held open; there is a sense of safety in this openness that does not rely on self-assertion.

Winnicott argues that all deep learning experiences are modelled on the example of the young child playing in the presence of a non-intrusive mother. When students are in the presence of someone who guards them without interference, they learn to trust their authentic responses to new situations. The implication of Winnicott's argument is that teachers need the patience and courage to avoid pre-empting the student's learning process, to avoid giving the student answers for which he or she is not prepared. Teachers need to stay present to the emerging dialogue rather than being distracted by their preconceptions and their own subjective fears and desires. While Winnicott (1990) insists that no one entirely escapes these subjective states, he argues that maturity is the ability to be aware of them and therefore learn from them when they arise (pp. 30–4). This awareness turns what might have been a distraction into a return to the here-and-now of the classroom.

Aware teachers work, like engaged students, on the crest of knowledge. They come across as genuine and passionate because they are good learners. Since the teachers live and breathe their knowledge, there is no final way to say what is known, for knowledge is continually being reformulated as life offers new connections. The deep form of knowing that teachers need is characterized by a simultaneous unknowing. To allow new connections to emerge from classroom dialogue, teachers must hold lightly those that they have previously made, allowing their knowledge to re-form around new starting points that arise in the class. This class is not the same as any other class.

Whereas feedback is commonly understood as an external form of evaluation, every response and every recognition in a dialogue is feedback. Feedback is a moment in the life of a system that does not demarcate boundaries between inside and outside (Bateson, 1972). The dialogue works because both teachers and students are simultaneously receiving and giving feedback, are simultaneously learning from and teaching each other (see Noddings, 1984, p. 177). It is the openness to receive that accounts for the effortlessness and lively energy of the engaged classroom. Aware teachers provide constant feedback through their openness to receive it.

As with feedback, the authority of aware teachers is not an external imposition on students but arises from their responsive attention to the class (see Arendt, 1961; Gordon, 1999; O'Byrne, 2005). Teachers can be trusted as leaders because they serve the needs of the class rather than allowing their subjective concerns and preconceptions to intrude. Embedded in the rituals and practices of the classroom, authority allows students and teachers to be open, rather than self-conscious or self-protective. The trust involved in organic authority allows teachers to be respectfully honest with students, helping them to develop a capacity for authentic work. This process highlights the teacher's facilitation of dialogue not as a non-confronting laissez-faire process of letting students do what they want, but rather as a process of challenging students to go beyond their preconceived ideas, expectations, and desires.

This discussion of the teacher's responsibility shows that aware teachers are characterized by the maturity to maintain open relationships, avoiding the premature closures that accompany the defensive desire for self-certainty. In short, teachers must have learned to tolerate unknowing and the uncertainties of life. This skill applies equally in their relations with students, their relations with their disciplinary specialties, and their relations with themselves. In all of these situations, they need to maintain faith in a process without finding false consolation in expectations (see Gaita, 2001; Murdoch, 1970).

Good teaching, then, is never just a matter of technique and strategy. It necessarily involves ethical questions about goodness. As Murdoch (1970) says:

> The self, the place where we live, is a place of illusion. Goodness is connected with the attempt to see the unself, to see and to respond to the real world ... [V]irtue is the attempt to pierce the veil of selfish consciousness and join the world as it really is. (p. 93)

As teachers, we can never finally master the responsibilities of the good teacher. Good teachers know that they are forever learning how to teach and that they need continuous support from others if they are to meet the world as it really is.

Team Teaching and the Teacher's Responsibilities

This discussion of the teacher's responsibilities allows us to appreciate the virtue of dialogic team teaching. The presence of other teacher colleagues as witnesses allows teachers to get out of themselves and see the world through the eyes of others (see Winnicott 1991, p. 61). Dialogic team teaching is based on an open flow of feedback that encourages teachers to be aware of how they are responding to the class. Teachers teach each other.

Many solo lecturers fear the prospect of team teaching because they imagine the other as judge of their vulnerabilities. This presumption fails to recognize the ontological transformation of dialogue: in dialogic team teaching, no teacher is in a position to judge the other, for all are carrying the other in themselves. In the same way, it is the teachers' carrying of students within themselves that guards against any tendency to unify as teachers against students. The witnessing in a dialogic classroom takes the form of support rather than judgment and surveillance.

The need for support is particularly clear in large classes. As Bligh (1975, p. 163) astutely remarks, it is not easy to move a tutorial style dialogue into a large lecture. The problem arises because of the multiple responsibilities of the teacher. If the class is to be dialogic, teachers must give their full attention to the responses of particular students while remaining aware of the dynamics of the whole class. At the same time they must be aware of the place of this particular discussion in terms of the needs of the whole class. They must balance the tension between the overall plans of the class and the course, and the suspension of purpose required for the dialogue to unfold. They have to continually adjust plans to meet the reality of this class and this day.

Solo lecturers tend to give monologic lectures because they have difficulty combining these responsibilities. The full potential of the classroom can present them with more possibilities than they feel they can handle; they fear that the different responses of students will throw them off course. By simplifying social relationships so that the teacher only has one task to do, the monologic lecture channels relational potential into narrow and pre-established parameters. When teachers give classes together, on the other hand, the mutual support they provide allows them to safely hold the classroom relations open. The potential of the class and the differences within the class are now resources rather than threats. The supportive relation allows lecture time and space to be used more flexibly and creatively. An attuned teaching team can readily and fluently carry within its relation the various responsibilities of the teacher. The dialogue between teachers allows them to think together and think differently at the same time.

Team Teaching a First-Year Course

To ground the rest of this discussion, we will now consider our own experience of teaching a large first-year sociology course. Our course, Relationships: Sociology and Everyday Life, attracts up to 400 students and is organized around short classic readings by famous sociologists and social philosophers. The course teaches students to apply this theory in analyses of social relations, from the intrapersonal to the interpersonal to the international.

The course is organized around large team-taught dialogic classes (between 100 and 300 students in each one), which are a cross between traditional lectures, tutorials, and seminars. Because these classes harness the dialogic potential of a large community, they develop a powerful energy that carries both teachers and students beyond their preconceptions. The value of students being able to listen to each other's discussions of important issues should not be underestimated. A key function of large classes, not easily replaced technologically, is the opportunity for simple presence, for the community that emerges from congregation. This community provides an enthusiastic and openhearted energy that counteracts many of the debilitating effects of the individualizing dynamics common in universities. Students learn to appreciate and respect their own possibilities when they are surprised by hearing their shy and private inklings enunciated by others.

The keys to the creative responsiveness of these classes are preparation and structure.

Preparation: Workbooks

To prepare students for the role they are to play as part of the team in large classes, we require them to keep a workbook. Workbooks are the course's lynchpin. Each week, before classes, students write about the readings and do an exercise that applies the readings to an everyday experience. We expect at least an hour's writing per week, and most students fill a large notebook during the session. The exploratory nature of workbook writing teaches healthy reading practices: instead of feeling scared and jealous of difficult texts, students learn how to work with them in a dialogic way.

The workbook is a supportive, disciplined working space that teaches students how to stay with and draw out their thoughts and hunches. The students' relation with their workbooks parallels the dialogic relations between teachers, between students, and between teachers and students. The workbook allows students to focus unselfconsciously on a particular line of thought, bracketing off the perfectionist self-criticism that inhibits the learning process. Because this free flow is captured in writing, students have the chance to reflect on it later, and develop it further and more rigorously, by asking themselves the same sorts of questions that their teachers would ask. The workbook produces a dialogic relation between students and their work, allowing them to teach themselves, to draw themselves out. By learning to trust this process, students develop patience, that is, a relationship to their own anxieties, fears, and frustrations, and a faith in the support provided by a steady work routine.

Like students, teachers must prepare themselves for class by working through the readings in their workbooks. We reread all readings each year, allowing our changing research interests and our new students to highlight different elements. We cannot teach unless the readings have come alive again to us. Like students, we prepare by recording our reading process and course reflections in workbooks. We also use our workbooks to record our reflections on, and plans for, the course.

Even though we have been teaching this course for many years, the rereading process allows us to reimagine the classes week by week, adapting the curriculum specified in our course handbook to the interests and needs of the year's particular group of students. Drawing on our archive of workbooks, we select appropriate exercises and activities, and augment them with new ones. To maintain student interest, we try to vary the types of activities week by week, choosing a sequence of activities that helps students develop their analytical skills and face the conceptual issues that are troubling them. Our first meeting of the week begins with new pages in our workbooks and ends, through a dialogue that neither of us controls, with lists of planned activities.

Each of us takes from this first meeting some special preparation to do for the class, such as an exegetical activity or the development of a resource for a class exercise. Then, on the day of each class, even if it is a "repeat" class, we meet again to talk through our plan, activity by activity, imagining it from the students' perspective, ensuring that our activities are fine-tuned and that we have a feel for the whole class. At a subsequent meeting, we include tutors in these processes of reflection and imagination, discussing the success of previous classes and sharing ideas for the coming ones. The teamwork in these meetings is essential to the success of our classes: our different perspectives and experiences ensure that we do not become inattentive to the needs of the course.

Structure and Freedom in Large Classes

Large classes are a dialogic opportunity for teachers and students to clarify readings, to draw out the implications of key concepts, to explore the empirical scope of issues, and to test the usefulness of ideas. In the course of our preparation, the class has been broken into structured components, none taking longer than twenty minutes. These segments usually include one or both of us giving short, prepared discussions on a key aspect of reading, but there are also collective discussions of passages from the readings and collective analyses of cultural phenomena that relate to the topic and theme of the week, as well as small group discussions, short writing exercises, and collective brainstorming sessions. The diversity of modes in the class recognizes the different ways in which students learn.

Structuring the class in twenty-minute components provides a supportive temporal quality to the learning process, allowing for patience and respectful relations. This structure helps teachers avoid a tendency to rush to an end, giving teachers and students time to relax, time to attune to each other's wavelengths and get a feel for the issues under discussion. The students' comments are the feedback we need in order to adjust what we'd planned to say and do. We go into each activity without needing a certain outcome, because we know there are regular opportunities to take stock and refocus. Whatever point the discussion has reached will offer possibilities for the next activity.

By itself, this modular structure might not produce a patient, holding environment. Anxious lecturers might have difficulty holding their nerve; self-conscious lecturers might have difficulty withholding their preconceptions. With team teaching, teachers can support each other in attentive and unselfconscious states. Their relation provides the organic structure that allows them to be fluent and responsive to the unfolding dialogue. The presence of a supportive witness heightens their awareness of any tendency to ask leading questions or give premature answers.

With the organic structure of the team-teaching relation, teachers can perform multiple activities simultaneously, remaining aware of how each moment relates to the whole class and the whole course. One teacher can fully engage in a particular line of discussion because he or she knows the other is listening to the place of that discussion in the broader setting of the class. The witness allows the speaker to fully attend to the students, who in turn find their thoughts drawn out because they are being heard with respect and without reserve. A peer observer from the Learning and Teaching Centre of our university made the following observation of a large class:

> Because Ann and Andrew were both actively involved throughout class, one of them could focus intently upon a student's comment, and respond in a way which deepened the student's analysis of a concept or idea, while the other scanned the room, looking out for other speakers and gauging the feel of the group to decide where to take the discussion next. This enabled them to be totally attentive and engaged with the student who was speaking, whilst simultaneously encouraging widespread participation – around one third of students contributed during the two-hour period. This dialogic approach to team teaching created for students the opportunity to engage in an extended, intense, high quality, analytic, creative, and scholarly conversation in which the whole group joined. The students' response to this approach throughout the class indicated its success in effectively engaging and stimulating them – I have not been in a lecture theatre before, as either a student or teacher, in which there was this level of sustained and active student participation in discussion. Through their dialogic approach, the teachers supported their first-year students in attaining a level of analysis that was extraordinary and inspiring, rivalling that which I had previously experienced in postgraduate discussions.

In short, by creating a potential space between themselves, teachers create that space in the classroom. As a student put it in an anonymous course evaluation, "I love the team teaching, seeing the teachers' own thoughts and relation together. This implicates me further as I feel more part of it. There are new voices, a growth of ideas and knowledge." By referring to "seeing the teachers' own thoughts and relation together," this student is drawing attention to the openness of the state that the teachers are experiencing between themselves. In the Winnicottian classroom, the students are this "between" – the reserve of potential upon which creative thinking relies. This is why students feel implicated in the team teaching and drawn out by the dialogue that they make possible.

Teachers working dialogically rely on students to draw them out, to help teaching find what is called for at this moment in the class. By watching teachers think out loud, students lose their fear of speaking unfinished thoughts. They learn how to suspend their desire to get everything right, and instead learn a love of the learning process. The dialogic lecture theatre models the state of being that is necessary to open thinking, maturity, and a life of learning. It is a model that students learn through their part in it. The peer observer commented:

> When Ann or Andrew responded to a student, they were actively engaging with the student's ideas, not merely continuing their own course of thinking. An understanding of the concepts unfolded in the room as the insights of students built upon each other. Students were making meaning and not simply coming up with the "right" or expected response. This was facilitated by the teachers' careful listening and encouragement of students to develop their own interpretations of the concepts being discussed. For instance, they responded to one comment by saying, "It's a bit more complicated than that isn't it?"; and to another student, "Do you want to say any more?"; and then again after the student elaborated, "More?," pushing the student further along in analysis. This conveyed the message that they were genuinely interested in students' contributions. While the approach seemed casual, the nature of their questions indicated careful and precise thinking and preparation.

Large Class Activities

To make this discussion more concrete, and evocative, we will describe a segment of a recent class. Offered in the third week of the course, this class focuses on the social theorist Émile Durkheim and on the conclusion to his book *The Elementary Forms of the Religious Life*. Team teaching allows us to draw on the different relation we each have with Durkheim. One of us is by background an anthropologist, trained through Durkheim's analysis of religion, while the other is a political theorist who first came across Durkheim, through his methodological writings, as a sociology lecturer. We highlight and use these differences by each focusing on different passages of the week's reading.

- Andrew begins with a very short introduction, locating Durkheim in the sociological tradition and giving a context for the book's conclusion by drawing attention to the key ideas of congregation and communion, effervescence, ritual, awe, and the sacred and profane.
- In their workbooks, students have been asked to choose and draw out the particular passage from Durkheim's reading that most interested them. They were also asked to connect this passage with an account of an everyday experience in their lives. In order to teach students how to go about their workbook preparation, we begin this task ourselves in the large class, putting on screens the passages that each of us chose.
- We ask students to underline interesting or puzzling words and phrases in our chosen passages, and, from their suggestions, we compile a list that we put on the board. This list, which comes from all of us and none of us, becomes the basis of a collective discussion of the passages. Instead of jumping to a comprehension of the two passages or the complete chapter or Durkheim's thought overall, we patiently work from the questions that present themselves. Taking a point of interest from the list, we ask students to draw out its implications, first by playing with its possibilities and then by identifying the questions it raises. When a student identifies something puzzling, we ask the class to address the question by identifying possible meanings and then by identifying what issues are at stake. As these are open questions that do not presume correct answers and do not ask for complete answers, all students are able to contribute.

The openness of this questioning process is aided by team teaching. Each of us is aware that space must be left for the other teacher, who will have different responses. This moment of pause is a respectful reminder of the potential of the whole class. When teachers are aware that the class is not their responsibility alone, they are less likely to give anxious students the ready-made answers they seek. To do so would be to pre-empt the dialogic process that can lead both teachers and students to ideas that they haven't yet had.

To further encourage dialogue, we, the teachers, do our own puzzling out loud, showing the process we use when making sense of what we do not understand. We ask each other and the students for help when we lose our train of thought or cannot see the connections between ideas. If one of us hears the other slipping into an old script, into esoteric jargon, into a leading question, the former, aware of what the students are experiencing, will pull the latter back into dialogue by asking him or her to explain, to elaborate, to give an example, to say what assumptions are not being made explicit. The teacher who had lost contact with the here-and-now is brought back to the class's need for living thought.

The timing of discussions like this can be difficult for solo teachers, who cannot watch the clock if they are to stay immersed in the moment of unfolding dialogue. But the presence of a teaching team gives one of the teachers the opportunity to periodically balance the value of the present activity with the needs of the whole class.

- After the collective discussion of the lists, Ann talks briefly about her chosen passage, starting with the words and phrases that she underlined and showing how she came to understand the potential of these words when she saw them in connection with a particular everyday experience. She highlights the differences in her readings of the passage over the years and her differences to Andrew's experiences. After she finishes, Andrew spontaneously asks her to reflect on whether Durkheim's own theory of social relations can be used to explore these different relations to a reading. Having heard Ann talk of her ambivalences about Durkheim, students are relieved to be invited to talk of their own struggles with this very difficult text. The class, however, is now in a position to make something interesting of what had simply been an obstacle to reading and thinking. By asking Durkheimian questions of these difficult experiences, the students raise the possibility of creating different reading relations.
- To change the energy of the class, we now show two short, videotaped interviews with musicians. We hope to surprise students by showing that Durkheim's analyses of religion in Australian Aboriginal societies can resonate with experiences of musical performance and the musician's life practice. This surprise is designed to open students to other possible situations where Durkheim could be relevant.
- Students are asked to talk in small groups about these interviews. We want them to have the opportunity to test, and help each other draw out, their first impressions.
- Ann then asks the students to talk about what they noticed in the interviews. As Ann and the students draw each other out, keeping the discussion as open and lively as they can, students are not paying attention to Andrew, who is listening intently and writing on

the board a list of the key terms that are emerging. Ann is entirely absorbed in the discussion with students, trying to get as deep as possible into the quality of the experience, without the desire to lead the discussion to any particular conceptual point. Andrew is thinking in a different way, about key terms that are used which connect to the broader themes in the class and the course.
- By this stage, two apparently unconnected lists are on the boards: one with keywords from Durkheim and one with keywords to facilitate understanding the musical experience. The class now has a chance to connect the conceptual and the experiential. We ask the students to scan the lists and identify connections that highlight the spatiality, temporality, and ontology of the experiences that Durkheim is identifying with the sacred. These ideas of space, time, and ways of being have been introduced in earlier weeks in the course in quite different contexts.

While one of the teachers is facilitating the discussion based on the lists, and on this class's content, the other is asking questions about this class's relation to the issues and questions that arose in the previous classes. Which teacher does which task changes fluently during this exercise. This non-linear process of talking about the current week by evoking earlier weeks continues throughout the course. As the weeks proceed there is a developing sense of richness. The different theorists enter the class as interlocutors: students can approach any particular experience from the different perspectives of the different theorists. The possibilities of previous classes are still emerging in later classes as new connections are made; the possibilities of the whole course are present in any particular class. This is Bohm's "new kind of mind com[ing] into being."

- By this stage of the two-hour class, teachers and students need a five-minute break to gather their thoughts and refresh themselves.

Small Classes

Because team-taught large classes perform many of the functions of traditional tutorials, they have allowed us to transform our small classes. The focus of these classes is now on what students can learn through learning how to teach. We encourage students to work dialogically, developing their academic skills by developing the patience, openness, and maturity that they have experienced from their teachers.

In weeks four to seven, groups of students are responsible for facilitating a segment of the class. Their role is not to present what they know, but to draw out the other students. These facilitations require students to develop skills in the teamwork of team teaching and also give them practice in opening issues for analysis. By encouraging students to imagine themselves as teachers who must be able to imagine themselves as students, these facilitations teach students how to sustain an open dialogue and keep the life in ideas. During the facilitation, the teachers take up the position of Winnicott's non-intrusive guardian, learning to listen by not speaking and creating a supportive space simply through their presence. The teachers contribute more actively during the feedback session in the second half of the class, in which students develop reflective skills, particularly in connection with the process itself.

In week nine, students bring a first draft of their final essay to the class and, through swapping drafts and talking to each other about them, learn to see their own writing through the eyes of others. This insight informs the new piece of drafting they bring the following week, where the process is repeated. This activity continues until week thirteen. The teachers again play the role of non-intrusive guardian, not dominating classes but giving them structure by reading all the drafts, answering questions, and giving general feedback on the writing process. By the time students submit essays, they have learned first-hand the patience, as well as the listening and reading skills, necessary for both collaboration and good writing.

This process is much more intensive student-centred work than conventional tutorials allow. The team-taught large classes make it possible.

Conclusion

Team teaching is often thought to involve no more than the addition of an extra resource or perspective. This view is limited because it maintains the exchange model of dialogue. A truly dialogic team teaching more radically transforms the learning experience. The relation between teachers allows them to support each other, to relax their fears, desires, and defences, and to be open to the possibilities emerging in the classroom. This support and openness in turn allows them to better fulfil their primary responsibility as teachers: to hold the learning relations in the classroom so that all participants feel safe in remaining open in the presence of doubts and questions.

The dialogic community that emerges from team teaching allows both teachers and students to be present to the learning process itself. It changes the space and the time of the classroom so that teachers and students are both teaching and learning. All those involved in the class are working at their creative edge, not simply repeating what they already know but finding words for the knowledge that is emerging for them. Moreover, the class allows students to learn first-hand the holding capacities and open states of being that are the basis of maturity and an ongoing life of learning.

ACKNOWLEDGMENTS

We would like to thank Dr Tracy Barber for her peer reviewing of our class.

This chapter is reprinted, with minor modifications for book format consistency, by permission of Taylor & Francis Ltd (www.tandfonline.com). The original work's full reference is as follows: Game, A., & Metcalfe, A. (2009). Dialogue and team teaching. *Higher Education Research & Development, 28*(1), 45–57. doi:10.1080/07294360802444354

REFERENCES

Arendt, H. (1961). *Between past and future*. London, UK: Faber & Faber.

Bateson, G. (1972). *Steps to an ecology of mind*. Frogmore, UK: Paladin.

Bligh, D.A. (1975). *Teaching students*. Exeter, UK: Exeter University Teaching Services.

Bohm, D. (1985). *Unfolding meaning*. London, UK: Routledge.

Brookfield, S.D., & Preskill, S. (1999). *Discussion as a way of teaching*. San Francisco, CA: Jossey-Bass.

Felman, S. (1982). Psychoanalysis and education. *Yale French Studies, 63*(63), 21–44. http://dx.doi.org/10.2307/2929829

Gaita, R. (2001, May 4). *The pedagogical power of love*. Keynote address at the Victorian Association for the Teaching of English, Melbourne, AU.

Game, A., & Metcalfe, A.W. (2007). The implications of dialogue: First year sociology. *UNSW Compendium of Good Practice in Learning and Teaching, 5*, 7–22.

Goetz, K. (2000). Perspectives on team teaching. *EGallery, 1*(4). Retrieved from http://www.ucalgary.ca/~egallery/goetz.html

Gordon, M. (1999). Hannah Arendt on authority: Conservatism in education reconsidered. *Educational Theory, 49*(2), 161–80. http://dx.doi.org/10.1111/j.1741-5446.1999.00161.x

Merleau-Ponty, M. (1974). *Phenomenology, language and sociology*. London, UK: Heinemann.

Metcalfe, A.W., & Game, A. (2002). *The mystery of everyday life*. Leichhardt, NSW, AU: Federation Press.

Metcalfe, A.W., & Game, A. (2006). *Teachers who change lives*. Carlton, Victoria, AU: Melbourne University Press.

Murdoch, I. (1970). *The sovereignty of good*. London, UK: Routledge & Kegan Paul.

Noddings, N. (1984). *Caring*. Berkeley, CA: University of California Press.

O'Byrne, A. (2005). Pedagogy without a project: Arendt and Derrida on teaching, responsibility and revolution. *Studies in Philosophy and Education*, 24(5), 389–409. http://dx.doi.org/10.1007/s11217-005-0967-3

Smith, B.L. (1994). Team teaching methods. In K.W. Pritchard & R. McLaren (Eds.), *Handbook of college teaching* (pp. 127–37). London, UK: Greenwood Press.

Winnicott, D.W. (1990). The capacity to be alone. In *The maturational processes and the facilitating environment* (pp. 29–36). London, UK: Karnac Books.

Winnicott, D.W. (1991). *Playing and reality*. London, UK: Routledge.

2 Complex Collaborations: Co-Creating Deep Interdisciplinarity for Undergraduates

SAL RENSHAW AND RENÉE VALIQUETTE

Introduction

> People who identify with knowledge take it personally, seeing the world and others only for what these say about themselves, as a mirror of themselves. People in dialogue, however, are able to hear the differences offered by others, because they are not personally affronted. They can imagine the experience of others and therefore understand how different perspectives can co-exist. Through the play of differences, they are making something that they share with others but which is no one's personal property. (Game & Metcalfe, 2009, p. 47)

Like so many of our colleagues, we have fretted over the state of undergraduate education for a generation of students who increasingly enter university already committed to a vocational path and incurious to other options. For many years now, these are the students who have populated our classrooms, filled with anxieties about work and financial security, and short on excitement for the imaginative possibilities of higher learning. We have lamented how far our students seem from Ken Robinson's dream of creativity as the basis for genuine education and imagination, and a key skill for anticipating "many possible futures" (Robinson, 2011). Such anxieties have led us to ask whether the seemingly rigid structures of higher education can flex enough to educate students for real world challenges without emptying their education of its transformative potential. If Robinson is right that creativity is as much an economic as a pedagogical imperative of twenty-first century education, in what ways can we redesign our curriculum to recognize such a reality?

These concerns have defined our fifteen years of collaboration as researchers and teachers of interdisciplinary gender studies, and have lead us most recently to the development of a unique concept course, Introduction to Interdisciplinary Analysis. The course embodies an innovative approach to interdisciplinary curricula and relational pedagogy, one that aims to balance the best of the expert/disciplined approach to knowledge with the expansive creativity of interdisciplinary collaboration. Each iteration of the course is anchored by a chosen theme. As of the writing of this chapter, we have run five versions of the course under the concepts DIRT, SLOTH, WATER, SECRETS, and GENIUS (see Figures 2.1–2.5 for interdisciplinary analysis course posters designed by Carol Szabicot, Nipissing University Marketing; full colour versions available at http://justcurriculum.nipissingu.ca).

DIRT ran in the spring session of 2013, using a block approach for delivery.[1] It was followed by SLOTH in the spring session of 2014, while WATER was our first offering for the fall/winter schedule in 2014–15. SECRETS ran in the spring session of 2015, and GENIUS in the fall/winter session of 2016–17. The course, which has received national recognition (see MacDonald, 2014), is the result of our own deep and long-standing collaboration – as co-planners, co-teachers, and co-thinkers – along with a desire to bring the inspiring power of shared knowledge to the classroom. In the following paper, we outline our work in co-planning and co-delivering this course in its various iterations, as well as highlight how deeply interdisciplinary curricula, taught collaboratively, can help students reorient their relationship to learning and thinking beyond narrow conceptions of applicability and vocational relevance.

Course Iterations: DIRT, SLOTH, WATER, SECRETS, and GENIUS

In addition to co-conceiving and co-developing this interdisciplinary course in its various iterations, the two of us also serve as the principal course directors and facilitators. The course is organized around alternating discipline-based guest lectures and interdisciplinary seminars. The curriculum for DIRT, for example, included lectures from twelve Nipissing faculty members across a range of arts and science disciplines, each of whom presented discipline-based material inspired by the framing concept. A biologist gave a lecture on soil contamination, an art historian on photographing the Alberta tar sands, a cultural theorist on *Dracula*, and nine others. For each offering, we co-teach and co-facilitate every other class, lecturing on the history and theory of interdisciplinarity

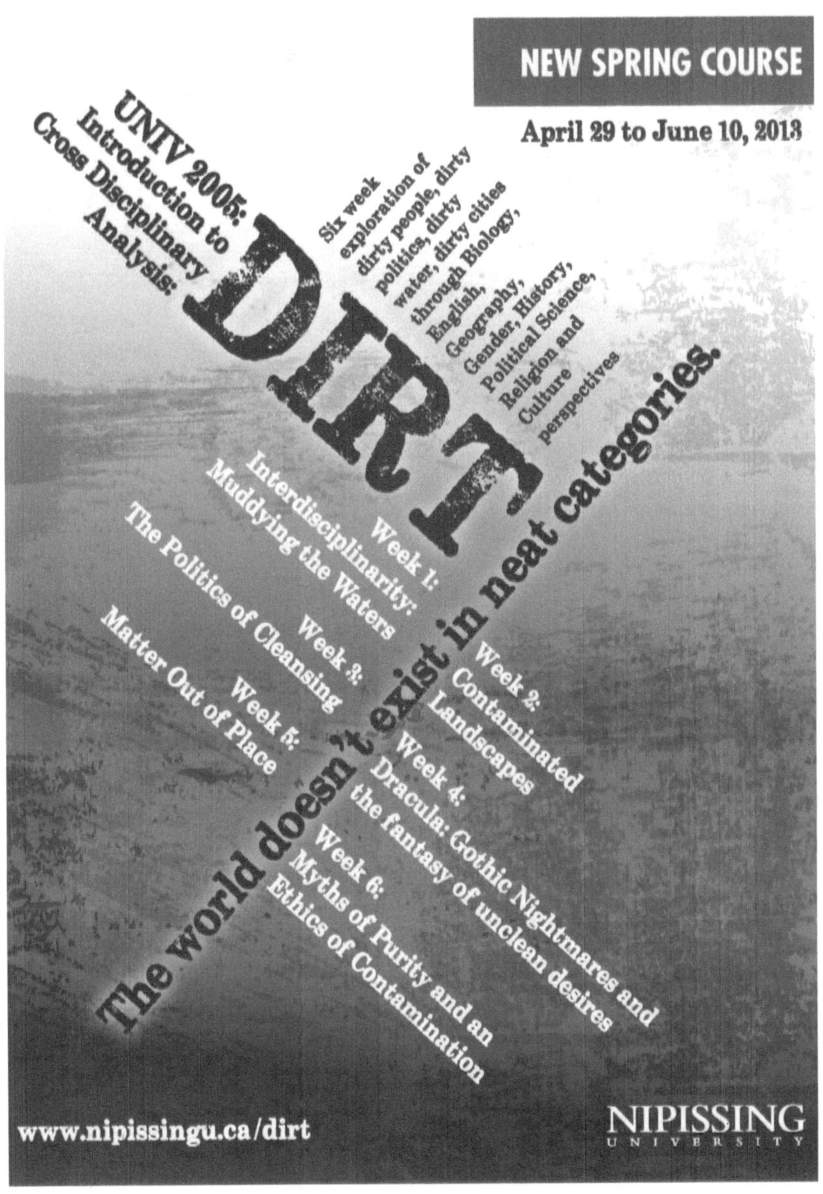

Figure 2.1. Poster advertising the interdisciplinary analysis course DIRT (2013).

Figure 2.2. Poster advertising the interdisciplinary analysis course SLOTH (2014).

Figure 2.3. Poster advertising the interdisciplinary analysis course WATER (2014).

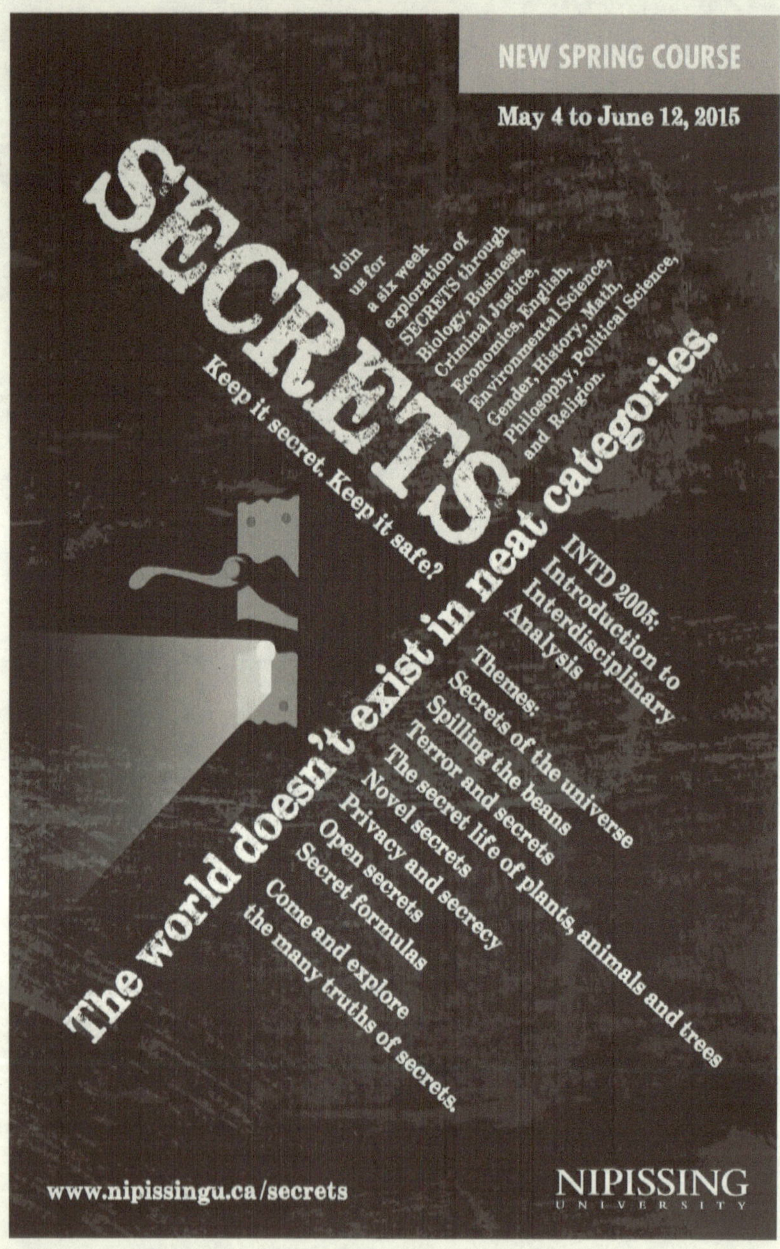

Figure 2.4. Poster advertising the interdisciplinary analysis course SECRETS (2015).

Figure 2.5. Poster advertising the interdisciplinary analysis course GENIUS (2015).

and facilitating an interdisciplinary engagement with the disciplinary content. Participating faculty members are invited to sit in on their colleagues' lectures, which many of them do, and students are encouraged to bring friends and family members to the guest lectures. The seminars are restricted to registered students and the facilitators.

The underlying vision for our interdisciplinary concept course is to offer students an opportunity to experience the way disciplinary knowledge is enhanced by encounters with other voices, from different perspectives, and with diverse forms of expertise. Deep interdisciplinarity, as we understand it, begins with the recognition that the disciplines themselves carry debts to a multitude of others, whether or not these debts are acknowledged, and that disciplinary borders have always been leaky. As Joe Moran (2010) suggests in *Interdisciplinarity*, "Order is simply a thin, perilous condition we try to impose on the basic reality of chaos" (p. 1). Deep interdisciplinarity means acknowledging the inherent messiness of the very ideas that shape and define the disciplines and rejoicing in that messiness, seeing it as the compost for innovation and creativity rather than the chaos of anarchy. In conceiving this course, we hoped that providing students with the opportunity for such delight might help reorient their approach to learning away from instrumentality and individualism, and towards curiosity and collaboration.

A shared philosophy of education, informed largely by critical pedagogy and post-structuralist[2] critiques of institutional power and knowledge production, as well as French feminist conceptions of immanent[3] relational ethics, provides the theoretical foundation for the organization of the course. Collectively, these theories have helped us develop an approach to collaborative teaching and learning that is more rhizomatic[4] than linear, more intersubjective than interactive, and more immanently responsive than reductively critical. This theoretical approach has led us to ask whether a deeply collaborative classroom can help foster a shared approach to knowledge creation, something Ann Game and Andrew Metcalfe call "a dialogic community" (Game & Metcalfe, 2009). Such an approach challenges the singular authority of the traditional expert/specialist model of teaching that remains essential to disciplinary thinking. Instead, students are invited to see themselves as active thinkers and learners whose efforts are essential to the project underway. Their role in the collaborative interdisciplinary classroom is not simply to retain, but to reach out, connect, and co-create, just as their professors are doing.

Our conception of relational pedagogy has inspired, formed, and been altered by the five iterations of our course. In the sections that follow, we will consider how co-planning and co-teaching these course offerings has shaped our understanding of "immanent otherness"[5] as a pedagogical concept. Further, we will ask how a pedagogy of immanent otherness can foster a relational learning experience that is both profoundly meaningful and vocationally applicable, teaching students the critical cognitive and literacy skills needed to meet the challenges of today's wicked problems,[6] while inspiring them to approach "difference" with excitement rather than fear.

The structure of this chapter aims to offer an easily navigable map for readers, but this formatting, much like interdisciplinarity itself, we recognize to be terribly leaky. Theorizing and practising co-planning, in our lived collaborative realities, is often hard to distinguish from the theorizing and practising of co-teaching.

Co-Planning and Co-Teaching in Context

The dominant curricula-planning model for post-secondary education remains one of prearrangement. Course directors alone decide what material will be covered and what knowledge will be acquired, and they alone are responsible for delivering this content. This model continues both because it is the traditional format and because it is perceived to be the most economically sustainable. The necessity of programming courses in this way has been relatively uncontroversial within the disciplinary setting. Students are understood to be building expertise in particular concentrations, and specific knowledge must be acquired to confirm such expertise; such is the necessary logic of disciplinarity. However, the push to translate this structure into instrumental metrics has greatly increased in recent years. In Ontario, for example, the Ministry of Education expects content to be articulated in terms of concrete course "outcomes," a trend that is quickly becoming ubiquitous across Western educational institutions. The drive to produce concrete outcomes is increasingly fuelled by a culture that views education in strictly instrumental terms – one that tells us from the outset what the students will learn, what will be discussed, communicated, established, understood, and *acquired*. This process can start to resemble telling the customer what he or she is buying. Knowing in precise terms that "I will learn X" is required for articulating how "I will apply X" in the workplace. Outcomes that name specific skills and content are preferred to ones that suggest non-linear, exploratory processes. For the many of us who hold on to the notion of a broad-based liberal arts and science education as not only valuable for cultivating informed and active democratic citizenries but also as instrumentally useful, the increasingly hegemonic outcomes-based model of curricula development is constraining.

This emphasis on utility and applicability feels somewhat out of step with the rise of interdisciplinary programming in the post-secondary sector over the last twenty years. Kathryn Shailer (2005) outlines this trend in *Interdisciplinarity in a Disciplinary Universe: A Review of Key Issues*, where she notes that "virtually every university [in Ontario] – even the oldest and most traditional – has introduced interdisciplinary programs, if not developed institutional policies regarding interdisciplinarity" (p. 4). However, Shailer is clear that "the trend toward interdisciplinarity should not be construed as irresistible nor as a major threat to disciplinarity, for during the same period a countervailing movement toward greater specialization has been at least as forceful in some disciplines" (p. 4). These twin trends of interdisciplinary programming and specialized, professional, outcomes-based education make for strange bedfellows. The latter requires that disciplinary education validate itself through utility and applicability; the former asks that disciplinary habits be challenged, stretched, and reimagined. Add to this picture the fact that the push for interdisciplinarity has, in its recent ascension, largely come from outside the university, from "governments, granting agencies, foundations, industry and other stakeholders in the production of knowledge" (p. 4), and the scene is further complicated. Put simply, it is not a question of professional schools and industry on one side and starry-eyed humanities scholars on the other. What is particularly compelling about our current situation is that aspirational education as the foundation of innovation makes good economic sense, hence the real reason that governments and industry are pushing for more interdisciplinarity. As Martha Nussbaum (2010) argued in the *New York Times*, "Even if a nation's only goal were economic prosperity, the humanities supply essential ingredients for a healthy business culture."

For the two of us, such debates comprise the context of our ongoing collaboration, one that involves co-planning and co-teaching, among other shared efforts. Discussions of how applicability and utility relate to creative, critical, and innovative thinking define the educational moment. Ignore this reality and risk irrelevancy. While at another time we might have happily defended broad-based liberal arts higher education as a good in itself, today such defences attract small audiences.

Among the most influential players in the post-secondary sector, the push is towards professionalization *and* interdisciplinarity. But how do we best integrate these seemingly discordant initiatives? Our discussions have consistently been attuned to this wider political and economic context, particularly as the enrolment trend at Nipissing University and elsewhere in North American universities has moved decisively from arts and sciences to professional programming. In considering such trends, we side with those who argue that the lack of emphasis on, and therefore access to, exploratory and non-instrumental curricula in professional programs *weakens* the quality of the education that students receive. Highly disciplined, vocational training that doesn't value interdisciplinary and exploratory education struggles to produce the kinds of thinkers and therefore, ultimately, the kinds of workers required to foster innovative and thus competitive economies. Recognizing the need for better cross-faculty and interdisciplinary collaborations, the question for us became, Is it possible to create curricula that draw on the best of a deeply interdisciplinary, exploratory, liberal arts education in order to strengthen disciplinary and professional training, and to reimagine the relationship between liberal arts and sciences and vocational application?

The Philosophy of Co-Planning

> In the beginning is the relation – as the category of being, as readiness, as a form that reaches out to be filled, as a model of the soul, the a priori of relation; the innate You. (Buber, 1937/1996, p. 78)

The immediate context of our collaboration is unarguably one of abiding relationality. For us, co-planning is not only made possible by a long-standing, interpersonal relation, it is also made more meaningful and more effective. The co-planning of the concept course would not have happened were it not for a foundation of deep and continuous relation, built on a shared background in post-structuralist theory, and our fifteen years of collaboration and co-teaching in the interdisciplinary gender equality and social justice program at Nipissing University. In other words, for us, co-planning begins with shared inspiration, with creative relational dialogue, and only subsequently moves towards expression as a focused concrete "product," that is, a course. At the core of this relational dialogue is a willingness to relinquish our respective positions as autonomous, independent, discrete experts – "experts" who are certain of what they know. Unlike an additive model of exchange, in which *my* idea is added to *your* idea, we aspire to a deeper form of intersubjective dialogue that first recognizes the illusion of autonomy and independence. For French philosopher and writer Hélène Cixous, this recognition might be described as a willingness to let go of our grip on being subjects or selves who know they know: "We all know how much we hold on to what we know or what we think we know. One has to know how not to possess what one knows" (Cixous, 1992, p. 67). In other words, this is a relation to self in which the idea that one is the individual possessor of knowledge makes little or no sense. For us as co-planners, knowledge and learning emerge in immanent community, and neither of us is the possessor of ideas, the teacher, or the student. We work towards a "self-less" relation to ourselves and to the other that fosters the possibility of deep learning. It is this space we aspire to create, at least some of the time, in our classrooms.

For Ann Game and Andrew Metcalfe, genuinely deep learning also emerges where the logic of self-conscious individuals defending their subjective positions has been loosened (Game & Metcalfe, 2009, p. 47). In being willing to relinquish our grip on the role of expert, that is, the disciplined, knowing self, we recognize that a space is opened for a different relation with others. Rather than "bouncing ideas off each other" – a notion of subjectivity that implies self-conscious autonomous knowers – the dialogic relation that forms the basis of truly deep learning implies a dynamic, emergent, and immanent notion of subjectivity, a notion built on the recognition that all subjectivity is really intersubjectivity. "The significance of this dialogic shift for educational theory is that participants change their cognitive capacities when no longer self-conscious individuals. People who identify with knowledge take it personally, seeing the world and others only for what these say about themselves, as a mirror of themselves. People in dialogue, however, are able to hear the differences offered by others" (p. 47). We share Game and Metcalfe's aspiration to create courses and classrooms that embody a dialogic of deep learning, and alongside them, we recognize that the same philosophical and ethical disposition has formed the essential and necessary bedrock of our own collaboration. With a spirit of humility and openness to the possibility that together we can be more than the sum of our parts, we have been inspired to take risks in co-creating as well as co-delivering curricula.

We began the planning of the first version of our concept course, DIRT, with only the vaguest sense of what it would look like as a finished product, let alone what students might accomplish by taking it. In other words, no concrete *telos* informed its development, and in this our debt to Deleuze and Guattari's (1987) notion of rhizomatic epistemologies, rather than Aristotle's linearity, are revealed. So too is a willingness to loosen our own grips on defending subjective pedagogic positions, for it is only in this loosened *inter*-subjective space that there is sufficient openness to encounter difference as an invitation to co-creation rather than a threat to autonomy. While it is probably true that nearly fifteen years of relational engagement is not incidental to creating the conditions of trust that would permit this loosened subjective grip, our experience of teaching the course five times has revealed that a prior relation is not a necessary precondition to deep learning. Like Game and Metcalfe, we can and have extended the circle of inclusive collaboration into the classroom. In this way, our co-planning and co-teaching efforts overlap and allow us to model for the students the relational openness required for deep learning.

The Practice of Co-Planning

The material conditions that gave rise to DIRT were, from our perspective, nothing less than profane. The last twenty years of announcing the death of the humanities and the arts, as we have already noted, has left no one in undergraduate education unscathed, and declining enrolments in anything other than vocational degrees has profoundly reshaped educational priorities in North America. At Nipissing University, the demand for vocational relevance across programming has grown every year, and alongside it the commitment to an exploratory, liberal arts degree is perceived to be, whether true or not, a luxury many students feel they can't afford. So, in large measure, our co-planning work for the interdisciplinary concept course was motivated by a desire to embrace, rather than abandon, the defining spirit of liberal arts education. By creating an open-ended and exploratory learning experience – one adapted to work within the bounds of professional and applied degrees – we hoped that students would be given the opportunity to de-instrumentalize their education. Taking our cue from the kinds of reimagining of general education being undertaken in many US colleges (see Hothem, 2013), we focused our attention on developing a course that, with sufficient buy-in from across programs and faculties, could do double duty. It could serve to fulfil our students' breadth requirements by balancing representation from the sciences, social sciences, and humanities, and it could also excite the students about the possibility of encountering knowledge outside their already firmly established disciplinary trajectory. In many ways this focus is a sleight of hand. While the course remains instrumental at the level of structure, that is, it is designed to fulfil students' breadth requirements (which is why the first offering, DIRT, appealed to so many of them), the curricula itself challenge the epistemic claims of an exclusively discipline-based, instrumental approach to education. In other words, while instrumentality gets students in the door, once there, they encounter an approach to discipline-based knowledge that recognizes difference not as threatening but rather as an open-ended epistemic opportunity. Nowhere was the success of this strategy more evident than with the three business students who, sullen and resentful at the start of DIRT, had become proselyting converts by the third class. Natalie, a business accounting major, articulates the shift succinctly:

> I would like to begin by saying that this is literally the most valuable course I have ever taken. Firstly, it has created an appreciation for disciplines that I haven't studied before, that I otherwise may have thought of as useless. It has opened my eyes to the possibilities within my education, and has fed a desire to learn … I think the course has rekindled my curiosity in the world and all the things I may one day come to know. I also think this course has provided a unique opportunity to see the way everything is connected, and I hope that I will not forget this lesson throughout my life. (Natalie, fourth-year business marketing student)

We'll say more about the transformative experience for students below, but what is striking about Natalie's response is how succinctly she encapsulates the importance of an engagement with disciplinarity at the same time that she celebrates the power of connection, in other words, of interdisciplinarity. Very early into teaching DIRT, we had confirmation that given the opportunity, students – even the accountants – would not only take the class but embrace the experience and recognize the relevance of exploratory interdisciplinarity to their disciplinary path.

In addition to responding to material and institutional conditions, co-planning the course has been an emergent and dynamic process, itself a reflection of the philosophy of immanence that underpins our general approach to creating conditions of deep learning. Each iteration of the course has undergone significant structural shifts from a broadly collaborative curriculum development process with DIRT, where all the presenting faculty "brainstormed" the classes, to the current structuring of GENIUS, where the work of shaping the topics and targeting specific faculty to teach has returned to us as the course directors. In reality, this shift is undeniably a contraction at the level of programming, and thus a move away from openness to difference and otherness, a withdrawal from transformative dialogue. It is less than ideal in that respect, but within the material constraints of the institution, constraints especially around time, it has also proven necessary. Moreover, with each iteration of the course we have developed greater clarity and expertise around what we can accomplish with interdisciplinary curricula delivered in this way. This development is precisely because the course flows endlessly from our relational dialogue about education, a dialogue our guest faculty are not necessarily part of because they come to us as representatives of their disciplines rather than as advocates for or exponents of interdisciplinarity. So, while we began planning DIRT with no sense of *telos*, the same is less true of the subsequent iterations. We do have a sense now of what we can and want to accomplish, but this sense is derived directly from our immanent embodied experience of delivering interdisciplinary curricula and our willingness to relinquish the identity of expert and allow ourselves to be transformed by the process. Relinquishing the expert role does not mean that we are not developing and accumulating expertise; we are. Rather it means that we resist at every turn the impulse to take on the identity of expert, something that more often than not forecloses on the possibility of the kind of deep learning that derives from relational dialogue. Just as we believe the course creates an occasion to approach the practice of encountering knowledge from a position of immanent openness, the same structure informs the planning process. So while we do direct and shape the curricula as course directors, we do so in ways that are considerably more open and inclusive than traditional course programming.

At least initially in the development of the first iteration of the course, DIRT, one of the most significant challenges in co-planning involved reassuring the guest faculty of the pedagogical value of an approach to learning that required them to simultaneously adopt and surrender the position of expert on the one hand, and to trust the expertise of interdisciplinary faculty who function as course directors on the other. So synonymous with education itself is the teleological model of course planning – in which the teacher has a clear sense of the terrain of knowledge the course will cover and has sketched out the waypoints in a clear and well-structured syllabus – that the invitation to be liberated from this process can actually be anxiety provoking. Were these faculty members being invited to be guest lecturers in a traditional sense, the same anxiety would likely not arise. They would be assured that, if not them, at least the professor whose class it "really is" was steering the ship. The process of co-planning, therefore, involves informing guest faculty that in this course the role of the course directors does not map neatly onto the solo professor model that has defined the modern university.

On the contrary, the anchoring professors in these interdisciplinary classes are in fact intermediaries between the disciplinary guest faculty and the students, and might better be described as collaborative facilitators. This structure has frequently given rise to mostly productive, if not always easy, conversations among faculty about the relationship between epistemology and pedagogy. Indeed, in the best of cases these conversations embody the truly dialogic spirit of transformative knowledge and deep learning that define Game and Metcalfe's approach to their very large, team-taught, dialogic first-year sociology courses in which an attitude of excitement and openness to difference overwhelms any impulses towards the self-protective but defended posture of the "expert" (Game & Metcalfe, 2009, pp. 50–3). Ultimately, in being liberated from the traditional structures of course design and course presentation, as noted above, we have found that the guest faculty have largely experienced their role in the team-taught course as an exciting opportunity to engage differently with students. As we move through the fifth iteration of the course, GENIUS, the word has spread, and much, though not all, of the disciplinary gatekeeping has fallen away. Faculty are less inclined to challenge the rigour of this approach to teaching and its value to students, a concern more frequently expressed with DIRT. As faculty have participated in delivery, and as they've heard the feedback from students who have taken the course, there is greater faculty, and therefore institutional, buy-in, and this support is by no means an inconsequential aspect of planning. It has required us as co-directors to trust the process and to allow each new version of the course to develop out of and take shape in relation to the immanent conditions in which it is emerging – conditions shaped by the individual and particular needs of the various stakeholders, namely the guest faculty, the students, and the institution.

In very pragmatic terms, the theme for each iteration of the course emerged as part of the ongoing dialogue between us. Over many years, we have compiled lists of topics we think may be inspiring and engaging, and we revisit and add to that list continually in response to contemporary issues in the culture at large, as well as in relation to the particular needs of our cohorts and the reactions of our colleagues and students as we try them out. Consistent with all the course topics is the requirement that they be easily taken up by faculty from across the disciplinary clusters, that is, the sciences, social sciences, and humanities. Thus, one of the unchanging structures for us is that each iteration of the course must balance the representation between these disciplinary groupings as one face of the way in which we are expressing and engaging with interdisciplinarity. The course themes must contain sufficient flexibility to not only allow, but ideally enhance, such representation. For example, while the concept of "evil" might work for the humanities and social sciences, it might be a strain for the sciences. On the other hand, a concept like "chaos" would likely work for all three.

The Philosophy of Co-Teaching

French-Algerian writer-philosopher Hélène Cixous's extensive work on "otherness" informs our curricula development and co-teaching practices at every level. In North America, Cixous continues to be primarily known for her contribution to Anglo feminist theory of the 1970s (see Cixous, 1976). She is recognized in France and across Europe, however, as one of the pre-eminent thinkers of our time, her many novels, essays, plays, and literary criticism now collected in the Cixous Archive at the Bibliothèque nationale de France. While she is read and loved by many Anglo and Québécois literary theorists, her work remains disciplinarily bound, limited largely to French and English studies. Despite being well recognized as a post-structuralist feminist, her work has received little critical attention within the broader Anglo-American community of post-structuralist scholarship, in stark contrast to her intellectual collaborator and interlocutor, Jacques Derrida. Despite publishing together, as well as writing about each other's work and ideas, there has been little uptake of the implications of Derrida's consistent affirmation of Cixous as his muse, interlocutor, and life-long intellectual companion. It is worth noting the ways in which collaborative intellectual relationships can themselves be disciplined into existing academic models that favour autonomous, discrete knowledge production, thereby obscuring the power of relational dialogue. Regrettably, one consequence of the repression of collaboration in this case is that the riches of Cixous's vast oeuvre remain under-acknowledged and under-applied, particularly in wider Anglo philosophical circles.

Cixous's work on otherness, as well as her broader metaphysics of immanence, comprises the theoretical grounding of our collaboration, both outside and inside the classroom. For Cixous, the otherness of other people, that is, their insistence on being more than "I" can know or anticipate, is a vibrant, fecund, and life-affirming aspect of social being: "I am for you what you want me to be at the moment you look at me in a way you've never seen before: at every instant" (Cixous, 1976, p. 893). Hell is not other people, by her account. On the contrary, "in one another we will never be lacking" (p. 893). Further still, for Cixous the notion of an "I," an "individual life," is a fantasy, an ideological fabrication perpetually undone by our interdependent, interwoven, interspecies reality. Cixousian metaphysics is one of immanence, not transcendence, recognizing existence as always a deeply intertwined, co-imbricated, and intersubjective affair. A metaphysics of immanence rests on the notion that for humans there is no way to get "beyond" the embodied, embedded, entanglement of existence, no way to get out of the fog of intersubjectivity. Cixous points out that "difference always operates between an us as an (im)possibility of resemblance. I notice the differences that compose 'difference' in the exchange of resemblances. Moreover difference is in the exchange. Moreover it moves – without stopping – from the one to the other. And it lives off the two. It is our incalculable resultant" (Cixous, quoted in Segarra, 2009, p. 56). For Cixous, this counter understanding of relationality is deeply feminist, because it rewrites women's historical consignment as immanent only to the extent that she cannot transcend her embodied existence by revealing that, in fact, immanence is the condition of all human subjectivity. Cixous helps to rewrite immanence as the very condition of fecundity. Immanence, on her watch, becomes the source of ontological richness, a seething, elemental, creative mess, one from which life itself is made possible. Rather than experiencing reality as disappointingly not in *my* control, Cixous contends that the messiness, unpredictability, and partiality that is immanence is the very condition of life:

> All that is stopped, grasped, all that is subjugated, easily transmitted, easily picked up, all that comes under the word concept, which is to say all that is taken, caged, is less true. Has lost what is life itself which is always in the process of seething, of emitting, of transmitting itself. Each object is in reality a small virtual volcano. There is a continuity in the living; whereas theory entails a discontinuity, a cut, which is altogether the opposite of life ... [Theory] is indispensable, at times, to make progress, but

> alone it is false. I resign myself to it as a dangerous aid. It is prosthesis. All that advances is aerial, detached, uncatchable. (Cixous and Calle-Gruber, 1997, p. 4)

In following Cixous, one does not lament the loss of transcendence; one revels in the vibrant, ontological possibilities that immanence grants, because we are all others in this together.

The Western epistemological impulse to colonize and domesticate knowledge, an impulse that has defined our institutions of higher learning for centuries, often renders knowledge lifeless, and thus less useful. The desire to transcend context, history, and situation, let alone other people, on Cixous's account is first, impossible, and second, boring and counter to life. Darwin, among others, tells us that life is always seeking new possibilities towards an unknown future; the only constants are difference and relation, change and intermingling (see Grosz, 2005). What does it mean to bring such insights into our classrooms?

The move from transcendence to immanence is central to wider post-structuralist efforts to dismantle the dominant epistemological framework of Western thought. The shift to immanence means changing our understanding of knowledge itself as well as of knowers. It is here, then, that we can begin to see the connection between Cixousian immanence and our own critical immanent pedagogy. For us, co-teaching begins with recognition of our immanence, that is, our embodied and embedded ontological entanglement. And the "our" here refers not only to us as co-creators and directors of the course, but also to the students and collaborating teachers. Co-teaching, as we aim to practise it, aspires to transform classrooms from environments of transcendental mastery and unquestioned expertise to ones of immanent relationality. Our philosophy of co-teaching begins with the recognition that taming knowledge, while often necessary and useful, can also mean limiting the potential of learning, pitting dogma against an ontological reality of immanence. Epistemologies and pedagogies of transcendental mastery do not prepare students for the so-called "real world," because the real world is an embodied, embedded, and entangled affair; the real world is itself already and always interdisciplinary.

The Practice of Co-Teaching

Practising our philosophy of immanent, relational co-teaching begins from the first moment of the first class as our own enduring entanglement sets the tone. Very quickly after meeting the students and introducing the course material, we are gently interrupting and querying each other, looking to each other to add to, finish, or reconsider statements that we've made. From the outset, we animate for the students a pedagogy of immanent otherness and the inter-relational requirements of interdisciplinary thinking and learning that we hope to cultivate in the class itself. Through our dialogue we demonstrate a relation to knowledge that is open and dynamic, focused on process and becoming rather than on arrival and being. The ideas we discuss are rarely presented as perfectly worked out and coherent. We listen to each other. We change each other's minds. This style of teaching can often catch the students off guard, for it immediately shifts away from the expert model with which they are most familiar. In short order, they realize that they've stepped into a very different kind of classroom, precisely because it is immediately and organically collaborative and dialogic. Unlike other forms of co-teaching, we typically resist the impulse to organize and structure the time by each taking on a particular aspect of the material we think will need to be covered. Rather, we model what our intersubjective, immanent, relational co-thinking and co-planning process looks like – something we believe is much closer to what their real world experience in the workplace will be like. To date, not a single student has dropped the course after the first day; more often, they bring their friends.

With our first guest lecture, we begin to extend these relational engagements to other faculty members. We regularly but politely interrupt them as they are lecturing and ask questions; we try to anticipate and query points, especially concepts that the students might not know. Not being at the front of the classroom ourselves, but rather seated with and among the students, makes it far easier for us to discretely assess which details might be outside their understanding. We model for them "informed ignorance," which is to say that we, the "experts," are happy to show them the limits of our own knowledge, making it safe for them to "not know" as well. At the same time that we make it acceptable for the students to "not know," we are also disrupting the formula of unquestioned expertise that remains the dominant structure for undergraduate education. No matter how many times we might, as solo teachers, tell our students we don't know everything; no matter how many times we literally say, "I don't know the answer to that question"; what we far more often do is communicate our disciplinary expertise. So, from the students' point of view, we *do* in fact mostly know or think we know. Such knowing is the necessary condition of disciplinary education. The interdisciplinary environment offers a liberating counterbalance to such a foundation. When other faculty are in the room, asking questions, offering their own perspective, and interjecting with details on how their own discipline approaches the issue being discussed, and sometimes *not* knowing things that perhaps the students *do* know, the classroom is transformed from one of knowledge delivery to one of collaborative learning. Bringing multiple, multidisciplinary voices into the classroom might seem like a small thing, but it is utterly transformative for undergraduate students. Every academic who has presented at or attended an academic conference has experienced such an environment – even in supposedly contained disciplinary spaces. Undergraduate students almost never get to have such experiences, and they are the poorer and less prepared for the "real world" because of it.

One of the most fascinating aspects of our course is the way in which the students, after a few guest lectures, become more knowledgeable in the interdisciplinary analysis of the concept (DIRT, SLOTH, WATER, SECRETS, GENIUS) than the guest lecturers themselves. Only the students and we, the course facilitators, know what has been discussed throughout the course, which shifts the expert/passive learner dynamic still further. The guest lecturers often refer to what they assume their colleagues might have already covered, but they don't actually know. Students, then, are perceived to be knowers by the guest lectures, and this perception also shifts the power dynamic of the classroom towards one of immanent collaboration.

One of the most powerful examples of this dynamic emerged in SLOTH, in which almost every guest lecturer, from the physicist to the political scientist to the religion professor, referenced the ancient Greeks and Aristotle. We discussed the meaning of such repetition in the alternating seminar classes as we reflected on the common epistemic foundations of Western disciplines. After two guest lecturers referenced Aristotle, the students started taking note, and the trend became something that we as a class were discovering, unbeknownst to the guests. Soon, a lecturer would make such a reference, and we would all look at each other knowingly. The students felt that they were detectives uncovering a secret formula, but by the end of the class they came to understand that what they were really seeing was the Western training of academics. They were discovering the ways in which knowledge is historically situated and contextual – a key lesson in critical and post-structuralist epistemology and pedagogy. While they were primed for such a discovery from the seminars, none of us could have predicted that the guest lecturers would animate this lesson so powerfully. The students knew that we didn't program this connection; they were seeing "the Matrix" in action and learning to read it themselves in the process, and we were their co-collaborators in this discovery.

The active role that the students play in the course, their role as co-learners and collaborators, is something that we particularly emphasize in the seminars. We do not know what will be discovered, learned, figured out in the course any more than they do. We are trained in interdisciplinary methodologies and pedagogies, but the curriculum is also built on the ideas of twelve other people. We don't know what our colleagues will teach, and therefore we don't know how it will all connect. In this sense, we are their co-explorers of the material being presented, rather than another set of experts. On reflection, we have come to see how critical this intermediary role is to deeply shifting the power dynamics of the classroom in the direction of collaborative, immanent learning.

> Many solo lecturers fear the prospect of team teaching because they imagine the other as judge of their vulnerabilities. This presumption fails to recognize the ontological transformation of dialogue: in dialogic team teaching, no teacher is in the position to judge another for they are carrying the other in themselves. In the same way, it is the teacher's carrying of students within themselves that guards against any tendency to unify as teachers against students. The witnessing in a dialogic classroom takes the form of support rather than judgment and surveillance. (Game & Metcalfe, 2009, p. 49)

While team teaching per se is not an innovation, the layering of the teaching role that comes with the addition of the anchoring course directors is. Having now delivered five iterations of this course, we have come to see the way in which the course directors' role is crucial to the transformation of the traditional power relations of the classroom and thus crucial to being able to move the conversation from dialogue as exchange to dialogue as co-created transformative collaboration. A further and unanticipated benefit of this model of collaborative teaching and learning turned out to be the liberating effect it had on the guest teachers. Many recounted their delight in this approach and their surprise at how dynamic and engaged the students were. Without the sole responsibility of course delivery, our colleagues had more opportunity to experience the frisson that good education promises. Without the structure of the expert model, the students also felt liberated from the inevitable silencing that can occur in the pressure of a disciplined classroom. Clearly, for us, the key to this opening up on both sides lies in an approach to teaching centred on creating a collaborative community in which the responsibility for the success of the class is shared among collaborators. As Game and Metcalfe (2009) say of their similar approach to dialogic teaching in large classes: "[B]y creating a holding space and a holding time that transform the classroom, it can produce a dialogic community among all participants in the classroom" (p. 46). Essential to our capacity to create a similar holding is the dialogic relation between us as both the course directors and course conceivers.

Disrupting the seemingly inherent and hierarchical power dynamics that structure the teacher/student relationship is one of the most significant preconditions for creating the possibility for deep learning in these classes. We have already noted the liberating aspect of teaching recounted by so many of the guest teachers whose sense of creative pedagogical possibility was unleashed by not feeling solely responsible for the class. Equally significant is the effect of the intermediary role of the course facilitators. Rather than occupying the traditional place of experts in the alternating classes, the facilitators meet students somewhere between ignorance and expertise, and model Plato's ideal as co-seekers of knowledge and wisdom. While those of us who teach might be well aware of the silencing potential of the expert/disciplined approach to pedagogy, even in the most generous of classrooms, we could not have anticipated how crucial the facilitators' role would be to the success of creating dialogic community. It profoundly affected how deeply the students felt themselves to be co-creators, and more importantly it unlocked their voices, as seen in the following two statements:

> One of the most gruelling tasks in university for students is talking aloud, not just for the sake of talking to accumulate participation marks, but actually engaging with the material and saying something of use or value to others. In an environment with one professor, or authoritative figure, lectures can race by without students having the slightest idea what it is they are meant to learn, and seminars can quickly stumble off topic with students voicing irrelevant opinions instead of bringing it back and engaging with the learning material. DIRT was different in that it amalgamated the popular classroom styles and created arguably the best possible learning

> environment. By having more than one professor in the room, colleagues could pull the reins if they felt a given lesson was perhaps too abstract, or too heavy. By having guest lecturers, a professor could have an allotted time in which a specifically structured and well-organized lesson could begin and end without many an interruption. (Cameron, fourth-year history major)

> The learning environment created by DIRT would not have been made possible without the presence of the other professors during the lecture. The combination of the consistent presence of one professor and input from all others, created a space that encouraged thought-provoking questions and meaningful conversation. The amount of professors in the room was a definite bonus; it was fascinating to watch them throw ideas back and forth, aiding one another in understanding the concepts presented by each other. This example set a standard for the students, and listening to multiple professors asking for clarification made the asking of questions much less difficult – the intimidation that most students feel was no longer there, for the hierarchies between professors and students, as well as among disciplines, was being broken down in front of our eyes. The other key component to the success of the course and its learning environment was the consistent presence of one professor throughout. This aided in clarifying the material, keeping focus within lectures, and posing deeper reflections on the subjects presented. The course and its atmosphere encouraged intellectual curiosity that lead to a critical and meaningful engagement with the material and with one another. (Julia, fourth-year combined major: history, gender equality and social justice)

By creating an environment in which we challenge each other's expertise as co-teachers and engage with the disciplinary material in ways that are respectful but inquisitive and dialogic, we create an atmosphere of openness and curiosity. Such dynamics also allow students to see themselves moving between expert one day and novice the next, just as the co-teachers and guest professors do. Students get to play expert if and when there is a guest lecturer in their discipline, but they are also given permission to not know in deeper ways than is typically permitted in their disciplinary courses. In this course, students don't choose the disciplinary subjects, and therefore they are not burdened with the same demand they get in other classes to master the material. They did not choose to take a course in biology. They chose to take an experimental interdisciplinary course. This dynamic enables a very different psychic structure from that of conventional undergraduate courses. Students are free to try to learn the material without the pressure of not getting it and potentially failing the entire course. We, the co-teachers and guest lecturers, take on the responsibility of the content, since the students can't anticipate in advance what they will have to know. It is only within such a safe environment that students can open themselves up to disciplines that scare them. It is for this reason, we suspect, that students are able to discover a love for a subject/discipline that they would never otherwise have considered. We regularly have students tell us that their favourite lecture was not what they expected it to be and that they will now consider taking a course in an area they had previously ignored or dismissed.

Our course, therefore, operates under the assumption that each of us can learn something meaningful at the introductory level of each discipline, no matter our disciplinary strengths and/or preferences. Not only does this structure help to empower the students as learners, it has the practical application of helping them discover unknown disciplinary passions. In addition to having a pedagogy of immanent otherness concerned with creating the condition for a more meaningful relationality, we want the course to ignite an intellectual imaginary in the students, an imaginary that pushes through, around, and in-between the borders of their disciplinary training. We want the world to seem bigger and more exciting with so much more to explore and learn. We watch them transform in a short time from learners with the focused gaze of disciplinary studies, necessarily aimed at the degree, the job, the finish line, to thinkers who can and want to look up, to move into the contemplative space where new ideas are made and shaped, the space of creativity and innovation. They are nervous about having to make interdisciplinary connections themselves, but seeing it modelled by us and their guest lecturers opens a safe space where they feel empowered to take that risk. The first time they make a new connection they are energized by the excitement of invention, and they become hooked on this excitement rather quickly.

Relational Dialogic Co-Assessment

Given the suspicion with which interdisciplinary scholarship is often received by disciplinary scholars, assessment must often bear the weight of undue scrutiny. It is here, perhaps more than anywhere else, that the credibility of the course is measured by those who question the rigour and intellectual legitimacy of interdisciplinary approaches to knowledge. We have often found that colleagues who are anxious about the intellectual content will first seek solace for that anxiety in knowing that students will have to engage in traditional research practices such as writing essays, and that they will indeed be tested. One way in which we assuage this anxiety on the part of the collaborating teachers is to invite them to collaborate on the final exam. Faculty members are asked to provide four short answer questions related to the readings and lecture that they provided. From these questions, and in response to the actual emphases that emerged in the interdisciplinary seminar classes, we collaborate with the students around the kinds of questions that will most meaningfully allow them to express what they, and we, have learned. In this sense, the spirit of dialogue continues with and alongside our different responsibilities as teachers and students. While the collaborative dialogic classroom displaces traditional power structures, the goal is not to erase the best of what they stand for. Hence the real challenge is to develop assessment tools that continue to facilitate the dialogic experience.

Of equal importance to the dialogic relational structure of the classroom are the student journals. Each student is required to keep a critical reflection and reading journal throughout the course, which helps to foster dialogue outside of the face-to-face opportunities. The journal entries combine the formal recounting of the disciplinary lectures with more creative entries for the interdisciplinary seminars. In assessing the journals, we are able to measure the degree to which students comprehend the disciplinary material. However, the journals also allow students another forum in which to share new ideas and new connections that they have made but were not able or comfortable to share in seminar. Details from the journals are collated and used during the seminars to help facilitate the sharing of ideas among all participants. This technique, which keeps the identity of the contributors hidden, has been essential to addressing imbalances in classroom power relations in which sometimes only a few students dominate the discursive space. Students who don't feel comfortable speaking in class can rest assured that the best of their ideas can still help to shape interdisciplinary discussions by way of the journals. In this sense, the journals extend into course assessment the students' role as co-creators of knowledge. The journals have proven to be even more essential in WATER and GENIUS. Where DIRT, SLOTH, and SECRETS were offered in condensed format – four days per week for six weeks – WATER and GENIUS were fall/winter iterations. The very different temporalities of the classes put more emphasis on the journals as a critical tool to hold open the space of dialogue.

The multi-professor classroom has also been very helpful in assessment. Having more than one professor in the classroom frees up spaces for engagement and observation that are simply not as easily available in single lecturer formats. As Game and Metcalfe (2009) note, "with the organic structure of the team teaching relation, teachers can perform multiple activities simultaneously, remaining aware of how each moment relates to the whole class and the whole course" (p. 52).[7] In this sense, assessment can itself be understood as relational and ongoing. Students co-produce the conditions of assessment in and through their engagement with us, each other, and the guest teachers. Further, having co-teachers anchoring the course significantly increases the opportunity to hold the space of inclusion for everyone. The structural emphasis on immanence that this co-teaching model permits means that we avoid setting up the conditions of individualism, which invites students to think of their success or failure as exclusively their problem. Co-teaching allows us to create a space in which, as much as possible, student success is our collective problem. Moreover the dialogic nature of the classes means we know well in advance if we are not succeeding in engaging everyone. This is a co-teaching, co-assessment model that sets students up to succeed rather than to fail.

Conclusion

The students' overwhelming affirmation of all iterations of the course has confirmed our hypothesis that a uniquely integrated classroom, one conceived in and as relational dialogue, can foster the kind of excitement for ideas that has long been the aspiration of liberal arts and science education. Students who entered the DIRT class in order to get their breadth requirements before graduating left saying that it had been a truly transformative educational experience. Indeed, their response to the experiment greatly exceeded our expectations, and revealed how hungry they were for such expansive opportunities. The course not only helped students to discover or reconnect to the excitement of collaborative and creative thinking, it also assisted them to acquire skills, attitudes, and capacities that will enable them to be better thinkers and problem solvers outside of the educational context. In other words, students' vocational aspirations were not sacrificed in order to make space for expanded knowledge and creative transformation.

The need to structure knowledge acquisition and creation in deeply collaborative ways has never been more critical. As societies face increasingly complex and critical social, political, economic, and environmental challenges, we need minds expanded by interdisciplinary encounters as much as we need minds trained in disciplinary expertise. As we noted earlier, a "both/and" rather than an "either/or" logic informs our approach. Professional study programs that remain disconnected from the resources of the arts and sciences are weakened in their capacity to create impassioned, creative, and flexible graduates. Deep interdisciplinarity, as we theorize it, begins in, models, and depends on relational thinking and learning, and helps to cultivate in students *and* faculty an openness to what we don't yet know, rather than an entrenchment into what we (think we already) do. Given the unpredictability and dynamism of contemporary society, deep interdisciplinarity is great job training.

Our interdisciplinary concept course in its various iterations is, in many ways, unapologetically pragmatic. Our economy needs employees who are eager to learn from others, have an appetite for new ideas and better solutions, and are curious about the world. These are the skills that post-industrial nations require to remain competitive. And these skills are best developed when interdisciplinary options complement a foundation of disciplinary studies. Refusing to translate the riches of interdisciplinary arts and science curricula into economic or instrumental terms often means that such wealth goes under-recognized. There is still room to debate the utility of higher learning in democratic societies, to make arguments that support education for its own sake or for democratic or social justice purposes, but we also need to make clear how important arts and science research is to strengthening applied and professional studies. Liberal arts and science research needs to be considered in exploratory, and not simply instrumental, ways. One approach to accomplish this goal is to design better means for students to access such riches within their increasingly professional and professionalized training. We need to stop telling students that it's an either/or scenario: either poetry or job security. Instead, we need to create more and better opportunities for students to realize the relevance of poetry to professional studies, to economic growth, and to employment opportunities, not to mention the relevance of economics to poets! We can do this while still arguing for the *intrinsic* worth of both poetry and economic theory to vibrantly democratic societies. The key to making such opportunities available, we believe, is to increase collaborative efforts – in planning and teaching – among us academics and within our own institutions. The more *we* plan, teach, and share classrooms, the more we can extend the benefits of immanent relational pedagogy and the riches of a broadly exploratory education to our graduates.

ACKNOWLEDGMENTS

We would like to express our gratitude to Dr Ann-Barbara Graff, then dean of Arts and Science at Nipissing University, for all her support in developing and launching the first iteration of our interdisciplinary concept course, as well as to all our guest lecturers whose contributions to the course have been for the love of teaching. Sal would like to acknowledge an eternal debt of gratitude to Drs Game and Metcalfe, in whose classroom she was an undergraduate student in the mid-1990s, at the time they began dreaming their collaborative classes into being. We would also like to acknowledge the fabulous design work that was done by Carol Szabicot and the internal marketing team at Nipissing University in producing the unique posters that were used to promote the five interdisciplinary analysis course offerings. (The colour versions of these posters can be found at http://justcurriculum.nipissingu.ca.)

NOTES

1 Spring semester courses at Nipissing University are offered four days per week, each session three hours long, over six weeks. This is the equivalent of a full-year credit. Fall/winter courses are offered in three-hour blocks, once per week, for thirteen weeks.

2 "Post-structuralism" is a term used primarily within Anglo circles to refer to a group of largely French theorists who came to prominence in the 1970s and 80s. Scholars such as Jacques Derrida, Michel Foucault, Gilles Deleuze, and Félix Guattari, as well as French feminists Hélène Cixous, Luce Irigaray, and Julia Kristeva, have all, at different times, been given the post-structuralist moniker. In general terms, these thinkers have been labelled post-structuralist because of the ways in which they address the structuralist positions prevalent in the 1950s and 60s. Where structuralists such as Claude Levi-Strauss in anthropology and Ferdinand de Saussure in linguistics sought out the essential underlying structures that determine human culture, post-structuralists took a decidedly more political approach.

If the structuralist seeks out a larger structural foundation that is consistent and unchanging, the post-structuralist approaches structure as historical, contingent, and shaped by power relations.

3 The terms "immanence" and "transcendence" have a long philosophical history, one that moves from theological uses to secular Western metaphysics. In contemporary continental thought, Gilles Deleuze has led the turn away from transcendental conceptions of knowledge and towards immanence. Immanence, for our purposes, refers to ways of thinking and learning that "remain within," that occur always in context, in relation, as opposed to transcendental knowledge, which is determined "from outside" with absolute objectivity. Immanent relational ethics, as we will explore in more detail throughout but particularly in the section "The Philosophy of Co-Teaching," begins with the idea of human relations as inextricably entangled.

4 Deleuze & Guattari (1987) use the image of a rhizome (a plant stem that puts out roots and shoots from its nodes as it spreads) to illustrate a philosophy that allows multiple entry and exit points. Rhizomatic learning therefore implies the acknowledgement that learners approach the learning space from diverse contexts; what they take away from a learning environment is often rhizomatic as well (as opposed to linear).

5 Binary dualisms are a key organizing structure of Western thought (Derrida, 1976; Cixous, 1976; Cixous & Clement, 1986). Within the dynamic of a binary dualism, one term, for instance, "man," is held up as the ideal term, while the second, "woman" serves as its "other." Meaning and value are created through an oppositional logic where "man" is affirmed as the ideal through the "othering" of woman. This logic is seen by theorists to function across a range of such pairings, from culture and nature (Haraway, 1988) to Western and Orient (Said, 1979). In dualist logic, difference is often viewed as deficient, and thus to be othered is to be devalued. In Levinasian and feminist critiques of this dynamic, the "other" is transformed from a position of loss to one of possibility. Rather than othering in order to affirm one's own authoritative position, Levinas and feminists such as Cixous find emancipation in otherness. The other, for Levinas, precedes the self and is the path to the infinite (Levinas, 1987). For Cixous, the otherness of relationality makes life and jouissance possible (Cixous & Clement, 1986). Immanent otherness as a pedagogical concept, therefore, refers to the idea that classrooms can be organized to transform the self–other relation from one of dominance and exclusion to one of fecund relationality.

6 The term "wicked problem," originally used in the 1960s in relation to intractable problems in social planning, has come to refer more broadly

to problems the complexity of which call for collaboration between vastly different stakeholders. They are typically problems that resist easy resolution, and while they can be experienced locally, such as homelessness in a particular city, they are often also simultaneously global: urban homelessness, for example, is a problem across the world. Other examples might include entrenched global poverty, climate change, mass extinction, deforestation, food security, and genetically modified organisms (GMOs). The complexity of these vast problems invites, in fact demands, interdisciplinary collaboration (see Brown, Harris, & Russell, 2010).

7 While Game and Metcalfe have pioneered a relational model of collaborative teaching with very large numbers, upwards of 300 students, our course is much more intimate. The average class size for all iterations of the interdisciplinary concept course has been twenty-five, and while we are intrigued by the possibilities of extending the size, we will also be attentive to the potential relational losses that we fear will come with larger numbers.

REFERENCES

Brown, V., Harris, J., & Russell, J. (2010). *Tackling wicked problems: Through the transdisciplinary imagination*. New York, NY: Routledge.

Buber, M. (1996). *I and thou*. New York, NY: Touchstone. (Original work published 1937)

Cixous, H. (1976). The laugh of the Medusa. K. Cohen & P. Cohen (Trans.). *Signs (Chicago, Ill.)*, *1*(4), 875–93. http://dx.doi.org/10.1086/493306

Cixous, H. (1992). Grace and innocence. In *Readings: The poetics of Blanchot, Joyce, Kafka, Kleist, Lispector and Tsvetayeva* (pp. 28–73). V.A. Conley (Ed. & Trans.). New York, NY: Harvester Wheatsheaf.

Cixous, H., & Calle-Gruber, M. (1997). *Rootprints: Memory and life writing*. E. Prenowitz (Trans.). London, UK: Routledge.

Cixous, H., & Clement, C. (1986). *The newly born woman*. B. Wing (Trans.). Minneapolis, MN: University of Minnesota Press.

Deleuze, G., & Guattari, F. (1987). *A thousand plateaus: Capitalism and schizophrenia*. B. Massumi (Trans.). London, UK: Continuum.

Derrida, J. (1976). *Of grammatology*. G. Spivak (Trans.). Baltimore, MD: John Hopkins University Press.

Game, A., & Metcalfe, A. (2009). Dialogue and team teaching. *Higher Education Research & Development*, *28*(1), 45–57. http://dx.doi.org/10.1080/07294360802444354

Grosz, E. (2005). *Time travels: Feminism, nature, power*. Durham, NC: Duke University Press. http://dx.doi.org/10.1215/9780822386551

Haraway, D. (1988). Situated knowledges: The science question in feminism and the privilege of partial perspective. *Feminist Studies*, *14*(3), 575–99. http://dx.doi.org/10.2307/3178066

Hothem, T. (2013). Integrated general education and the extent of interdisciplinarity: The University of California Merced's Core 1 curriculum. *Journal of General Education*, *62*(2–3), 84–111. http://dx.doi.org/10.1353/jge.2013.0016

Levinas, E. (1987). *Time and the other* (Rev. ed.). Pittsburg, PA: Duquesne University Press.

MacDonald, M. (2014, April). The subject was dirt: Nipissing's first undergrad interdisciplinary course. *University Affairs*, *55*(4), 23–7.

Moran, J. (2010). *Interdisciplinarity* (2nd ed.). New York: Routledge.

Nussbaum, M. (2010, October 17). Cultivating the imagination. *The New York Times*. Retrieved from http://www.nytimes.com/roomfordebate/2010/10/17/do-colleges-need-french-departments/cultivating-the-imagination

Robinson, K. (2011). *Out of our minds: Learning to be creative* (2nd ed.). West Sussex, UK: Capstone.

Said, E. (1979). *Orientalism*. New York, NY: Random House.

Segarra, M. (Ed.). (2009). *The portable Cixous*. New York, NY: Colombia University Press.

Shailer, K. (2005, July). *Interdisciplinarity in a disciplinary universe: A review of key issues.* The Working Paper Series, presented to the Academic Colleagues of the College of Ontario Universities. Retrieved from http://legacy.wlu.ca/documents/8216/Interdisciplinarity_final_Shailer.pdf

3 Undisciplined Debate: Coursing through Dialogue

SUSAN SRIGLEY AND SARAH FIONA WINTERS

An Invitation to a Conversation

In October 2011, Sarah Winters attended an Arts and Science Council meeting at Nipissing University at which two colleagues, Nathan Colborne from the Department of Religions and Cultures and Herminio Teixeira from Political Science, gave a presentation on the "dialogue course" they were teaching. These dialogue courses were an initiative of our dean at the time, Craig Cooper, and Nathan and Herminio were two of the first faculty to act on it. They had brought their disciplinary expertise together to create a new course, Religion and Politics, and in their presentation they talked about how to "woo" a fellow faculty member with whom you might like to teach. Sarah enjoyed this evocation of the language of courtship, but she had no such faculty member in mind, nor any idea of what course she might like to teach.

Susan Srigley was also at the dialogue course presentation, and she had previously co-taught a course, Ideas of Love, several times at Thorneloe University (Laurentian). For that course, the two professors were from the same discipline (religious studies), and Susan's co-teaching colleague was male. Analysing the story of Abélard and Héloïse from the perspective of both genders became an intense debate and one that always delighted the students. Sarah had also had previous experience team teaching: in 2006, her first year at Nipissing, she was assigned to the six-credit, first-year English course Introduction to English Studies, which at the time was team taught by four faculty members. While she found teaching her portion of the lectures intimidating, she found listening to her colleagues' lectures illuminating. But it had been several years since the department had reorganized its program, and she had not co-taught since. The Nipissing dialogue courses sounded different from both these experiences, however, structured as they were around a conversation between two people from two disciplines. As the invitation to the follow-up workshop on the courses put it:

> [R]epresenting the diversity of perspectives in our own lectures and encouraging the expression of a variety of outlooks among our students does not quite match the intensity of a discussion with a colleague whose expertise in another field brings insight, disagreement, and genuine interdisciplinarity to a course. (Dialogue Workshop, 2012, p. 7)

That workshop took place in February 2012, during the same semester that Sarah was teaching in a classroom in which the course scheduled right before hers was Religion and Literature: Flannery O'Connor. Sarah knew the professor for this course, Susan, mostly by sight and reputation only, although she had seen her present on women mystics a few years previously. Sarah and Susan exchanged some pleasantries during the ten-minute interval between courses, while Susan packed up after her lecture and Sarah set up for hers. Nathan and Herminio's presentation came back to Sarah: the most important element of a dialogue course, they had emphasized, was your relationship with the other instructor – the chemistry. Sarah was finding the pleasantries to indeed be pleasant, and something told her that Susan would be a very easy colleague to "click" with in terms of potential co-teaching.

Sarah had for some years been wondering how to teach a course on the Bible as literature at Nipissing. The advertisement for the position that she had been hired for had listed that particular field alongside children's literature, but there was no such course on the books when she arrived, and the time had never been right to create one. She had taught such a course only once before: The Bible and Literature at the University of Toronto in 2000. Because her background was in literature and religion, she wanted to teach a course like that again. Who better to teach it with than the professor who taught religion and literature? In the end, her approach at wooing was not that premeditated a moment: as Susan packed up one day halfway through the term, Sarah simply blurted out something along the lines of "Would you maybe be interested in teaching a dialogue course with me on the Bible as literature?" It was not much of a formal wooing, but Susan agreed to the proposition at once.

The Bible: Religion versus Literature

The faculty in the Department of Religions and Cultures had always wanted to develop a course on the Bible: students were clamouring for new courses, and many of them had expressed a desire to see further studies in biblical texts and traditions. But as a relatively small department with courses focused on religion and culture, and no biblical scholars among us, a traditional biblical studies course was not an option. Other than our course Gender, Sex and the Bible, we lacked a course devoted to the study of the Bible itself and its cultural and literary role in Western civilization.

One of the primary challenges in teaching biblical texts to undergraduate students is their general lack of historical knowledge. Teaching the Bible in religious studies at the university level means introducing students to the academic study of religion: studying the Bible is not the same as a Bible study. Students need to become familiar with the history of the texts; the languages, culture, and geography; issues of translation; and the theological debates surrounding their inclusion into the canon. In Susan's experience teaching religion, students are either acquainted with the texts through a faith tradition, or they do not know any biblical history and tradition at all. For religious students, studying the Bible as an ancient text with a dramatic history and in conversation with biblical criticism can be a challenging experience, and may be felt as a potential threat to their faith. The non-religious students might be equally suspicious about studying the Bible, although for different reasons. In either case – whether a student is religious or not – the problem is a predetermined view of the texts.

One of the best thinkers Susan has used to help students approach the biblical texts more openly is the Jewish philosopher Martin Buber (2000), who wrote extensively on the Bible and produced his own translations of the Hebrew Bible. Buber instructs his readers on the beauty of biblical poetry, and he tries to evoke the awe of an encounter in reading it. In Buber's approach, the reader is not simply an observer or a listener, but a participant: "Do not believe anything a priori; do not disbelieve anything a priori. Read aloud the words written in the book in front of you; hear the word you utter and let it reach you" (p. 5). Buber maintains that reading the Bible is in itself a dialogue in that the reader encounters and relates to the text, the other, and God. But this requires, says Buber, the reader's willingness to open up to what is there: "He must read the Jewish Bible as though it were something entirely unfamiliar, as though it had not been set for him ready-made. He must face the Book with a new attitude as something new" (p. 5).

While the academic study of the Bible can sometimes appear to be difficult, or feel confusing for students of faith, Buber's argument suggests a scholarly process of reading the texts in a richer and more participatory way, rather than simply inheriting the stories as something to be believed. The idea of active participation – including questioning and doubt – in religion is an extremely compelling concept to students who have a religious background, and also for those who don't. Instructors want to find a way to make the texts meaningful and real to students so that the texts speak to them where they are. It is no surprise then that students can sometimes find their way to reading the Bible more easily through their love of Harry Potter, or music, or art. One of our texts, *The Writing on the Wall: High Art, Popular Culture and the Bible* by Maggi Dawn (2012), provides examples of more accessible cultural routes, whether the students are religious or not, to the biblical stories that feed and inspire more contemporary ones. The concept for our course as a study of the Bible focused on the Bible's cultural reverberations and allowed us to help students with little or no biblical background move from the contemporary cultural icons that they recognized back to the biblical texts themselves and their history. Regardless of the students' biblical backgrounds, the reading of the texts in this way made them new and often surprising.

The English Department was intrigued to hear that Sarah was proposing a dialogue course, but both intrigued *and* pleased that it was to be on the Bible. It is commonplace to hear English faculty lament the ignorance of biblical stories, imagery, and ideas among our students, an increasing number of whom appear to have been brought up without any formal exposure to this text. While it is also commonplace to bewail a lack of knowledge of Greek myths, at least our students can take a course in such from the classical studies program. Years ago, Nipissing had offered a Bible as Literature course, but when the faculty member who taught it left, a corresponding gap was left in the program.

Northrop Frye (1982) has called the Bible a "huge, sprawling, tactless book sit[ting] there inscrutably in the middle of our cultural heritage" (p. xviii) and the "imaginative framework … within which Western Literature has operated down to the eighteenth century and is to a large extent still operating" (p. xi). While nothing can compensate for a childhood and adolescence immersed in this imaginative framework, formal instruction in it is better than no exposure at all. As an example of the latter, Sarah offers the following anecdote. She teaches a class for non-majors on the Harry Potter books, and in one lecture she presented a series of quotations in the form of a quiz, as in "Who said this?" Almost all of her seventy students knew that the answer for "THEN YOU SHOULD HAVE DIED! ... DIED RATHER THAN BETRAY YOUR FRIENDS, AS WE WOULD HAVE DONE FOR YOU!" was the character Sirius Black (Rowling 2000, p. 275), but not one of them knew that the answer for "Greater love hath no man than this, that a man lay down his life for his friends" was Jesus Christ (John 15:13, King James Version). Yet clearly the former text, now a not insignificant part of the imaginative framework within which Western literature is operating and will continue to operate for some time, is written from and within the biblical framework. As Rowling herself has said of *Harry Potter and the Deathly Hallows*:

> They're very British books, so on a very practical note Harry was going to find biblical quotations on tombstones ... But I think those two particular quotations he finds on the tombstones ... sum up, they almost epitomize, the whole series. (Rowling, quoted in Petre, 2007, n.p.)

The trouble with having to identify and explain allusions is that one is left with less time to analyse the work that those allusions do in the text, or the questions they invite. For example, in the case of Sirius, what does it say about his character that his own death takes place in a battle rather than as a pure self-sacrifice?

The Bible is important to the study of English literature as more than just a source of allusions, however; it is also important as a source of methodology. In one of the course lectures, Sarah was able to bring up for the students the definition of the term "hermeneutics," defined by *The Oxford Dictionary of Literary Terms* as:

> The theory of interpretation, concerned with general problems of understanding the meanings of texts. Originally applied to the principles of exegesis in theology, the term has been extended since the 19th century to cover broader questions in philosophy and criticism. (Baldick, 2008)

On the same PowerPoint slide she showed them the same publication's definition of "exegesis":

> The interpretation or explanation of a text. The term was first applied to the interpretation of religious scriptures (or oracles and visions), but

> has been borrowed by literary criticism for the analysis of any poetry or prose. Literary scholars have likewise inherited some of the procedures of biblical exegesis, for instance the decoding of allegories (see typology). (Baldick, 2008)

(Since the lecture was on typology, the "see typology" moment was one of the most satisfying Sarah had ever experienced as a lecturer.) The discipline of literary studies is historically entwined with the interpretation of the Bible, and all English literature students should know that. As Sal Renshaw and Renée Valiquette argue in their chapter in this volume:

> Deep interdisciplinarity, as we understand it, begins with the recognition that the disciplines themselves carry debts to a multitude of others, whether or not these debts are acknowledged, and that disciplinary borders have always been leaky. (Chapter 2, p. 38)

For Sarah, this was perhaps the most deeply interdisciplinary moment of teaching in the course.

In effect, while the dialogue courses are a form of interdisciplinary teaching, enhancing student learning alongside other forms of co-teaching such as the interdisciplinary pilot courses taught by Renshaw and Valiquette at Nipissing University, they offer a distinctly dialogic approach to student learning. Co-teaching the course as professors from different disciplines certainly enhances the student experience: students in all of Nipissing's dialogue courses witness the flexibility between disciplinary boundaries and are introduced to new ways of reading and approaching the texts. More significantly, however, we believe that the students are able to access a deeper level of educative experience by participating in a class where two scholars pursue the study of a subject through conversation.

Two interconnected levels of dialogue happen in the course we teach: the dialogic approach we take in the classroom between both professors/disciplines and the students, and the dialogue that occurs between Sarah and Susan as we teach and learn together. A finding from the study by Bacharach, Washut Heck, and Dahlberg (2008) that "[f]aculty unanimously report having had an enriching experience in which they learned new material and instructional strategies" (p. 15) was certainly our experience. One of the most memorable examples of this experience came during a class late in the term. Sarah was showing a video clip of Boney M performing "Rivers of Babylon" while teaching the Psalms. As she explained some of the verses that had been redacted from the song, we looked more closely at Psalm 137 to discover what had been changed in the lyrics. Susan had been working on a talk she was invited to give at the University of Notre Dame, and there was a line in a Flannery O'Conner story she was discussing about a child's head being smashed upon a rock, precisely the line that had been excised from the "Rivers of Babylon" song. The discussion of the Psalms and Boney M with the students led to a new connection and insight for Susan's research and her interpretation of a Flannery O'Connor story. But the revelation in that class was not just Sarah and Susan's; the students also experienced it alongside us, and they were, we think, just as transformed by it. They were able to see how inquiry draws us out, the ways research can deepen and how it occurs, and where new ideas can take us. Hence the data from the previously cited Bacharach et al. 2008 study also recognizes that co-teaching significantly increases student participation.

Educator and philosopher Paulo Freire explains that in dialogic pedagogy

> [k]nowledge of the object to be known is not the sole possession of the teacher, who gives knowledge to the students in a gracious gesture. Instead of this cordial gift of information to students, the object to be known is put on the table *between* the two subjects of knowing. They meet around it and through it for mutual inquiry. (Shor & Freire, 1987, p. 99)

Our approach in the class was never presented as simply two disciplinary takes on the subject of the Bible. The very mode of the course was exploratory, so that the different disciplinary approaches by the professors allowed for a greater investigative scope into the subject. Freire maintains that despite the idea of "mutual inquiry" of teacher and student as "two subjects of knowing," the educator must nonetheless have considerable knowledge of the subject, and thus disciplinary knowledge is always a necessary starting point for dialogic pedagogy. But just as "knowledge of the object to be known is not the sole possession of the teacher," we would also argue that neither is it the sole possession of the discipline. This insight refers to our experience of the special dialogic nature of co-teaching with a colleague from another discipline. While Susan is trained in the discipline of religious studies and brings that knowledge base to the course, her interactions with

Sarah, both inside and outside the classroom discussions, challenged her assumptions of knowledge of the texts we were studying and teaching, and vice versa. Thus, while the premise of the course was originally conceived as a discussion of the subject matter from the perspective of two disciplines, the disciplinary boundaries were themselves perpetually challenged by our openness to thinking within each other's disciplines alongside the students.

Creative Conflicts: Planning the Course

In chapter two of this volume, Renshaw and Valiquette write:

> For us, co-planning is not only made possible by a long-standing, interpersonal relation, it is also made more meaningful and more effective. The co-planning of the concept course would not have happened were it not for a foundation of deep and continuous relation, built on a shared background in post-structuralist theory, and our fifteen years of collaboration and co-teaching in the interdisciplinary gender equality and social justice program at Nipissing University. (Chapter 2, p. 41)

For us, the process was very different: we hardly knew each other before we started planning the course, we were from different disciplines, and we didn't share a particular theoretical framework apart from interpretation of texts through close reading. In our case, a friendship emerged from the course rather than the other way around. Our creation and co-teaching of this course had not been previously informed by any research in the scholarship of teaching and learning, and any theoretical conceptions of what was happening emerged out of the experience of the class itself.

When we sat down in the summer of 2013 to plan the course, we immediately ran into our first and last two conflicts. The first conflict concerned the title of the course: Sarah wanted to call it The Bible as Literature. Susan pointed out that the word "literature" immediately made it a literature course, not a dialogue one, and that she wanted to include a lot of art and religious practice. Sarah saw the logic of this argument and accepted the alternative title, The Bible as Cultural Text. The second conflict was more serious: which translation of the Bible would we assign for the course? As an English professor, Sarah wanted the King James or Authorized Version (KJV) of 1611, the version that has informed the words of almost every literary text written in the following three centuries. Indeed, for some time Sarah had wanted to offer a course not on the Bible *and* literature, as she had done at the University of Toronto, but on the Bible *as* literature, in particular the King James Bible as literature. However, Susan argued for the New Revised Standard Version (NRSV) as both a more scholarly edition and a more accessible and accurate conveyer of the Bible's content for our students. In the end, this decision yielded one of the best aspects of our lectures, as Sarah would often place a few verses from the NRSV on one side of a PowerPoint slide and the same verses from the KJV on the other side, and invite students to comment on the poetic effects of the two different translations. For example, she followed the juxtaposition of the NSRV's "The light shines in the darkness, and the darkness did not overcome it" and the KJV's "And the light shineth in darkness; and the darkness comprehended it not" (John 1:5) with a slide on the various meanings of "comprehend" from *The Oxford English Dictionary*. Such an approach ended up being more appropriate to the discipline of English literature than using only the KJV would have been.

But this approach also ended up being more appropriate to the dialogic nature of the course, as Sarah realized later upon reading Richard Dawkins on the King James Bible. In an opinion piece for *The Guardian*, Dawkins (2012) argued that every state school in the United Kingdom should possess a King James Bible on the grounds of its glorious language, declaring, "A native speaker of English who has never read a word of the King James Bible is verging on the barbarian." But his next argument represented a continuation of his usual anti-theist position in his claim that children should read all the violent stories in the Bible in order to put them off religion for good: "'Sophisticated' theologians (what is there in 'theology' to be sophisticated about?) now treat these horrors as parables or myths, which is just as well." What is there in theology to be sophisticated about? One might as well ask, What is there in literature to be sophisticated about? Using a scholarly and accurate translation such as the NRSV allowed Susan to bring her theological sophistication to the subject matter more easily than using the KJV, glorious record and source of seventeenth-century English that it is.

In general, course planning went smoothly. For the evaluation scheme, we decided on an in-class essay, a midterm test, an essay, a final exam, and a participation mark. We agreed to each grade half the students for the test and the other half for the in-class essay, but to both grade all students' final essays. The students' initial reaction to this scheme was one of alarm: would they be graded fairly? We were able to tell them when we handed back their essays that for almost all the essays we graded, we were only 2 per cent apart in our final grade. Thus if one of us gave an essay a 70 per cent and the other a 72 per cent, the essay received a grade of 71 per cent. This similarity in grading was one of the confidence-boosting aspects of the course for the instructors; it reassured us that, however subjective the grading of essays can seem to be in the humanities, a certain objectivity is inherent in the grading too. Each student also received back two sets of final comments, as well as two marked-up copies of the graded essay. This richness in evaluative feedback was one of the great advantages of the course for students. We were able to do this double grading because the course was capped at forty students. (When we first submitted our plan to the dean's office, we were told our cap was eighty students. Upon responding to the dean that our predecessors, Nathan and Herminio, had their course capped at forty students and that faculty had been encouraged to take on the dialogue courses with the promise that all requirements for extra resources would be met, our cap was brought down to forty. In retrospect, this interaction foreshadowed the current institutional attitude towards the initiative.)

The choice of readings and creation of the coursepack seemed effortless. The planning for the actual lectures took place every week, and our delivery methods varied. Sometimes we each took ninety minutes of the three-hour lecture; sometimes we timed it carefully in advance so that we would each speak for about fifteen minutes before swapping. Interestingly, perhaps surprisingly, a few students expressed dislike of this latter approach, claiming that it was "confusing" to see us swap the lectern so often. While we each always knew what the other would be talking about, we didn't always know what she would say, thus allowing us to experience the pleasure of being a student in the other's classroom – albeit perhaps the most opinionated and talkative of students. Our PowerPoint digital slideshow presentations, which we would sometimes keep separate and sometimes merge, ended up being quite long at times: our record is ninety-seven slides focusing on the books of the prophets and history.

We did not tailor our part of the lectures to the students from outside of our discipline at all, each trusting the other's lectures to do that. Both of us agreed that we learned almost as much from the other's lectures as the students did. In Sarah's case, the lectures filled a gap caused by her own lack of formal education in religious studies. She grew up Catholic and then wrote her PhD dissertation on the Christian poetry of John Donne, George Herbert, Christina Rossetti, and Gerard Manley

Hopkins; consequently, she picked up some theology and history of Christianity in the process, but she had never been taught religion in a classroom after high school. One of the elements new to Sarah that Susan brought to the course was her knowledge of Judaism; for example, while Sarah's lecture on Abraham and Isaac focused on the way that story was used by Wilfred Owen for his sonnet "The Parable of the Young Man and the Old," Susan's lecture on the story illuminated the differences between the Jewish and the Christian interpretations (and she also presented Islam's interpretation).

Susan also contributed to deepening Sarah's appreciation of the Bible by introducing the visual element. The cultural texts that Sarah taught were either written (fiction and poetry) or musical (*Joseph and the Amazing Technicolour Dreamcoat, Jesus Christ Superstar*, Madonna's "Like a Prayer"). Susan brought in images ranging from the catacombs of Rome and the facades of cathedrals to medieval and renaissance paintings to, especially, the modernist paintings of Marc Chagall. Before the course, Sarah had a superficial knowledge of this painter; now she not only knows his work, she knows the Bible better through his work. Susan also introduced Sarah (and no doubt some students) to the rich world of podcasts on religious themes (Sarah's favourite was Joe Carter on the legacy of the African-American spiritual) and to current big names in religion, such as Cornel West and Nadia Bolz-Weber, through the use of videotaped speeches and interviews. Since Sarah brought in fanvids, introducing Susan to a whole new world of fandom and its connections to religious adoration and worship, we were both exposed to the other's use of YouTube in lectures and ended up giving the inaugural lecture for Nipissing University's Centre for Interdisciplinary Collaboration in the Arts and Sciences (CICAS) on "You Teach? YouTube!" in September 2014.

Sarah loved all of Susan's arts connections and related readings during the lectures, as did the students, and Susan loved all of Sarah's poetry and language analysis. But Sarah did have one disappointing revelation. Our in-class essay gave the students two sections in which they had to write on a selected topic: one section gave them a choice between some lines from Rossetti's "Goblin Market" and some from the Old Testament book of Isaiah; the other gave them a choice between Blake's and Chagall's paintings of *Moses and the Burning Bush*. Almost without exception, students wrote better answers on the images than on the texts, a result that made Sarah reflect wryly on the future of her discipline.

Debating Jesus

Since one debate clearly stood out as a highlight of the course, and because it offers a concrete example of our approach to teaching the dialogue course, we will outline our experience of an in-class debate that we orchestrated on the topic of the two natures of Jesus, as drawn from the biblical texts. One week, during planning for our lecture, Sarah suggested that we have a debate. The pedagogy preceded the content here: Sarah did not know what our debate would be about; she just thought it would be entertaining for the students, while at the same time modelling what academics in the humanities do. *They Say, I Say: The Moves that Matter in Academic Writing* by Gerald Graff (2013) is now an assigned textbook for Nipissing's academic writing courses, and a debate is a live version of "You say, I say." Disagreeing with each other courteously, while enjoying ourselves, was another way to model for students what we want to see them do in class and in their essays.

The topic for the debate arose from its timing in a lecture on the Gospels: Is the Jesus of the Gospels Human or Divine? The debate over that question comprises a large part of the history of Christianity, and was thus a suitable topic in which Susan could engage. Debates over whether any element of a literary text is either *a* or *b* also comprises a large part of the history of literary criticism, and was thus, similarly, a suitable topic in which Sarah could engage. We realized that we could debate this topic, then point out to students that orthodox Christianity decided on "both" as the answer, while literary criticism often responds to any "either/or" question with a "both/and" celebration of ambiguity.

Having decided on the topic of the debate, we then had to pick sides. Both of us were willing to argue either side, but we settled on Susan arguing for the human and Sarah for the divine. This decision was surely the right one, as students might well have expected us to take the opposite stances based on our disciplines.

We decided to structure the debate as follows: Susan would frame it with the history of the debate in Christianity, including the Apollinarian, Nestorian, and Monophysite heresies; then she would make her argument with slides for Jesus being human, followed by Sarah presenting her argument with slides for Jesus being divine. Next we would each stand at a lectern with only our Bibles in front of us, face each other, and argue. At the end of the debate, we would invite students to join in, and then Susan would complete the framing by showing the

Figure 3.1. Co-instructors Srigley and Winters engaged in the formal debate session. Photo by Jeff Scott, Schulich School of Education, Nipissing University.

conclusions of the debate in the history of Christianity. The whole exercise was planned to take about an hour, with the debate proper occupying half of that time. We were both nervous about this plan since it involved the situation "You bring up a passage and interpret it according to your position, and I will respond; then I will bring up a passage, and you will respond," and we did not know in advance which passages the other would bring up. This leap into the unknown was like a combination of improvised theatre and an oral PhD examination (see Figure 3.1).

Once Sarah had agreed to argue the "divine" position, she had to choose whether to argue that Jesus was God or *a* god. She picked the latter as far more appropriate for both her discipline in general and her research in particular. While literary criticism could explore the Gospels to examine if the text presents Jesus as the God of both the Judaism that precedes the text and the Christianity that proceeds from it, such interpretation is more suited to a theologian or a historian of religion.

Examining the Gospels for the construction of Jesus as *a* god, however, draws upon ideas not just from theology and religious history but also from comparative mythology and archetypal criticism. Moreover, Sarah's research within the field of children's literature centres on the mythopoeic literature of J.R.R. Tolkien, C.S. Lewis, and J.K. Rowling, all three of whom create heroes who combine Christ-like divinity with the numinous qualities of other myths, such as those of Norse, Celtic, and Greek traditions. The arguments Sarah marshalled to present her case that Jesus in the Gospels is a god like Dionysius or Balder are the same arguments she uses to argue that Aslan and Harry are gods like Dionysius, Balder, and Jesus.

One student objected to this approach, writing in the course evaluations: "It would have been nice to hear about the actual Divine side of the debate, not just god." The student did not give reasons for this request, but we assumed that either the student was interested in theology and wanted a religious studies approach rather than a literary one, or the student was a Christian. One of Sarah's slides for the lecture concerned C.S. Lewis's letter to his friend Arthur Greeves in which he recounted his 1931 conversation with J.R.R. Tolkien. Lewis (already a theist but not yet a Christian) asked Tolkien (a devout Catholic) why he should believe in Christ. Tolkien replied by pointing out that Lewis was profoundly moved by the dying god (Balder, Adonis, Bacchus) in myth, and that

> the story of Christ is simply a true myth: a myth working on us in the same way as the others but with this tremendous difference that it *really happened* and one must be content to accept it in the same way. (quoted in Hooper, 2004, p. 977)

Sarah then quoted Lewis's later comment on "Christianity as myth":

> I myself, who first seriously read the New Testament when I was, imaginatively and poetically, all agog for the Death and Rebirth pattern and anxious to meet a corn-king … [saw that] one moment particularly stood out. A "dying God" – the only dying God who might possibly be historical – holds bread, that is, corn, in His hand and says "This is my body." (Lewis, 1947, p. 183)

By framing her argument in this way, Sarah hoped to make it clear that reading Christ as *a* god was one way of reading him as God. But perhaps that particular student found her approach heretical.

Susan guided the students through art and scripture to make a case that Jesus was human rather than divine. For example, she used a painting by Hans Holbein of the dead Christ (see Figure 3.1), which nearly broke the faith of Russian novelist Fyodor Dostoevsky, to argue for Jesus's human nature. Illustrating her arguments with this painting and others, Susan took students through all the biblical texts in which Jesus's human characteristics are displayed, including his anger at the money changers in the Temple (Matthew 21:12), references to him growing in years and wisdom (Luke 2:52), and especially his suffering and death on the cross (Matthew 27:50). She concluded with one of the most searing representations of his humanity: his anguished cry from the cross asking why God had forsaken him (Matthew 27:46).

Some students with religious backgrounds may have been familiar with the doctrinal statement that affirms the full humanity and divinity of Jesus; however, according to Susan, this creedal formulation had never been clearly stated in the Gospels, and the doctrine was the result of interpretation (hermeneutics) and debate, not to mention considerable historical drama. We think we captured something of this process in our debate, allowing the students to enter this ancient forum through some of their modern cultural lenses. To simply be told something is not the same as navigating the process of how ideas are formed. Students joined in the conversation, intrigued by the painstaking detail of the debate, with some wanting to quickly get to a conclusion that would settle the question. At one point, when a student voiced a position on the two natures that had been deemed a heresy, Susan shouted out to the student with an accusatory (yet playful) gesture, decrying her as "heretic!" and the dramatic exchange heightened.

We reminded the students that the debate itself is ancient, just as the texts are ancient. To teach the history of Christian thought requires a reimagining of the formation of the biblical writings and the controversies over their inclusion in the canon, as well as the theological debates surrounding the articulation of doctrine. In this instance, our debate on the two natures of Jesus encompassed not only an interpretation of scripture, but more significantly, the investigation of several different historical interpretations of scripture as they wrangled out a doctrinal understanding of Jesus. The students were therefore invited to participate in an ancient debate with their professors, rather than simply being presented with the biblical texts and the doctrinal position that historically won the day. Instead, they witnessed a moment from a historical epoch and experienced the evolution of biblical and theological reasoning.

During her presentation, Susan used a quotation from Gregory of Nyssa (one of the early Church Fathers responsible for the doctrine of the Trinity in the Nicene Creed) that described the manner in which the debate over interpretations of Jesus pervaded every corner of society:

> Every place in the city is full of them: the alleys, the crossroads, the forums, the squares. Garment sellers, money changers, food vendors – they are all at it. If you ask for change, they philosophize for you about generate and ungenerate natures. If you inquire about the price of bread, the answer is that the Father is greater and the Son inferior. If you speak about whether the bath is ready, they express the opinion that the Son was made out of nothing. (Placher, 1983, p. 68)

Our intention was to recreate this type of dialogue, controversy, and debate in the classroom, not just between the professors but by engaging the larger "crowd" of students. Another fascinating element in this debate, and borne out in Gregory of Nyssa's description, is that this conversation was not the specialized purview of theologians and religious leaders, nor was it confined to scholarly debates: it garnered the attention of Christians at all levels of society. The students were therefore granted an opportunity to weigh in and observe how and why these questions mattered to everyone. Students also learned that theological ideas and doctrines did not appear out of nowhere but were the subject of intense debate and argument. By participating in this debate they also gained valuable insight on how good arguments are made in essays, using the textual evidence to support their claims.

Our approach towards the debate highlights specifically the point that Shor and Freire make about dialogue in teaching:

> Dialogue is the sealing together of the teacher and the students in the joint act of knowing and re-knowing the object of study … [I]nstead of transferring the knowledge *statically*, as a fixed possession of the teacher, dialogue demands a dynamic approximation towards the object. (Shor & Freire, 1987, p. 100)

Nowhere was this point more evident in the dialogue course than when we engaged in our debate. In fact, the debate represents most clearly and literally what it means to be engaged in knowing jointly rather than transferring knowledge from professor to student. One of our strongest impressions of the class was that students seemed genuinely compelled by our ability to engage each other in discussions that took us out of our disciplines and required us to rethink our own ideas and assumptions. The "Jesus debate" became the embodiment of our weekly discussions writ large. As mentioned earlier, we did not prepare this class together, choosing instead the spontaneity of hearing each other's arguments for the first time in the company of the students. We were not limited to biblical proof texts; the Christian cultural tradition as it had unfolded was also incorporated into arguments. Hence the students experienced the tradition of biblical exegesis and – from the course title – the Bible as a cultural text; their view of the debate was expanded by the inclusion of the Bible's cultural extensions. Poetry, paintings, literature, and philosophy were incorporated into our debate. The class became participants in knowing, rather than the recipients of knowledge. By the end of the debate, the class was high spirited and their experience of learning transformed. Students wrote on the evaluations: "I loved the debate class, very interesting to gain two different perspectives" and "I loved the debate class and wish there were more classes like that one."

The debate introduced some unexpected moments for us, since our disciplinary backgrounds coloured our approach to the question. One of the most stunning instances of how our disciplines affected our reading of the Bible came when Susan realized that Sarah's interpretation of the Bible had been indelibly influenced by the canon of English literature. (She had already noticed this earlier in the course during the lectures on Genesis, in which Sarah kept referring to John Milton's *Paradise Lost.*) In this case, the poetic cultural appropriation of the Bible became the lens through which she read it. Susan's approach, on the other hand, tended to focus on an almost social-scientific reading of the biblical text, likely influenced by her graduate school's identification of the religious studies department as a social science rather than a humanities discipline. This type of disciplinary difference subsequently emerged in the debate when Sarah chose to look at the question of the divinity of Jesus in relation to the myth of the dying god in literature rather than as a theological debate with regards to Jesus's doctrinal or salvific status. It was this sort of moment that gave rise to the title for our chapter: our debate in its spontaneity and dialogue was "undisciplined" in the best possible way.

Student Reactions

Were the students happy with the course as a whole? Yes, many were. Some, however, feared the lack of disciplinary boundaries and worried about increased expectations from two professors. But the courageous knew that something special was happening and that they were learning how to know in new ways. What did the evaluations say? We were interested to know whether the dialogue courses represented a model of learning that students wanted, as well as what they had learned from our course. We asked students the question, Would you take another dialogue course? One student replied: "Hands down. Such a neat experience, and I brag to my friends about it regularly." Despite the emphasis on the proverbial "experience," this student witnessed *something* happening that wasn't just about the students, but that nonetheless gave them something to think about. "I find it really neat to see the cogs turning in one professor's brain as the other talks, looking for connections and such." This observation is a clear acknowledgment of understanding the *process* of understanding – modelled by the two professors who appeared not to be simply teachers but also co-learners. The academic conversation that we engaged in was not a mere performance; it was not a gimmick or a technique. According to another student, one of the most valuable aspects of team teaching was having "two different opinions about the material," which the student described as a kind of "constant debate." Ultimately, the students both participated in and experienced the pursuit of understanding. This experience happened because the professors were genuinely involved in the mutual effort of knowing in common.

For most of our students, The Bible as Cultural Text was their first experience of a dialogue course. Responses to this model of teaching included the following:

> "The idea of the dialogue course made the class interesting. It was great to see how the two disciplines interact with each other."
>
> "Unique and refreshing. I greatly enjoyed the dialogue between professors and the increased range in subject matter and perspectives. You two have great academic chemistry!"
>
> "Loved the two-teacher dialogue approach. Having two profs provides a lot more insight!"
>
> "I think that the dialogue course really complemented your already dynamic teaching style. I hope you will look into engaging with other disciplines in your future courses!"

Learning in and through Friendship

One theoretical understanding of co-teaching is informed by the work of Diana Glyer (2007) on collaboration within the Inklings, the group of Oxford academics and others, including C.S. Lewis and J.R.R. Tolkien, who shared ideas and drafts with each other from the early 1930s to 1949. We are not of course creative writers, but teaching draws upon some of the same skills as creative writing does; moreover, the Inklings were not just creative writers. Both Lewis and Tolkien were English professors, both were religious, and Lewis wrote and published books and articles on religion and literary criticism that are used in both our disciplines. Glyer's four categories of co-writer are resonator, opponent, editor, and collaborator. Of these, her treatment of editor and collaborator applies to the Inklings' writing to such an extent that it is difficult to apply those categories to teaching, so we focus here on the remaining two categories: resonator and opponent.

The *resonator*, defined broadly, "refers to anyone who acts as a friendly, interested, supportive audience" (p. 48). The resonator's "primary gift … is encouragement" (p. 48). This role is more important for writers than for teachers, since, as Glyer phrases it, "without it, the writer may lack the courage to start or the persistence to finish" (p. 48). The teacher, on the other hand, is contractually obliged to both start and finish, whether encouraged or discouraged by his or her students or co-teacher. Nevertheless, acting as and having a resonator constituted one of the great pleasures of the dialogue course for us both. Glyer's subcategories for resonator are praise, pressure and perseverance, the wager (friendly competition), "think of a subject" (the generation of new ideas), modelling, anticipation and accountability, practical help, and promotion. Of these, the four that apply the most directly to our experience with the dialogue course are as follows: praise, the generation of new ideas, modelling, and anticipation and accountability.

The first of these subcategories, praise, was also the most purely enjoyable. Students often withhold their praise (as well as their criticism) until they fill out the student evaluations at the end of the semester; co-teaching means instant feedback at the end (and sometimes during) a lecture. We both experienced the generation of ideas for new projects: Sarah was inspired by Susan's lecture on another O'Connor story, "Parker's Back," to think about the sacred nature of fan tattoos, such as the popular *Deathly Hallows* one of the cloak, the stone, and the wand, and from there to contemplate larger questions of fandom as a religious practice. Susan was inspired by Sarah's dramatic rendering of "Goblin Market" and her rich analysis of its biblical themes and images.

Modelling manifested itself in a somewhat amusing way, through the design of the PowerPoint slides. Up until this lecture, Sarah had used the basic template of white background with black font. She was charmed by the thought Susan put into her design, for example the use of the "Trek" design for the lectures on Exodus (the stripy yellow background evokes desert sands). Now Sarah spends time on all her PowerPoint slides for other courses, thinking through the pedagogical and aesthetic consequences of the design. (Practical help was also involved in this aspect of the course, as Susan talked Sarah through a few issues regarding the embedding of video within slides, something made rather more challenging since the former uses a Mac computer and the latter a PC running Windows). We told the students this learning of Sarah's was taking place while the course proceeded, and they enjoyed seeing us as students of each other.

Glyer's "pressure and perseverance" differs from her "anticipation and accountability" in the nature of the relationship between the collaborators. For example, in the "pressure and perseverance" model, one collaborator can become almost aggressive in putting explicit pressure on the other, as in this anecdote recorded in Tolkien's letters, and quoted by Glyer:

> "Tolkien explains that when he produced text that was not up to par, Lewis would say, 'You can do better than that. Better, Tolkien, please!' Tolkien writes 'I would try. I'd sit down and write the section over and over.'" (Glyer, 2007, p. 55)

We certainly did not speak to each other about our lectures in that way (surely that would be a disaster for most colleagues); rather, our relationship proceeded along the lines of anticipation (accountability, writing to a deadline, does not really apply to the contractual obligation of delivering a weekly lecture). Anticipation, writes Glyer, includes "working deliberately to attract certain kinds of compliments and avoid known forms of criticism" (p. 64). We had no known forms of criticism, as we did not criticize each other, but we learned that the kind of compliments we might receive from each other differed from the kind of compliments we might expect to receive from students. In the case of individual teaching, anticipation of weaker students' boredom or confusion may cause a teacher to play up the entertaining aspects at the expense of the intellectual; but the anticipation of a colleague absorbing that same teacher's lecture helps by keeping the most talented and able students (those closest to the colleague in ability) at the forefront of the teacher's mind. In other words, this kind of anticipation keeps a teacher honest.

Glyer's second category of collaboration is the *opponent*, a role exemplified most in the Inklings by C.S. Lewis who, as Glyer points out, attributed his aggressive style in arguing to his academic training. Glyer quotes Lewis writing to E.M.W. Tillyard (with whom he co-wrote the 1939 book *The Personal Heresy*):

> We have both learned our dialectic in the rough academic arena where knocks that would frighten the London literary coteries are given and taken in good part; and even where you may think me something too pert you will not suspect me of malice. If you honour me with a reply it will be in kind; and then, God defend the right! (Glyer, 2007, p. 77).

Neither of us learned our dialectic in this rough way; moreover, our gender may also differentiate us from the all-male Inklings in the matter of aggressive disagreement. However, we did model this style in our debate. It is simpler to play-act disagreement than to engage in it sincerely; so far we have found it easier to make up a disagreement than to find a real one.

The Future of Innovative and Dialogic Pedagogy

One may ask whence came the call for this kind of pedagogical innovation? What led two university professors to create a "dialogue" course shared between their disciplines? Did they want to boost enrolments or introduce an innovative pedagogy to their departments (in order to boost enrolments)? The drive to attract and retain students is indeed a persistent motivation for humanities programs at most undergraduate institutions these days. Without negating the fact that innovative pedagogy can be a very good thing for professors and students alike, the underlying drive for administrators remains financial. And a financially driven desire for educational reform often limits the real innovation that academics could be pursuing in their teaching.

There is no shortage of studies on the current state of undergraduate education. Richard Arum and Josipa Roksa's book *Academically Adrift: Limited Learning on College Campuses* highlights the persistent demand for adaptive pedagogy that meets the requisite "student experience," which is identified as primarily social. As Arum and Roksa (2011) point out: "In a recent study of undergraduate student culture at a Midwestern public university, Mary Grigsby notes that 70 percent of students reported that social learning was more important than academics" (p. 59). Without rejecting academic learning entirely, students identify it as "work" as opposed to social learning, which is "fun" (p. 59). A similar survey in Susan's classroom recently produced the same response. Increasingly these studies indicate that the onus is falling on the faculty to create programming that will address and meet student needs: "Scholarship on teaching and learning has burgeoned over the past several decades and has emphasized the importance of shifting attention from faculty teaching to student learning" (p. 131). However, recall for a moment Freire's comments about dialogic pedagogy (discussed earlier), in which he posits that student learning occurs in *conversation with* the teacher, *between* the two as a gift to mutually explore. It is not initiated or driven by the student. While a focus on student learning is not immaterial to our pursuit of innovative pedagogy in the dialogue courses, it cannot be the guiding focus. As Flannery O'Connor points out in her essay "Total Effect and the Eighth Grade," "ours is the first age in history which has asked the child what he would tolerate learning" (Fitzgerald & Fitzgerald, 1961, p. 137).

These cries for innovation in education and a renewed focus on student experience and learning are nonetheless rooted in the concern for financial stability in post-secondary education. If the students don't like what they're learning, they simply won't show up. Reduced to serving "clients" who pay for services, education understood according to this model remains subject to economic demands rather than educative ones. If it isn't "fun," the students won't come. This outlook puts remarkable pressure on faculty, who are compelled to create courses that attract students while at the same time maintain academic rigour. How do these new interdisciplinary and dialogue-style courses at Nipissing University fit into its mandate? Even though these courses continue to have high enrolments and have garnered significant student interest, administrative support remains non-committal, and in most cases the senior administration is unwilling to allow two faculty members to teach one course, no matter the cumulative benefit or appeal to students. In the standoff between innovation (which directly affects recruitment and retention) and financial efficiency, cost remains the determining factor.

Still, a number of references to the advantages of developing interdisciplinary programming at Nipissing University can be found in the final report on enrolment management and planning, *Strategic Enrolment Management Strategy and Implementation Plan*, prepared for the university by Higher Education Strategy Associates (HESA) (2015). As the report notes, "A promising approach to program innovation lies in the development of new, inter-disciplinary and inter-professional programs" (p. 37). Clearly, the report acknowledges the benefit reaped from interdisciplinary programming, even though it tends to view cross-disciplinary courses as cost-saving measures for small departments. But ultimately, the proposals of the "education strategists" (who should not be confused with educators) perpetuate the assumption that the humanities disciplines should find a way to become *useful* in post-secondary education.

Stefan Collini (2012) laments this trend in his book *What Are Universities For?* He states, "In present circumstances any invitation to *characterize* the work of scholars in the humanities is almost immediately construed as a demand to *justify* it" (p. 61). Consequently, the pedagogical motivations for interdisciplinary programming by faculty continue to be at odds with the propositions made by education strategists, evidenced by the attempt to make a humanities degree more useful by pairing it with business courses, as the following passage in the HESA (2015) document shows: "Inter-disciplinary and inter-professional programs could be helpful, too, in changing the conversation from, 'what can I do with a degree in History or English,' for example, to 'how will my degree help to prepare me for work and life in the future?'" (p. 37). No matter how much positive encouragement is given to program innovation, the bottom (economic) line remains efficiency, which invariably trumps all discussion of pedagogical worth. Every suggestion to explore interdisciplinary pedagogy in HESA's strategic enrolment report is matched by a need to monitor at the departmental and program level the "net cost per credit and net cost per student" (p. 41).

Without suggesting that costs are irrelevant to the running of a university, if we are discussing pedagogy, the primary direction must be academic. Even in that pedagogical focus, the propensity towards utility should not become the automatic recourse for justifying these courses. Innovation in learning and real experimentation in teaching cannot flourish when the goal is to minimize risk and maximize student enrolment. As Paulo Freire notes, dialogic pedagogy should not be seen as a "*mere* technique, which we can use to help us get some results" (Shor & Freire, 1987, p. 98). Nor should dialogue be understood as a "tactic we use to make students our friends. This would make dialogue a technique for manipulation instead of illumination" (p. 98).

Our dialogue course came to an end in December 2013. Since then, we have been inspired to continue collaborative work, both with each other and with other colleagues. We both took part in the SLOTH interdisciplinary course described by Renshaw and Valiquette in chapter two of this book. We each attended the other's lecture, and Sarah was able to draw upon parts of Susan's lecture for her own, since Susan's came earlier in the syllabus. Sarah also co-lectured with her English Department colleague Gyllian Phillips in the GENIUS iteration of the interdisciplinary course in Muskoka. We have both taken part in the CICAS initiative established by Ann-Barbara Graff and Pavlina Radia in 2014. We hope to teach our course The Bible as Cultural Text again in 2018 after our sabbaticals.

But will it be a dialogue course? As Jacqueline Ferguson and Jennifer Wilson write in chapter seven of this volume (citing an article by Scruggs, Mastropieri, and McDuffie [2007]), "[Co-teaching] has been discussed as most ideal when administration supports the undertaking and teachers choose their collaborative partners, are trained in collaborative techniques, and are given time to plan and discuss content and activities to be used in the classroom" (Chapter 7, p. 165). We first taught the course under three of these four ideal conditions. We had support, choice, and time, and while neither of us was trained in collaborative techniques we presumably picked some up as we went along. Three years later, however, we have lost one of those three: our administration no longer supports the undertaking of dialogue courses. We were told that the current word from above is "no collaborative teaching." Although we created the course as one that we could each teach alone, neither of us wishes to, partly because we both feel the Bible calls for at least two voices but also because we loved the pedagogical experience, and the students loved the educational experience. The future of innovative and dialogic pedagogy, the future of co-teaching, the future of collaboration in education should not be left solely in the hands of the administrators of the institution and its financial advisors. As all the voices in this collection attest, the potential good that emerges out of collaborative teaching requires at least the occasional leap of faith, as well as landing at a run that does not falter before the finish line.

REFERENCES

Arum, R., & Roksa, J. (2011). *Academically adrift: Limited learning on college campuses*. Chicago, IL: University of Chicago Press.

Bacharach, N., Washut Heck, T., & Dahlberg, K. (2008). Co-teaching in higher education. *Journal of College Teaching and Learning*, *5*(3), 9–16.

Baldick, C. (2008). *The Oxford dictionary of literary terms* (4th ed.). Oxford, UK: Oxford University Press.

Buber, M. (2000). The man of today and the Jewish Bible. In M. Buber & N. Glatzer (Eds.), *On the Bible: Eighteen studies* (pp. 1–13). Syracuse, NY: Syracuse University Press.

Collini, S. (2012). *What are universities for?* London, UK: Penguin Books.

Dawkins, R. (2012, May 19). Why I want all our children to read the King James Bible. *The Guardian*. Retrieved from https://www.theguardian.com/science/2012/may/19/richard-dawkins-king-james-bible

Dawn, M. (2012). *The writing on the wall: High art, popular culture and the Bible.* London, UK: Hodder & Stoughton.

Dialogue Workshop. (2012, January). *Newsletter, Faculty of Arts and Science, Nipissing University*. Retrieved from http://www.nipissingu.ca/academics/faculties/arts-science/Pages/Arts-and-Science-Newsletters.aspx

Fitzgerald, S. & Fitzgerald, R. (Eds.). (1961). *Flannery O'Connor: Mystery and manners—Occasional prose*. New York, NY: Farrar, Straus & Giroux.

Frye, N. (1982). *The great code: The Bible and literature.* Toronto, ON: Academic Press Canada.

Glyer, D. (2007). *The company they keep: C.S. Lewis and J.R.R. Tolkien as writers in community*. Kent, OH: Kent State University Press.

Graff, G. & Birkenstein, R. (2013). *They say / I say: The moves that matter in academic writing*. New York, NY: Norton.

Higher Education Strategy Associates (HESA). (2015). *Strategic enrolment management strategy and implementation plan, Nipissing University*. North Bay, ON: Nipissing University.

Hooper, W. (Ed.). (2004). *Collected letters of C.S. Lewis: Vol. 1. Family letters, 1905–1931*. San Francisco, CA: Harper Collins.

Lewis, C.S. (1947). *Miracles*. New York, NY: Harper Collins.

Petre, J. (2007, October 20). "J.K. Rowling: 'Christianity inspired Harry Potter.'" *The Telegraph*. Retrieved from http://www.telegraph.co.uk/culture/books/fictionreviews/3668658/J-K-Rowling-Christianity-inspired-Harry-Potter.html

Placher, W. (1983). *A history of Christian theology*. Philadelphia, PA: The Westminster Press.

Rowling, J.K. (2000). *Harry Potter and the prisoner of Azkaban*. Vancouver, BC: Raincoast.

Scruggs, T.E., Mastropieri, M.A., & McDuffie, K.A. (2007). Co-teaching in inclusive classrooms: A metasynthesis of qualitative research. *Exceptional Children*, *73*(4), 392–416. http://dx.doi.org/10.1177/001440290707300401

Shor, I., & Freire, P. (1987). What is the dialogical method? In I. Shor & P. Freire (Eds.), *A pedagogy for liberation: Dialogues on transforming education* (pp. 97–102). Westport, CT: Bergin & Garvey.

4 Forming ICE in Pre-Service Teacher Education

BLAINE E. HATT AND ROB GRAHAM

Introduction

In the late 1990s and first decade of the 2000s, England, and later Northern Ireland and Scotland, became highly focused on promoting creative and cultural education in public schools. In 1999, the British National Advisory Committee on Creative and Cultural Education (NACCCE), chaired by Sir Ken Robinson, issued a report stating that many who had contributed to the research for the study believed "that current priorities and pressures in education inhibit the creative abilities of young people and of those who teach them" (NACCCE, 1999, p. 6). In sum, creative education was envisioned as "a balance between teaching knowledge and skills, and promoting the freedom to innovate and take risks" (p. 8), and creative development was directly related to cultural education.

In 2012, TED Talks posted their top twenty most-watched videos, and Sir Ken Robinson's February 2006 talk, "Do Schools Kill Creativity?," topped the list at nearly 13.5 million views (Robinson, 2006). Now, more than a decade later, that talk has been subtitled into fifty-nine languages and internationally has had nearly thirty-one million views. Robinson has added several other popular TED Talks to his repertoire, but none have approached the views that his seminal 2006 talk generated.

Between 2002 and 2006, Blaine Hatt facilitated a course for pre-service teachers titled Creative Activities in the Classroom. As such, he was familiar with the work of Vygotsky (1930/2004), Guilford (1950, 1959), Gardner (1993), Amabile (1996, 1998), Csikszentmihalyi (1998), Michalko (1998), Runco (1986), and Runco and Pritzker (1996), among others. It was easy to add Robinson to the list of informed and informing researchers on the topic of imagination creativity education. It is worth noting that the idea espoused by Robinson – that children possess innate creative ability and/or capability – was earlier voiced by Friedrich Froebel. In the late nineteenth century, Froebel stated that this "formative and creative instinct … has existed in all children in all nations and in all ages of the world" (quoted in Quick, 1894, p. 404). Despite Froebel's contention, issues of creativity and cultural development concerning the whole of education did not gain international prominence as an educational phenomenon until the late twentieth and early twenty-first century.

It was against this background, and fortified with an ever-growing knowledge of imagination creativity education (ICE), that Hatt came to Nipissing University in the summer of 2006; in the winter of 2008 he began the process of assembling a team of colleagues from within the Faculty of Education who were interested in forming ICE as an option course for pre-service teachers.

The Collaborative Process: Moving from "Me" to "We"

The team was intentionally assembled to represent a wide range of knowledge and attitudes, and a variety of curricular and cross-curricular interests. It was also important that each member could and would be genuinely committed to cross-disciplinary application of the principles and practices of imagination and creativity, and that each would be passionately committed to her or his areas of expertise and to an interconnectedness with other curricular areas. For instance, Hatt's pedagogical practice was grounded in curriculum instruction, physical education, coaching, and secondary literacy (language, literature, and multi-literacies). In addition, Hatt had extensive experience in educational leadership as a secondary school principal (grades 7–12). His experiential base and commitment to life-long learning were integral to all that he had done as an educator, and were integrative components that he brought to the process of inviting colleagues to join with him in forming the ICE team.

Anna-Marie Aquino brought onboard her strength and expertise in primary/junior division literacy and elementary educational leadership. When approached with the idea of joining a collaborative team that had the goal of forming ICE as an option course for pre-service teachers at Nipissing University, she was immediately and enthusiastically supportive. So too were Elizabeth Ashworth, Rob Graham, and Kathy Mantas.

Ashworth's background was a blend of visual arts and English language arts; Graham's expertise was in the field of technology-enhanced learning, and his extensive classroom experience was working with junior and intermediate students, including those with special needs; and Mantas's foci were in the areas of visual arts, holistic and artful education, and language arts (second language learning).

Other faculty, although not part of the original team, were consulted throughout the course of the project. In the third year, we expanded the expertise of the ICE team with the addition of Julie Corkett (literacy and special education) and Dan Jarvis (numeracy and visual arts instruction). Notwithstanding, the inaugural team consisted of five who were passionate about individual areas of instructional expertise and the connectedness of interdisciplinary teaching and learning; committed to the collaborative process of researching, designing, planning, and implementing a new option course; and highly supportive of forming ICE for the benefit of our pre-service teachers.

In our initial meeting as the ICE team, the collective power of *we* became immediately apparent. The amalgam of ideas and the shared opportunity to take an imaginative concept and craft it into an original, creative optional course were deeply engaging. The critical exploration of what might be brought an air of exhilaration to our meeting and infused our discourse with a genuine expression of candid thought and deeply held feeling. In essence, Wenger, McDermott, and Snyder's (2002) notion of a community of practice made up of individuals with a common interest and a desire to share, connect, and build on existing knowledge was being realized. Seemingly disconnected ideas or impressions flowed into a confluence of imagined potentiality. However, none of this was accomplished without effort.

One of the first challenges we encountered was co-constructing a common understanding of what imagination creativity education (ICE) meant and what it would look like in a course design. This task prompted an investigation of theories and principles surrounding imagination and creativity. Towards that end, we examined Vygotsky's (1930/2004) principles of imagination: imagination is based on experience, experience is based on imagination; emotions influence imagination, imagination influences emotions; and imagination becomes reality, reality becomes imagination. Vygotsky's principles align with and amplify Hume's theory (as cited in Streminger, 1980) that imagination is composed of three distinguishing and different functions: cognitive, aesthetic, and artistic. We further examined Gardner's (1993) theory of Big "C" creativity (creativity is limited to a few exceptional individuals); Amabile's (1996) theory of small "c" creativity (creativity resides in varying degrees within each individual); and Csikszentmihalyi's (1998) theory of flow in the psychology of discovery and invention, and its connection with the three dimensions of divergent thought – fluency, flexibility, and originality.

We then explored our professional and pedagogical orientations to teaching and learning. We soon realized that when it came to ICE, we, as facilitators, were very student-centred and endorsed a constructivist and inquiry-based approach to education. We also agreed with Freire's notion of the dialogic atmosphere (Shor & Freire, 1987, p. 99) as essential in ICE. Our research, exploration, and consensus building greatly informed the following course description for Exclusion to Inclusion: Imagination and Creativity in the 21st Century Classroom (EDUC 4286):

> EDUC 4826 is a study of imagination and creativity development for K–12 learners. It is an introduction to alternative education with a focus on the interdependent relationships among philosophy, psychology, methodology, technology, and education to inspire imaginative and creative teaching. The goal is to foster an attitude that values other ways of knowing, doing, and expressing, and to challenge the teaching world taken-for-granted. The course will offer first-hand experience including a variety of imagination and creativity activities relevant to the classroom. The course duration is 36 hours and is worth 3 credits.

In addition, and in support of the course description, we fashioned a series of learning expectations that would keep us as facilitators and our pre-service teachers focused on the goals and aspirations relating to imagination creativity education. The ethical standards for the teaching profession were also embedded in the learning expectations for this course. Furthermore, the group was mindful of the International Society for Technology in Education's (2007) *Educational Technology Standards for Students*. We combined these and other standards, and the course was built upon the following learning expectations that students would:

- Have opportunities to develop and increase skills and effectiveness as imaginative and creative educators
- Understand and implement Ministry of Education curriculum expectations and district school board policies and guidelines in a manner that meets the needs of all learners

- Create learning environments that nurture imagination, foster creativity, inspire, and engage the learner
- Identify, select, and plan education programming specifically suited to the imaginative needs and creative potential of all learners
- Recognize the integral nature of imagination and creativity in the education process
- Demonstrate a level of competency in modelling imaginative and creative pedagogical experiences for K–12 learners
- Employ the most current and effective cognitive and non-cognitive instructional methods related to education in all divisions

Clearing the Approval Hurdles for Forming ICE

We established the cornerstones and laid the foundation for our option course. Our next step was to present a proposal for the new ICE course to the Faculty of Education and obtain its support. This task necessitated additional research and careful attention to the Guidelines for Curriculum Changes in adding a course. In researching courses of a similar nature at other Canadian universities, we discovered that only three western Canadian universities offered a full or partial course focused on imagination and/or creativity. It became very obvious to us as researchers and developers of ICE that Nipissing University was in the enviable position of getting ahead of the imagination creativity wave. By adopting an option course in imagination creativity education and then expanding that course offering as a requisite for all pre-service teachers, our university could well be the vanguard in Ontario in advancing a new paradigm in education for pre-service teachers, in-service teachers, and most especially, public school students. Forming ICE for all pre-service teachers at Nipissing became for us not merely a possibility but a necessity, especially if we were to lend credence to Robinson's claim that by ignoring ICE in the classroom, schools would continue to stifle creativity.

We introduced the proposal for a new option course in October 2008 to our Faculty of Education, and a few members spoke against the implementation of ICE. We were surprised at their response, particularly since we thought that all our colleagues would be the strongest proponents of ICE. However, those who were not in favour of the proposed course generated a resistance to the introduction of imagination creativity education that we had not considered. This development was the beginning of an incredible learning experience for us as members of the team. We had launched the project with a great deal of utopianism, passion, some knowledge, and a belief that we were receptive to individual and collaborative learning. What we realized was that, whereas our team's openness was to the sort of new learning that supported our commitment to ICE, some colleagues perceived the proposed course as being potentially in opposition to such learning. We had been presented with an alternative perspective, one that reminded us that imagination and creativity were considered by some to be instinctual in all effective teaching, and hence one that challenged us to engage in deeper research, reflection, and rethinking of the foundational principles of ICE. Despite the objections, the majority of faculty voted in support of the new course proposal, and ICE was one step closer to becoming a reality.

After approval from the Faculty of Education was obtained, the proposal for the ICE option course was forwarded to Nipissing University's Academic and Regulations Curriculum Committee (ARCC) for its approval. ARCC gave approval in November, and the proposal was forwarded to the Senate Executive Committee for its review and approval before moving on to Senate. The Senate Executive Committee gave its assent in December 2008.

At the January 2009 Senate meeting, unlike what had happened at Faculty Council, there was little discussion of the motion, and no dissent was expressed. As a result, imagination creativity education (ICE) became a bona fide option course slated for implementation in the 2009–10 academic year. In announcing the results of the motion to our Faculty Council meeting participants in February 2009, our then interim dean stated: "We spend a great deal of time in this Faculty emphasizing literacy and numeracy; it's now time we focused on imagination and creativity."

Pedagogical Considerations for Implementation of ICE: The Glue that Binds Us

Once ICE had cleared all the approval hurdles, the ICE team began in earnest to finalize the course outline and prepare for implementation of the course in September 2009. A distinguishing feature of the course was the team-teaching approach that was an integral component of the instructional delivery system. As educators representing the various curricular fields of literacy, technology, fine and performing arts, we were determined that our approach to ICE would be interdisciplinary.

Our pre-service teachers would have the distinct advantage of being instructed each week by a team of educators devoted to the knowledge that students learn best and most lastingly when they experience the deeply intertwined reality of interdisciplinary, creative, hands-on, and imaginative problem-based learning.

Towards that end, we developed a series of topics that would guide us as we worked towards a realization of imagination creativity education as a pedagogy for ourselves as facilitators of ICE, for our pre-service teachers, and for the students that our pre-service teachers would have opportunity to educate during their practicum placements. The following topics were set forth:

1. The missing link: Imagination and creativity in the classroom
2. The imaginative and creative process
3. Cognitive skills: Knowing and expressing
4. Non-cognitive skills: Knowing and expressing
5. The attributes of imaginative and creative teachers and students
6. Teaching for imagination and creativity
7. Creative activities for imaginative development
8. Educational technology in the imaginative and creative classroom

In addition, we established a weekly teaching schedule that would accommodate our team-teaching approach to EDUC 4826 and highlight the unique characteristics of our collaborative approach to teaching ICE.

The idea of collaborative (team) planning, instructing, and evaluating subject areas is not new in public education. As a course of action, collaborative teaching and learning is common in primary (K–3), junior (grades 4–6), and intermediate (grades 7–10) division classes, but not as common in senior (grades 11–12) division classes, where a course-specific, or silo, mentality persists in the presentation of content or skills-based material. The same delineation of applied skills, academic content, and acquired attitudes exists at the university level.

There are certain exceptions in course offerings at the university. Some courses are offered by a team of instructors, each responsible for her or his section of the content material, which is presented individually and consecutively as a component of the overall course. However, it is highly unusual for a team of four university professors to be assigned to concurrently or collaboratively teach one course. Integral to our pedagogical approach to ICE were collaborative instruction; learning environs aligned with class activities; facilitator and learner conference sessions; open assignments; facilitated workshop sessions; and teacher, peer, and self evaluation of individual learning and course assignments. These were unique experiential-based learning techniques that we as a team offered to our pre-service teachers in the inaugural year of ICE.

To facilitate organization of the teaching component of the course, Ashworth initiated a meeting with the then interim dean and his executive assistant to discuss our preferences for teaching/timetabling the thirty-six–hour course. We, individually and collectively, were committed to collaborative learning. We believed that just as collaborative ideation and planning had resulted in the approval and implementation of the course for the 2009–10 academic year, our pre-service teachers' learning would be exponentially increased by having three or four different professors collaboratively facilitating each learning situation. Specifically, we were committed to integrating the arts, literacy, and technology into all, or at least the majority, of our classes.

Aquino would not be remaining as an on-site member of the team as she was returning to public school education and assuming the role of principal of one of the elementary schools in the local district school board. Taking the lead on our request to team-teach ICE, Ashworth received approval for the four remaining members to each be granted nine hours of instructional time for the course. Team teaching was the mode of instructional operation for ICE. Of necessity, we each put far more instructional hours and facilitation time into the course than was allotted. But that didn't matter to any of us, because we were living the realization of a unique innovation in teaching and learning for our pre-service teachers and for us as instructors. We had taken an idea from imaginative inception through creative innovation to implementation, and so time, effort, and energy were worthwhile sacrifices.

Strategic Resource Acquisitions and Promotion of ICE

Prior to the course beginning in September 2009, we, as the ICE team, focused on ways that we could more fully lay the groundwork within the university for the introduction of the course. In February 2009, we decided to pool our resources and apply for faculty funds allocated for the course print and materials budget. Once our funding was assured, we designated a certain amount for print materials and the remainder for consumable and resource materials to support the interdisciplinary activities and assignments associated with the course.

We also examined the potential of related conferences and publishing. In March 2009, we submitted a presentation to the New York State Federation of Chapters of the Council for Exceptional Children (NYS CEC) titled "Exclusion to Inclusion: Imagination and Creativity in the 21st Century Classroom" (Ashworth et al., 2009). This presentation described the following elements: the rationale for developing and implementing an option course in imagination and creativity for pre-service teachers; the process of developing the course; strategies, instructional approaches, and assessment tools; and examples of a course outline to assist in planning. In October 2009, Ashworth, Graham, and Hatt journeyed to Buffalo, New York, and introduced ICE to a large audience of international educators.

In May 2009, Mantas and Aquino introduced the course at the Ministry of Education/Faculties of Education Forum at the Ontario Institute of Studies in Education/University of Toronto (OISE/UT) conference held in Toronto, Ontario, with a similar seminar titled "Imagination and Creativity in Education" (Aquino et al., 2009). In a follow-up performance in May 2010 at the Ministry of Education/Faculties of Education Forum at the OISE/UT conference in Toronto, Mantas, Aquino, and Ashworth presented a more detailed experiential-based seminar on ICE titled "Curriculum Integration in Pre-Service Teacher Education through Imagination Creativity Education" (Aquino et al., 2010). In that same month, Mantas and Ashworth took the lead on a team submission at the Canadian Society for the Study of Education (CSSE) 2010 conference in Montreal titled "Ice-breaking the Mold of Pre-Service Teacher Education: Sharing Experiences of Creating, Implementing and Team Teaching a Course on Imagination Creativity Education (ICE)" (Mantas et al., 2010). They also presented a seminar the following year at the National Art Education Association (NAEA) in Seattle, Washington (Ashworth & Mantas, 2011). Whether the conference venue was provincial, national, or international, each seminar or presentation on ICE was well attended. The reception accorded each proffering of ICE was incredibly positive, and the feedback strengthened our resolve to continue to advance imagination creativity education in as many ways as we could envision.

In November 2008, one of us was tasked by the ICE team to write to Dr Kieran Egan, creator of the imaginative education program at Simon Fraser University, and introduce him to our newly proposed option course, Exclusion to Inclusion: Imagination and Creativity in the 21st Century Classroom. We inquired about his availability as the keynote speaker in our inaugural ICE conference slated for mid-April 2009. In his reply, Dr Egan expressed disappointment that he was unavailable, as he was scheduled to be out of the country during the month of April conducting a series of workshops, but he enthusiastically endorsed our initiative and wished us every success in our conference. While waiting for a response from Egan, we approached our university president and asked for $1500 as seed money to launch the conference, which was granted. We now had the funds necessary to initiate the conference.

We had planned the ICE conference as a launch for the optional course and as a possible fit with the centennial plans for the 2009 celebration of "100 Years of Teacher Education in North Bay and Nipissing University." The Centennial Planning Committee ultimately selected our ICE conference, titled "Infusing Imagination and Creativity into Teaching and Learning," as one of their three signature events to commemorate the centennial celebrations of teacher education. They also indicated that, as a signature event, the conference would receive special funding to help defray expenses.

The inaugural ICE conference was opened with an introduction to ICE by members of the team. In our remarks, each member of the ICE team (ICE mates) specifically addressed one of the five tenets of imagination and creativity that had emerged from our literature review, discussions, conference proposals, and ICE conference planning. Ashworth spoke to the value of collaboration and a multidisciplinary approach to ICE. Mantas posited that imagination and creativity are not qualities reserved for those in the arts, but that all educators and students possess the capabilities to develop these attributes. Aquino addressed the notion that initiatives related to literacy and numeracy have been overemphasized and that imagination creativity education is a largely unexplored and necessary domain. Graham stated that developments within the field of educational technology and the Internet offer many opportunities for educators to provide their students with engaging and relevant project-based learning experiences that develop skills related to imagination and creativity. Hatt concluded with remarks focused on accountability and efficiency as being two present-day driving forces within education that tend to discourage courses and teaching practices that develop and allow for imagination and creativity.

In all, the conference featured fifteen Nipissing University Schulich School of Education presenters in addition to Ms Chris Prefontaine, our keynote speaker, who combined to offer eighteen workshop sessions to an audience of over seventy pre-service teachers and a few in-service teachers. The feedback from those in attendance was extremely positive. One presenter wrote: "Thanks to all those who made the day possible ... It was a wonderful vision that played out perfectly." One pre-service teacher who attended four sessions protested, "There were too many good choices." Imagine that for a complaint!

In our debriefing after the ICE conference, there were a number of achievements to be celebrated. The centennial committee had high praise for the success of the conference. The president was particularly pleased with the profile of success that the conference brought to Nipissing University and jokingly remarked that he was even more pleased that we didn't have to access the money that he had allocated to us. We were grateful to Nipissing faculty who championed our cause in ways other than course delivery. For example, one colleague did an exceptional job assembling a conference organizing team who then planned, designed, and delivered an extremely successful conference.

Positive feedback is of course always welcome, but we also noted areas for improvement. The timing of the conference was not the most advantageous for catching the attention and participation of pre-service teachers. It was too close to final exams, and pre-service teachers were exhausted from the rigour of studies during the academic year and in many cases were overextended financially. In addition, our timelines for engendering faculty participation as workshop presenters were too tight; some of our colleagues felt that with CSSE and American Educational Research Association (AERA) conferences looming in May, they could not adequately prepare for the ICE conference. We also felt that we needed a more streamlined process for conference registration and for tracking volunteer services before, during, and after the conference. We reviewed the academic calendar for pre-service teachers, paying particular attention to practicum sessions for the concurrent and the consecutive BEd programs; the professional development calendar for in-service teachers in northern Ontario school districts; and the annual scheduling of major national and international conferences. As a result, we determined to schedule ICE conferences for November in succeeding academic years. We also met with financial and organizational support staff at Nipissing and made plans to design a more efficient system for publication and promotion of the conference, and for registration of presenters and participants.

ICE Is Formed at Nipissing University

Exclusion to Inclusion: Imagination and Creativity in the 21st Century Classroom (EDUC 4826) officially began as an option course in

September 2009 for twenty-five registered pre-service teachers. It is worth noting that option courses are expected to be taken in addition to required BEd courses, and that pre-service teachers in 2009 paid a registration fee of $750 to take an option course. Option courses are interest-based, add-on courses, and as such are revenue-generating for the faculty and the university. As you might well imagine, the additional cost to pre-service teachers greatly restricted the number of enrollees in most option courses, with the exception of Religious Education in the Roman Catholic Separate Schools (EDUC 1526), which was a requirement (of most Catholic boards) for pre-service teachers wishing to teach in a Catholic school. The annual enrolment in this course was quite high, as a number of pre-service teachers wanted to maximize their opportunities for employment. However, over time, unrest grew among pre-service teachers about having to pay additional fees for courses that they deemed to be equivalent to elective courses, which bore no additional cost. Option courses, while of high interest to a number of pre-service teachers, were seen as financially restrictive and exclusionary rather than inclusionary. Added to that was the discontent among pre-service teachers that the majority of option courses were taught by contract faculty, as opposed to full-time or tenured faculty.

ICE was the notable exception, with a team of four full-time instructors facilitating the course offering. In order to be viable, an option course was required to have a minimal enrolment of twenty students. This number was somewhat fluid in that course enrolments were totaled and averaged across the number of option courses being offered in any given academic year. Ironically the high enrolment in the Catholic religion course benefited other option courses. In fall 2009, the practice of averaging enrolment across all option courses was de-emphasized, and greater responsibility was placed on each option course to be a stand-alone entity.

One of the great benefits of ICE for pre-service teachers was the change of venues for instructional and experiential purposes. For example, the Weaver Auditorium with its large space at the front was chosen for in-class presentations. The effect and affect of an imaginative and creative approach to teaching literacy and numeracy was accomplished in an evening class in Aquino's elementary school. Children and their parents were actively engaged in this workshop as they volunteered their evening time to participate. Room A246, a classroom especially equipped with various types of educational technology, was the site for an intense hands-on workshop using technology to enhance teaching and learning. The arts classrooms of F301 and F304 provided much needed space for in-class demonstration sessions and for working on various assignments. The White Water Gallery was an exceptional location for a gallery walk, an appreciation of fine art including musical entertainment.

Another benefit to participants in the course was that assignments involved choice and flexibility. All assignments were open-ended and increased in level of difficulty and degree of challenge as the course progressed. Learners decided on the mode and content of their assignments, and by the end of the course decided how their major assignment would be evaluated. The facilitators collaboratively decided on the types of assignments and the criteria for evaluation of each assignment, with the exception of the final project.

The team developed five assignments for the course: (1) a metaphor of inquiry for education, (2) an answer to a "what if?" question, (3) a switch in point of view, (4) a reflection on imagination and creativity from practica placements, and (5) a learner-designed final project, based on personal perceptions of imagination creativity education. For most assignments, pre-service teachers had the choice of working individually, in pairs, or in groups. They could choose any format through which to complete and share their various assignments; that is, they could create a traditional work of art, a video, a performance, or use another suggested format. Students were asked to document their progress, via process notes and drawings, and to do self- and peer-assessments before assignments were team evaluated.

A great advantage for pre-service teachers in the preparation of their assignments was that the team of facilitators modelled each assignment (with the exception of the final project), and then each assignment was critiqued and evaluated by course participants (facilitators and pre-service teachers). We decided to blend theory and best practice by bringing aesthetics, literacy, and technology into every class. We planned, implemented, and assessed activities and assignments together as a way to infuse our individual strengths into the course. In-class activating and acquiring activities varied from class to class. We performed mime metaphors in an auditorium where pre-service teachers observed and deconstructed our performances. We handed digital video cameras to small teams of pre-service teachers and had them plan and record a short video regarding a perceived barrier to ICE. We varied the locations of our classes, from an art room or technology room at the university to a pond-side setting, a school classroom, and a local gallery.

We held studio classes just before each assignment was due, and during those classes we conferenced with each pre-service teacher. It was during these conferences that we got to know our pre-service teachers as individuals and gained an understanding of their thoughts and feelings regarding the course. For the most part, the comments were very positive. The majority of teacher candidates found the course to be engaging, motivating, hands-on, applicable, exciting, and different. These types of comments, however, were accompanied with others expressing discomfort. For example, some students used "challenging" and "a bit up in the air" as course descriptors. Some of the unease arose because many of our pre-service teachers had never experienced a holistic or learner-centred course in all their years of schooling, including university. Because the majority of our pre-service teachers did not have an art background, the course activities and assignments were sometimes challenging for them, and some expressed concerns regarding their successful completion of assigned tasks. We dispelled such concerns by emphasizing that the purpose of this course was to gain personal insight and confidence from a multiplicity of imaginative and creative endeavours, and to learn ICE concepts through holistic activities that would benefit them and their future students in a variety of ways.

The Darker Side of Collaboration

Thus far we have chronicled some of the challenges with collaboratively developing a course that is team taught by subject-specific scholars. As noted by Wenger, McDermott, and Snyder (2002), the element of inspiration that can be cultivated and found within a community of practice is a by-product of bringing practitioners together into a collective in which their lived professional experiences and stories can be shared. While there was a level of comfort, insight, and knowledge – both tacit and explicit – that was regularly harnessed during the many meetings and planning sessions, there was also a darker side to the collaborative process that emerged during the teaching. In this sense, creating a community of practice is not an easy or seamless undertaking.

The complexities of a socially and collaboratively constructed knowledge in a higher educational context, combined with the considerable stress-related challenges of today's actual teaching practice, are likely to result in what Yanow (2000) regards as "clashes of practice" (p. 260). The added dimension of having four scholars from four divergent disciplines attempting to find their place in the conversation, as well as teaching in the evenings, at times resulted in apprehension and tension, although never in animosity or a dismissal of the merits of team teaching.

Reynolds (2000) reminds us that there is a "darker side" to the notion of community and collaboration that must be addressed. As the ICE team, we didn't walk on the "dark side," but we did realize that the process of developing this course, and the facilitating of it, was not without tension, not without apprehension, and not without negotiation and reciprocity. Based on our experiences with this course, we learned that creating a community of practice requires a continual process of analysis, reflection, and synthesis. This process is made more challenging when post-secondary scholars bring their extensive field experiences, research, and theories of practice to bear on a team-taught course. It must not be assumed that these same scholars will intuitively and comfortably know how and when to find their space and place in the context of a team-taught learning environment. This point is emphasized in Ashworth's recent reflection:

> Personally, I found the large-group planning was great, especially with us being from various backgrounds; however, I found large-group team teaching did not work as well as when two of us were teaching together. It seemed we were overwhelming our small-ish class when we were all present. As well, I found large-group marking was also hard: it took much time and was like "too many cooks." (Personal communication, 15 February 2015)

Overall, as a team, we believed that we succeeded in helping learners realize that they possessed strong abilities and capabilities which enabled them to be imaginative and creative. They all came to learn for themselves the difference between teaching creatively and teaching for creativity. Furthermore, they each developed the competence and confidence to introduce ICE in their classrooms for the educational benefit of their students and for themselves as teachers. In regards to the latter, a number of our pre-service teachers reported that in some classrooms they encountered resistance and at times strong opposition from their associate teacher (AT) or a school administrator when introducing ICE strategies in a lesson or unit. However, they also reported the need in such situations to negotiate permission for a trial run of a content or skills-based lesson infused with strategies and/or learning activities grounded in the praxis of imagination creativity education. When such permission was obtained, they reported a discernible increase in student engagement in the lesson to the extent that approval was granted by their AT and/or school administrator to continue with this pedagogical practice.

Year Two ICE Fissures

As a team, in May 2010, we celebrated our successful integration of content and methodology by presenting at the Ministry of Education/Faculties of Education conference a paper titled "Curriculum Integration through Imagination Creativity Education (ICE)." Unfortunately, our celebration was short lived as teaching assignments were confirmed from the dean's office. We were informed that ICE as a course offering in 2010–11 would feature only one facilitator. The course, if approved based on enrolment, had been assigned to Hatt for the fall term. We were collectively very disappointed, as we felt that we had already proven the educational viability of a collaborative team approach to teaching a course at the post-secondary level.

The student feedback and course evaluations were impressively positive in all categories, especially in instructional planning, delivery, approachability, and support of facilitators. Ashworth and Hatt had had a lengthy meeting with our then new dean in the early spring of 2010, and she spoke very positively of the achievement of ICE, most notably the collaborative team approach to facilitating the course. However, the timetables for Ashworth, Mantas, and Graham had been heavily front-loaded; there was no instructional time allotted for any of them to dedicate to ICE, and there was no flexibility in their fall schedule to allow for collaborative engagement in ICE. To their credit, they still wanted the ICE team to remain intact, and thus committed to doing all that time and circumstance would allow them to do to advance the cause of ICE. Despite all of its success, imagination creativity education as an option course had fallen prey to the complexities of timetabling and financial constraint.

Our professionalism being what it was, we regrouped as an ICE team and planned a series of workshops to be conducted by team members and invited guests. We strategically placed these workshops throughout the course to gradually increase our pre-service teachers' awareness of the interconnectivity of the arts, special education, creative writing, technology, literacy, and numeracy. We infused each workshop with teaching and learning strategies and activities grounded in imagination creativity education. In addition, we planned our next ICE conference, slated for early November 2010, which would be titled "Dare to Inspire!" We opted for the same format that had proven successful at our inaugural conference. Our keynote address would be presented Friday evening by Dr David Booth, internationally renowned scholar in literacy, professor emeritus at OISE/UT, and recently appointed as the first to serve in the Elizabeth Thorn Endowed Literacy Chair at Nipissing University. On that Saturday, we offered twenty-three eighty-minute workshops in four timeslots throughout the day.

We continued on as an ICE team, scheduling meetings as often as we could and generally keeping each other informed of happenings within and outside the university as it related to ICE. One of the great successes of the second year of ICE from the pre-service teachers' perspective was the variety of in-class workshops and studio presentations provided by individual members of the ICE team and invited colleagues from the Schulich School of Education. In addition to presentations by existing team members Ashworth (visual arts), Mantas (holistic and arts-based education), Aquino (integrated literacy and numeracy at the elementary level), and Graham (collaborative uses of technology), other faculty members also participated, including Corkett (ICE with special education students) and Gosse (creative writing). The unique aspect about each of these faculty presenters was that they dedicated their time, effort, energy, and, in some cases, resources to the pre-service teachers in ICE without financial remuneration.

The Move Back to "Me" from "We"

Hatt tried, to the best of his ability, to replicate the collaborative energy and enthusiasm of the ICE team in his facilitation of the ICE course during its second year. Despite the effort and energy that he put into arranging a variety of evening offerings within the course, interviewing and conferencing with individual participants in the course, providing ongoing feedback and encouragement on personal achievements and course assignments, he could not help but feel deflated at times. The option course from the students' perspective was a unique success in their educational experiences, and provided them with the knowledge, skills, and attitudes needed to fully implement ICE in their student's day-to-day learning. None of his pre-service teachers had experienced the initial, collaborative offering of ICE, so for them, their ICE experience was singular. However, for Hatt, in comparison to the inaugural year, he rediscovered, to his dismay, the powerlessness of "me" in comparison to the powerfulness of "we."

The third offering of the ICE course in 2011–12 was heavily modelled on the form and format of the 2010–11 offering. There was little difference in the evening class sessions. Hatt again sought presentations from ICE mates and colleagues from within the faculty. Once again, without financial remuneration, they participated to the benefit and betterment of the pre-service teachers enrolled in ICE.

In early November 2011, we hosted another ICE conference titled "Light the Flame." Corkett and Hatt served as co-organizers of the conference. The keynote speaker on the Friday evening was Bob Barton, an accomplished novelist, internationally known drama educator, and a sessional instructor at OISE/UT. The pre-service teachers who were enrolled in the ICE course provided all the volunteer services required for the conference, including acting as on-site guides, introducing workshop presenters, and providing technical support when needed. Sixteen workshop presentations in four timeslots throughout the Saturday event were offered to the eighty-five attendees. One particular highlight of the conference was a presentation facilitated by the instructor of, and the graduate students enrolled in, the Nipissing University master's level course Modelling Methods for Program Development for Gifted Learners (EDUC 5656).

However, as individual ICE team members pursued independent educational goals in an effort to obtain tenure or promotion, their commitment to ICE was understandably, yet increasingly, reduced. ICE had again registered outstanding feedback from the pre-service teachers involved in the 2011–12 course, but the collaboration and collegiality that had hallmarked the work of the ICE team and its educational accomplishments just two years previously had all but disappeared. To a person, the initial members of the ICE team were philosophically and pedagogically committed to ICE, but the individual effort required to achieve professional career goals in academia necessitated a high degree of concentrated personal time, energy, and effort. Something had to go, as it were, and ICE was cracking.

In 2012–13, a new format for informing pre-service teachers about option courses was put in place by the administration. Previously, option course facilitators met pre-service teachers in prescheduled information sessions during the first week of the fall term so that they could benefit from a personalized introduction to the course and receive direct answers to their questions. Now it was decided to put all the option course descriptors on a single page flyer and mail it out with all the other introductory print information pertaining to the bachelor of education degree program. The rationale for this decision was that interested pre-service teachers would register in advance for option courses. However, the result of such action was immediate and negative. ICE went from a traditional annual enrolment of twenty-two to twenty-six pre-service teachers to an enrolment of twelve. Other option courses, notably international teaching, also experienced a 50 per cent decline in registrants. Objections and protests to the new method of promoting and registering for option courses were ineffectual. The only concession granted was that option courses adversely affected by a drop in registrations would continue for the 2012–13 academic year because workload assignments had already been made for courses scheduled to be offered.

In fall 2012, Hatt organized the annual ICE conference to take place in November. He enlisted the support of the pre-service teachers in the ICE course for all volunteer services needed to ensure the hosting of a successful conference. On Friday evening, in thankful appreciation, the original founders of ICE reassembled and launched the conference. They spoke to the principles of imagination creativity education that would be realized in the workshop presentations addressing the theme of the conference, "ICE for Life!" Jack Lockhart, a retired teacher, principal, and internationally recognized artist, delivered the keynote address, followed by our traditional reception hosted in the main foyer.

The Saturday format of the conference proceedings was changed primarily because of a decline in workshop proposals from within the Schulich School of Education. Twelve workshop sessions were scheduled for eighty-five participants in three time slots and followed up in the fourth time slot with a concluding keynote address by Dr David Booth, a former keynote address participant. Despite what might be perceived as a reduction in faculty support for the conference, the cast of workshop presenters had a very positive impact on those in attendance. In addition, for the first time in the short history of ICE conferences, proposals had been received and accepted from instructors from two other faculties, Arts and Science, and Applied and Professional Studies. Nipissing University PhD candidates also presented workshops at the conference, as did the founder and executive director of Paradigm Education Academy of Creative Enlightenment

(PEACE) School, a charitable, not-for-profit private school featuring an arts-infused academic program founded on the principles of imagination creativity education. Overall, the non-education faculty members accounted for 50 per cent of the workshops presented at the conference. This statistic was heartening because it evidenced a widening of the appeal of the ICE conference beyond our Schulich School of Education.

The feedback on the conference and the workshop presentations was again overwhelmingly positive, as was the end-of-term feedback from pre-service teachers on the ICE course itself. Despite all the personal, professional, academic, aesthetic, and artistic successes that ICE had achieved, its death-knell had unfortunately been sounded. For the academic year, 2013–14, administrators held to their practice of disseminating information on option courses and registration through a single page flyer included among the many pages of the packet introducing pre-service teachers to the bachelor of education program. In 2013–14, only six pre-service teachers registered for Exclusion to Inclusion: Imagination and Creativity in the 21st Century Classroom (EDUC 4286), and the course was cancelled.

Research Matters: A Rejuvenated Focus for ICE!

In 2013–14 there was no pretense of informing pre-service teachers about option courses that had once been available to BEd students and were still listed as available in program literature. The then interim dean, citing a backlash from previous students opposed to paying the additional fee for an optional course, had decided to cancel all option courses with the exception of the Catholic religion course.

Nevertheless, from the breaking away of old ICE, new ICE is forming at Nipissing University. Graham and Hatt, through an approved and internally funded research project, have been deeply engaged in analysing the data obtained from pre-service teachers as they entered the bachelor of education program. Specifically, we asked pre-service teachers six questions regarding their perception of imagination creativity education (ICE) before they began any instructor-led learning in the program. The data have proven to be very rich, and we are in the process of concluding a series of three papers in which the informing perspectives of pre-service teachers are central to an enriched understanding of imagination and creativity and their fusion within education.

In addition, with the recent provincial restructuring of the BEd program into a two-year model in Ontario, imagination creativity education (ICE) has been reclassified from an option to an elective course. ICE now stands as one among several elective offerings, without extra cost, that will be made available to pre-service teachers in the fourth term of their BEd program. Given the past achievements of our team, there is reason to be optimistic that ICE will again be forming at Nipissing University!

ACKNOWLEDGMENT

This chapter was written in consultation with Dr Elizabeth Ashworth, Dr Anna-Marie Aquino, and Dr Kathy Mantas. We thank them for providing insightful feedback for the completion of this work.

REFERENCES

Amabile, T.M. (1996). *Creativity in context: Update in the social psychology of creativity*. Boulder, CO: Westview Press.

Amabile, T.M. (1998). How to kill creativity. *Harvard Business Review*. Retrieved from https://hbr.org/1998/09/how-to-kill-creativity/ar/1.

Aquino, A., Mantas, K., Ashworth, E., Graham, R., & Hatt, B.E. (2009, May). *Imagination and creativity in education*. Seminar presented to the Ministry of Education/Faculties of Education Forum 2009 (OISE/UT), Toronto, ON.

Aquino, A.M., Mantas, K., Ashworth, E., Hatt, B.E., & Graham, R. (2010, May). *Curriculum integration in pre-service teacher education through Imagination Creativity Education (ICE)*. Seminar presented at the Ministry of Education/Faculties of Education Forum 2010 (OISE/UT), Toronto, ON.

Ashworth, E., Hatt, B.E., Aquino, A.M., Graham, R., & Mantas, K. (2009, October). *Exclusion to inclusion: Imagination and creativity in the 21st century classroom*. Seminar presented at The New York State Federation of Chapters of Exceptional Children (NYS CEC), Buffalo, NY.

Ashworth, E., & Mantas, K. (2011, March). *Reflections on art education and a pre-service option course on Imagination Creativity Education (ICE)*. "Best practices" seminar presented at the National Art Education Association (NAEA) 2011 National Convention, Seattle, WA.

Csikszentmihalyi, M. (1998). Society, culture, and person: A systems view of creativity. In R.J. Sternberg (Ed.), *The nature of creativity: Contemporary psychological perspectives* (pp. 325–39). Cambridge, UK: University of Cambridge Press.

Gardner, H. (1993). *Creating minds: An anatomy of creativity seen through the lives of Freud, Einstein, Picasso, Stravinsky, Eliot, Graham and Gandhi*. New York, NY: Basic Books.

Guilford, J.P. (1950). Creativity. *American Psychologist*, *5*(9), 444–54. http://dx.doi.org/10.1037/h0063487

Guilford, J.P. (1959). Three faces of intellect. *American Psychologist*, *14*(8), 469–79. http://dx.doi.org/10.1037/h0046827

International Society for Technology in Education. (2007). *Educational technology standards for students*. Washington, DC: Author.

Mantas, K., Ashworth, E., Hatt, B.E., Graham, R., & Aquino, A.M. (2010, May–June). *ICE-breaking the mold of pre-service teacher education: Sharing experiences of creating, implementing and team teaching a course on Imagination Creativity Education (ICE)*. Presented at the Canadian Society for the Study of Education 2010 Conference (Concordia University), Montreal, QC.

Michalko, M. (1998). *Cracking creativity: The secrets of creative genius*. Berkeley, CA: Ten Speed Press.

National Advisory Committee on Creative and Cultural Education (NACCCE). (1999). *All our futures: Creativity, culture and education*. Retrieved from http://sirkenrobinson.com/pdf/allourfutures.pdf

Quick, R.H. (1894). *Essays on educational reformers*. London, UK: Longmans, Green, and Co.

Reynolds, M. (2000). Bright lights and the pastoral idyll: Ideas of community underlying management education methodologies. *Management Learning*, *31*(1), 67–81. http://dx.doi.org/10.1177/1350507600311006

Robinson, K. (2006). TED Talk: Do schools kill creativity? Retrieved from http://www.ted.com/talks/ken_robinson_says_schools_kill_creativity?language=en

Runco, M.A. (1986). Predicting children's creative performance. *Psychological Reports*, *59*(3), 1247–54. http://dx.doi.org/10.2466/pr0.1986.59.3.1247

Runco, M.A., & Pritzker, S.R. (1996). *Encyclopedia of creativity*. San Diego, CA: Academic Press.

Shor, I., & Freire, P. (1987). *A pedagogy for liberation: Dialogues on transforming education*. Westport, CT: Bergin & Garvey.

Streminger, G. (1980). Hume's theory of imagination. *Hume Studies*, *6*(2), 91–118. Retrieved from www.humesociety.org/hs/issues/v6n2/streminger/streminger-v6n2.pdf

Vygotsky, L.S. (1930/2004). Imagination and creativity in childhood. *Journal of Russian and East European Thought*, 42(1), 7–97. (Original work published 1930)

Wenger, E., McDermott, R.A., & Snyder, W. (2002). *Cultivating communities of practice: A guide to managing knowledge*. Brighton, MA: Harvard Business Review Press.

Yanow, D. (2000). Seeing organizational learning: A cultural view. *Organization*, 7(2), 247–68. http://dx.doi.org/10.1177/135050840072003

5 From Shafts to Drifts: Collaborating to Strengthen Integrated Teaching and Learning

ASTRID STEELE AND ELIZABETH ASHWORTH

Introduction

We have been afforded the privilege of writing about our collaborative efforts in subject integration within our faculty of education. Over the past few weeks we have spent considerable time talking about what that writing might look like, intuiting that presenting our work in an objective and traditional scholarly style would fail to convey the spirit of the collaboration. Our work together has been a series of conversations – long and short, philosophical and logistical, methodological and reflective – that speak directly to the subjective, lived experience of being collaborative. These conversations are a form of narrative inquiry.

According to Shacklock and Thorp (2005), narrative inquiry involves "production, interpretation and representation of … lived experiences [that are] assemblage[s] of life fragments" (pp. 156–8) that reveal layers of meaning. Similarly, Bruner (1987, 1991) and Richardson (1997) suggest that lived experiences are best understood through a blend of personal stories. We met just over five years ago, and since then our collaborative efforts have been "life fragments" – in informal meetings between classes, during dog walks in the bush, while paddling on our annual canoe trips – all for the purpose of planning, teaching, and assessing art and science teacher education. Youens, Smethem, and Sullivan (2014) suggested that collaboration works best when collaborators "engineer an interactive space" (p. 101). Throughout our professional partnership, we have worked on our collaborations (for example, assignments, articles, and presentations) in a variety of spaces. These locations include our offices, classrooms, the university cafeteria, local restaurants, hiking trails, camping sites, and canoe routes, all of which provided space for intellectual interaction.

We invite you to experience the essence of our collaboration as a conversation between two colleagues. Ellis and Bochner (2000) included dialogue as a format for sharing personal and academic stories. This chapter is presented as a dialogue that is a "blended representation" of the many conversations that we have had as both our collaboration and our friendship evolved. Through a narrative dialogue, we describe how we became collaborators in teaching and research, share our conceptual framework and literature review for our collaborations, and provide details about how we co-plan, co-teach, and co-assess within our education program. As well, we include a discussion about future collaborations within and outside our university classrooms.

Beginnings

Astrid: Liz, I've been doing a lot of thinking about the art/science integration collaboration that we assign our teacher candidates (TCs) every year. The more I read about integration, the more complex my thinking becomes about what that whole project signifies to us and to our TCs.

Elizabeth: Yes, I've also been looking back at some of the art projects and the reflections that the TCs wrote, and I think that we should probably have some more conversations about integration and how we worked together to achieve that. After all, we're going to be starting a new, two-year teacher education program next year, so it's a good time to reflect on our own teaching and learning.

A: Well, we can start by going back to the beginnings of the integration project and how we came to be collaborators. I know that my personal background created a lot of spaces where science, art, music, and other subject areas could intersect in really positive ways. I've been part of a number of very exciting and successful teaching and learning collaborations in my career, and so have wanted to share those experiences with the TCs here. That's why I was really open to a collaboration between my science methods course and your art methods course.

E: Sadly, I didn't consider a partnership with another professor to expand teaching and learning beyond the walls of my classroom. Looking back, the choice to work on my own came naturally: as a former secondary school teacher, I was used to planning, implementing, and assessing assignments alone. I had worked within a traditional high school timetable that was set up to promote the segregation of subject areas and provided little opportunity for teachers to create integration opportunities. When integration happened in my classroom, it was when I, alone, merged subject areas within assignments: for example, blending art and English in a project focusing on William Blake's poetry while teaching the physics of the camera and the chemistry of the darkroom during my photography course. Students began asking questions about learning content from other subject areas within my visual arts lessons – evidence to me of positive lateral learning. Astrid, I think the idea for our collaboration came when we discovered that we were independently giving a similar integration assignment to the same group of TCs.

A: It also helped that we are friends. That made the initial connection much smoother, and the subsequent bumps were a little easier to talk about from positions of friendship and respect.

E: Absolutely! This is not my first time team teaching with another professor. A few years ago, I was one of five professors who planned and taught a course at this university. We all had much classroom and university teaching experience along with a wide range of subject expertise areas. I think, collectively, we had been teaching for over one hundred years! It was invigorating to plan a new course with my colleagues: we met regularly, bounced ideas off each other, and worked as a group for some tasks and individually for others. We were equitable in how we divided the responsibilities for weekly lessons and assessment of assignments. We were flexible about locations for teaching and moved teacher candidates around the campus; for example, some classes were held in traditional classrooms, others outside.

A: That sounds like a positive, collaborative experience.

E: Well, as we taught the course, I found that five professors were, perhaps, too many for a successful collaboration. There were times when all of us were present for a lesson, and I think that overwhelmed the learners. Most classes, however, were taught by one or two of us, and we could focus on the individual strengths that we brought to the course. I preferred those particular lessons. I found that the most difficult time was when we did group assessments of the course work because there were too many "cooks': we all had different lenses regarding how assignments should be marked, and these differences got in the way of smooth assessment and evaluation sessions. The assessments took far too much time to complete and added much frustration to an otherwise positive experience.

A: Hmm ... food for thought about what works and what doesn't for collaboration. What is the optimal number for collaboration? Does the level of collegiality matter?

E: I think, in our case, we work well as a partnership. Because we are friends, the discussions are easy, and our successful co-planning, co-teaching, co-assessment, and research practices over the past few years demonstrates what works for us. We look forward to working with each other within and beyond our university.

A Collaborative Framework

A: You know, Liz, collaboration between a science education professor and a visual arts education professor could be seen as incongruous.

E: It's strange how some may perceive our subjects to be so disparate, but think about what we do outside the classroom: you're a science professor who does ceramics, and I'm an art professor who does photography – a medium that includes physics and chemistry. In a way, we've been blending the two disciplines naturally in our hobbies.

A: And we were both secondary school teachers in public education systems that required us to be adept at teaching in multidisciplines and with multi-grades, often with limited resources. I think that I suspected early on that the distinction between disciplines is largely a construct created by, and for, educators in the secondary panel and beyond. Lucas (1980) called it "disciplinary chauvinism," and Siskin (1994) talked about protection of subject areas. Venville, Wallace, Rennie, & Malone (2000) referred to disciplines as artificial learning compartments – really an elitist system that tends to separate teachers as well as subject areas!

E: Calling teachers elitists is pretty strong language. The separation of disciplines in higher education is complex. It's related to how knowledge is constructed and how secondary and post-secondary school curricula are designed. I like how Venville et al. (2002) described the functioning of a school as its "grammar." They said, "Grammar underpins the culture of schools and is reinforced by the customs, rituals, ceremonies and artefacts of everyday school life ... Once established, the grammar of schooling is difficult to change" (p. 54). So, really, the separation of disciplines seems to be a fundamental part of their identity.

A: Yes, disciplines in education are often referred to as "silos," full of disciplinary content and standing independently in each field of study. But we both worked in mining towns for many years, and sometimes I think that a mine might be a much better metaphor for how curricula are organized. I was intrigued by Schroeder's (1999) allusions to mining when discussing how subjects are traditionally taught in ways that can be detrimental to integration, where he stated that "specialization often results in what is popularly described as functional silos or mine shafts … which effectively curtails communication and collaboration between areas" (p. 9).

E: Mine shafts?

A: Bear with me while I think through Schroeder's metaphor. Years ago, when I visited the museum in Timmins, Ontario, there was a sculptured model of the city illustrating several landmarks, including mine headframes. Beneath those landmarks the model displayed an elaborate "honeycomb" of underground shafts and drifts that dwarfed the city above. Well, we're both familiar with mining headframes above the surface, and with mine shafts and drifts down below.

E: Yes, we know them from our years of teaching in Ontario mining communities: you in Timmins, and me in Red Lake, Ontario, and Lynn Lake, Manitoba. I had a tour of an underground mine in Lynn Lake, and it was labyrinth of connected tunnels.

A: Shafts are vertical mine tunnels, and drifts are horizontal passages that branch off from the shafts (see Figure 5.1). Sometimes drifts connect two or more mine shafts. Gutiérrez (2008) described traditional, formal learning as "vertical" and informal learning as "horizontal." Metaphorically, that would support the idea that teaching, learning, and even knowing not only have multiple connections within a single area of study, or discipline, but also have many connections and links to other disciplines. The mine sites become the metaphoric sites for collaboration among educators.

E: So, any individual subject could have its own shaft and drifts. Instead of collecting "surface" knowledge, the subject is explored deeply by digging down into the content "ore body." The drifts are different areas of focus that branch out from the shaft into the ore, such as a design "drift," or an art history "drift" in a visual arts course. I think that the mining metaphor provides a rich meta-language for reflecting on our art/science collaboration project here at our faculty of education.

A: Maybe our experiences suggest that formal learning can be supported to occur both vertically and horizontally, that is, both in individual

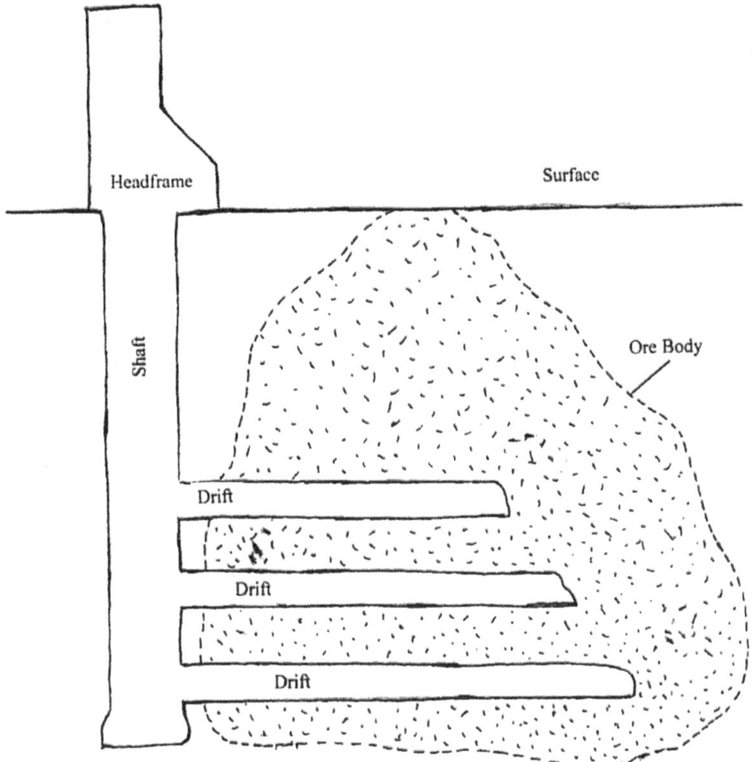

Figure 5.1. Diagram of an underground mine.

subjects and through integration between them. For our integration assignment, we first integrated art and science concepts, and later added language in the form of reflections and environmental education considerations into the requirement of the constructions being made from recycled materials.

E: So, in keeping with that metaphor, the assignment connections would be like a more complex "education mine," where the art and science "shafts" and "drifts" are accompanied by language and environmental education "shafts" and "drifts." Some subject "drifts" may connect with one or more other subject "drifts," depending on how much integration occurs (see Figure 5.2).

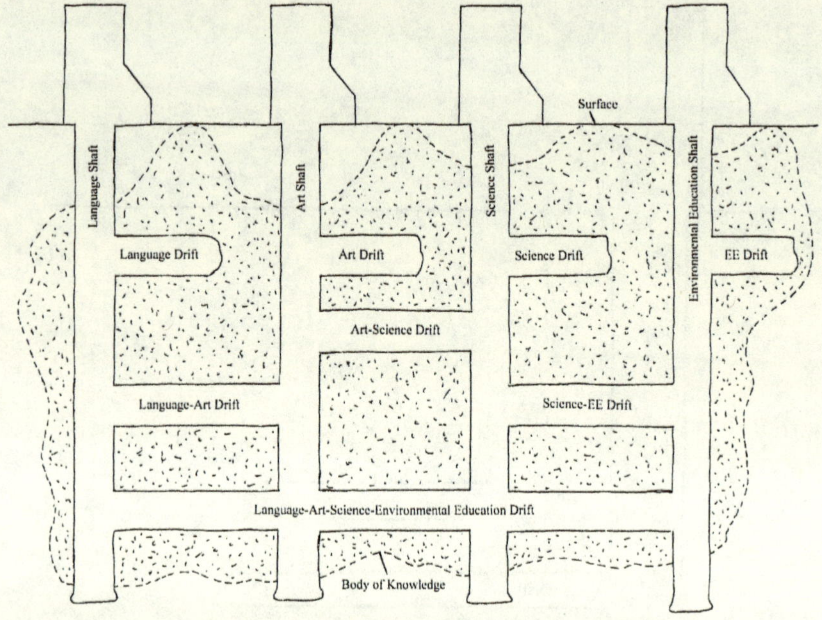

Figure 5.2. Art/science integration assignment "mine" diagram.

A: Yes. But keep in mind that the "mine" wouldn't necessarily be limited to just four subjects. Any integration could involve two or more subjects. An important question that needs attention is, Why would we bother with a collaboration that integrates curricula? It's a departure from our comfortable norm, and, as you and I know from experience, it's a lot of work. What are the benefits of collaborative subject integration for our TCs and for us as teachers?

E: Much has been written about the benefits for students learning through interdisciplinary approaches; these benefits can generally be put into two categories. The first has to do with higher levels of student success through increased interest and engagement, because students tend to see integrated learning and projects as more relevant and meaningful to them, and hence more worthy of their time and attention (Drake & Burns, 2004; Drake, 2007). Integrated learning also tends to require higher-order thinking skills, such as problem solving (Hargreaves, Earl, Moore, & Manning, 2001).

A: And the other category? Let me guess: it has to do with how the brain works.

E: Yes, brain research for education is a relatively new field, but some really important results are emerging. For one thing, our brains don't work in distinct subject areas; instead our brains' neurons make countless connections and process information in rich and complex ways (Jensen, 2005). So teaching subject-specific lessons often doesn't make optimal use of students' brainpower, not to mention that "intelligence is a function of experience; and the brain stores most effectively what is meaningful from the learner's perspective" (McGeehan, 2001, p. 8). Those findings are strong endorsements for integrated learning.

A: They make sense intuitively for educators like us who have spent decades helping students learn across all sorts of subject areas. Which brings us to the second part of the question, What are the benefits for us as teachers?

E: Well, much more seems to have been written about the barriers to integration than about the benefits for teachers. For example, there are obstacles like traditional school organization and culture, inflexible classroom scheduling, parental pressure, and subject-based qualifications (Venville, Sheffield, Rennie, & Wallace, 2008; Venville et al., 2000, 2002). The most common barrier, for which Wallace and his colleagues made a very strong case, is inadequate teacher planning time (Wallace, Sheffield, Rennie, & Venville, 2007).

A: That's quite a list, but it makes sense. Those were some of the drawbacks for me when I taught at the secondary school level. But surely there must be some advantages for teachers as well?

Connecting Collaboration and Integration

A: Drake (2007) talks about the opportunity for teacher creativity, which would hold for an individual working alone or for those working in a pair or group, and the literature I mentioned earlier seems to imply that teachers benefited from increased collegiality. I'd like to think that working collaboratively also strengthens a teacher's pedagogical knowledge and pedagogical content knowledge too (Shulman, 1986). It seems to me that, based on our experiences, we might be able to add to the list of benefits for teachers who integrate curriculum, and particularly for those who do so in a collaborative environment.

E: It strikes me that, in our case, our collaboration is akin to an integration of our separate skills, knowledge, and experiences in education. Maybe for us collaboration and integration merge.

A: I agree that, in our case, the difference between collaboration and integration has become somewhat indistinct. A group of mostly Australian education researchers have, over the years, done quite a bit of work on curriculum integration and teacher collaboration. I've already mentioned their names: Venville, Sheffield, Rennie, Malone, and Wallace. Emerging from all their research into integrated curriculum projects in schools is the importance of collaboration. In a significant portion of their work, they found that one of the conditions necessary for *integration* to occur among subject areas was that collaboration had to be viable, accessible, and desirable for all the teachers involved. Indeed, these researchers outline the necessary conditions for successful collaboration among teachers. Remember, integration in the elementary years of schooling, where students have only one teacher, is a simpler undertaking than in the middle and secondary years where students have multiple teachers. In the "mine shaft," or separate-subject years, collaboration becomes more complicated.

E: What are some of those necessary conditions for collaboration? I'm guessing that enthusiasm and motivation to work with someone else both have to be there. And likely an agreeable administration?

A: Enthusiasm and motivation, a strong understanding of subject matter, administrative support, and dedicated time in the schedule to work together to plan and implement the integration were all reported factors (Venville et al., 2008; Wallace et al., 2007).

E: I can see how, for us, integration and collaboration are similar. The conditions for one are the same as the conditions for the other. In a sense, our collaboration is really an extended integration of our combined experiences in our subject areas and our pedagogical skills. Our experiences and skills are the mine shafts that reach down into our disciplines of art and science education.

A: And the drifts are the connective tunnels that enable us to see and work with the interconnectedness of our disciplines and to connect to other disciplines, such as language arts/English and environmental education.

E: We can take that a step further and consider the nature of our particular mine drifts – the extent of their connectedness, their dimensions.

A: Are you suggesting that there might be different kinds of mine drifts? Different kinds of connections? Different collaborations or integrations? Didn't Drake do some work with typifying integration?

E: Yes, Drake and Burns (2004) looked at the different forms of curriculum integration and identified three main types: *multidisciplinary, interdisciplinary*, and *transdisciplinary*, with a number of subcategories in each.

A: Let's think about how our collaborative integration project might fall into those categories.

E: I think our project actually falls into two of the main categories because of the nature of our program, in which our TCs often simultaneously wear both student and teacher hats. When the TCs create an art construction based on a science topic, the project falls most closely into the *multidisciplinary* integration category. The subjects remain fairly distinct (Drake, 2007) within the assignment, with specific expectations for the science portion and the art portion, and these are then assessed separately. It's sometimes referred to as "parallel curriculum" (p. 33). That is the portion of our collaboration that we manage individually, although we do share what we are doing with the TCs.

A: I see that. But what about the reflection paper that the TCs have to write, or the requirement that they use recycled materials? Those two pieces are not attached specifically to either discipline.

E: That's where the *interdisciplinary* category comes into play. The reflections that the TCs write for us focus on their understanding of pedagogical and content knowledge that span subject areas. The lines between subject areas become somewhat blurred in interdisciplinary integration (Drake, 2007). When the TCs consider themselves as teachers of integrated curricula, they have to take a broader perspective, which requires them to think about designing and implementing integrated curricula across disciplines in ways that will engage their students.

A: In a similar way, the requirement to use recycled materials involves appreciating the science behind recycling, repurposing, and reusing, as well as the aesthetics of using various unusual and creative media. That is certainly an interdisciplinary component of the project. You mentioned a third kind of integration?

E: Drake (2007) identifies *transdisciplinary* integration, which doesn't begin with any subject areas. Rather, students focus on an issue or theme that is relevant and of interest to them, and then they use whatever knowledge and skills necessary to tackle the issue.

A: That sounds very intriguing for students and their teachers, but I don't think that our art/science project falls into the transdisciplinary category.

Co-Planning

E: Astrid, I think we've digressed a bit. Can we go back to our initial thinking about why we began our art/science project?

A: I think we both had a common vision of what we wanted our TCs to know and be able to do when they leave our faculty of education. We both felt that the educator skills associated with curricular integration are very important. They are discussed in general terms within our program but are not fully explored or practiced. We both believe that it is important to model concepts for our TCs, and to have them experience integration first-hand.

E: And we both have strong environmental sensibilities concerning excessive consumerism by teachers and students, coupled with recognizing the heightened creativity that comes from having limited resources, like requiring TCs to use only recycled materials in their art constructions.

A: True, and I get at those environmental issues through the STSE expectations in the current science curriculum used in Ontario, Canada (Ontario Ministry of Education, 2007, 2008a, 2008b). STSE is the acronym for how science and technology impact society and environments. I strongly encourage the TCs to find contexts for the science and technology learning and teaching that they do, as a way to realize that there are usually social and environmental repercussions, both good and bad, when science and technology are in play.

E: Yes, you actually have the TCs create a fishbone organizer for the STSE elements of a specific science topic such as flight or space. The organizer is a framework for their thinking in science methods, but it also generates ideas for the TCs when they are considering how to represent something like flight artistically.

A: My practical side was also thinking about the logistics of our collaboration: our timetables and course schedules have to mesh appropriately, and for that we need administrative support.

E: That is no small feat, is it? Gaining and maintaining administrative support was one of the key components to enable our collaboration. Without our Dean's support, our timetables and those of our TCs would not have been coordinated. We had to align our separate courses in terms of teaching and setting assignments so that when the time came, we could coordinate the integration between our two courses.

A: We also had to agree on due dates and assessment tools early in each semester, as these become part of our course outlines.

E: I agree that much goes into the actual planning of the project. Our planning meetings have been formal and informal, long and short, within and outside our university. Sometimes we reflect together, other times we reflect on our own; we share thoughts online or in person. Regardless, from inception to assessment, we have worked together (see Figure 5.3).

A: We may have found a way to work like that, but our education program still functions in the separate "mine shaft" paradigm. We have to find a way to combine two separate courses that happen to share the same students.

E: Indeed, we begin from a state of separateness. We set the foundations early, separately, in each of our courses, and then merge our classes for the last assignment. That way, they have some knowledge of content and skills in both art and science before doing the integrated project. In the first part of the art education course, I introduce them to the basics of traditional media, such as drawing, painting, sculpture, and printmaking, with design elements and principles mixed into all media (Ontario Ministry of Education, 2009, 2010).

A: In my science education class we talk about and engage in science learning experiences that are inquiry-based and hands-on, and which provide meaningful contexts for student learning in grades 4 to 10. We also review a wide range of basic science concepts that fall under the categories of life systems, structures and mechanisms, matter and energy, and earth and space systems (Ontario Ministry of Education, 2007). We touch on really diverse topics, which is important since many of our graduates will be teaching science concepts that they haven't tackled since their own secondary school years. And of course, the revised Ontario science curriculum addresses the wise use of energy and other local and global resources.

E: I think the group project, which focuses on separate content and skills, is one of the drifts that connect across our two curricular mine shafts to offer opportunities for integration and collaboration.

A: True. In their science education course, the TCs do mainly group work; however, in art education, the art/science integration project is the only group assignment that they do. The remainder of the course is individual sketchbook activities and portfolio preparation. I think it's good for them to see us collaborating for the integration assignment as a model for their future practice in the classroom.

E: It would be wonderful if the model worked well in classrooms at all levels. There are substantive differences in how integration and

Figure 5.3. Co-planning meeting at our university. Photo by A. Steele.

Figure 5.4. One of our off-campus collaboration locations. Photo by E. Ashworth.

collaboration can work at the elementary, secondary, and higher education levels: one teacher versus two or more collaborators, and how that changes the landscape of integration. It's hard to avoid the mine shaft model, and to create drifts between subjects beyond the elementary grades.

A: Creating a space for drifts to exist between the subject shafts is something that can be difficult for educators for a number of reasons, many of which we've already mentioned. But I think that there is yet another element in play in our collaboration. It has to do with where we met to co-plan the assignment. I'd say that more than half of our co-planning time was spent off-campus, often outdoors, whether we were sitting on your deck, or walking our dogs in the woods. I wonder if that impacted our collaboration?

E: It certainly fits with the idea that integrated learning and thinking are how we function in the "real world." Perhaps by removing ourselves from the physical setting of the institution, with its mine shaft focus, we were also removing ourselves from some of the perceived barriers to collaboration and integration, and awakening our creative selves (see Figure 5.4).

A: Certainly some of my best thinking is done while walking in nature. That definitely doesn't happen in my office! Maybe creating drifts requires creative space.

Co-Instruction

E: Astrid, let's discuss how we worked together to create those drifts between art and science.

A: Well, it seemed easy to plan collaborative activities, but what was more difficult, based on our course schedules, was the concept of co-teaching.

E: Ideally, we would be timetabled into the same time slot in adjoining classrooms with connecting doors to move freely between lab and studio. Realistically, we have to make do with combining two separate courses with common TCs at different times of the day or week in classrooms separated by a long hallway. So, we organized our courses to accommodate our collaboration.

A: It has helped that our classrooms are in the same part of the university, and we know when we are both teaching our common TCs. I feel comfortable dropping into your class, and I know you feel the same about mine. We connect, check on the progress of the integration assignment, share observations, and make plans to discuss any issues later outside of class time.

E: In fact, visiting each other's classrooms while the TCs are present should not be just a spur-of-the-moment action because we find ourselves in the vicinity of the rooms. If we really want to model collaboration for our TCs, there should be an intentional decision involved in those visits, which speak to our commitment to interdisciplinary teaching and learning. In a way, we are collaborating in a model just short of team teaching.

A: Sadly, we have not yet had the opportunity to team teach, because our shared groups of TCs do not have their art and science education courses back-to-back or even on the same day.

E: At least for smooth implementation, we agree on the art/science project's description, including specific details, so that all components are clear for both of us. We also support each other's parts of the projects, and know enough about each other's segments to help in our individual classes.

A: I have a working knowledge of design, and you have a basic understanding of STSE concepts and expectations. If the TCs have questions during any part of the assignment, both of us may answer them in either class.

E: One of our assumptions leading into this integration assignment was that our TCs would obtain their "integration learning" elsewhere, whether they discuss integration in general – within their teaching methods course – or have experienced some form of integration in their own schooling. Neither of us spends much time discussing general integration concepts with our TCs, because we each have limited hours of course time in which to teach science education and art education, respectively; therefore, learners work "intuitively" on integrating these subjects.

A: The integration goes beyond our two subjects as well. The TCs also blend in language and environmental expectations for a multidisciplinary experience. They begin with science, apply design within their constructions created from recycled materials, and write reflections about integrations in general, merging art and science, connections to subjects beyond our disciplines, the process of creating their constructions, and related applications in their future classrooms (see Figure 5.5).

E: Overall, we want our TCs to have this integration experience, but the experience is for us too. We teach separately, but the opportunity to drop into each other's lessons helps to move the collaboration beyond just planning. Neither of us feels awkward answering questions from learners within the other's classroom; it is all part of the integration.

A: Although we have not had the opportunity to team teach in our respective courses, we have done so for conference workshops on a few occasions. It would be nice, in the future, to team teach lessons in a formal sense, in a common room and time period, for a more authentic collaborative instruction experience.

E: For us, personally, and as a model for our TCs and our colleagues.

A: In fact, over the past couple of years, colleagues in our faculty, university, and beyond have noticed what we are doing through our collaborative efforts and are curious about how it works. This curiosity has led to invitations to share our work in workshops, presentations, and publications.

Co-Assessment

E: Something else to consider, Astrid, is how we worked together to assess and evaluate our TCs' work and our own practice.

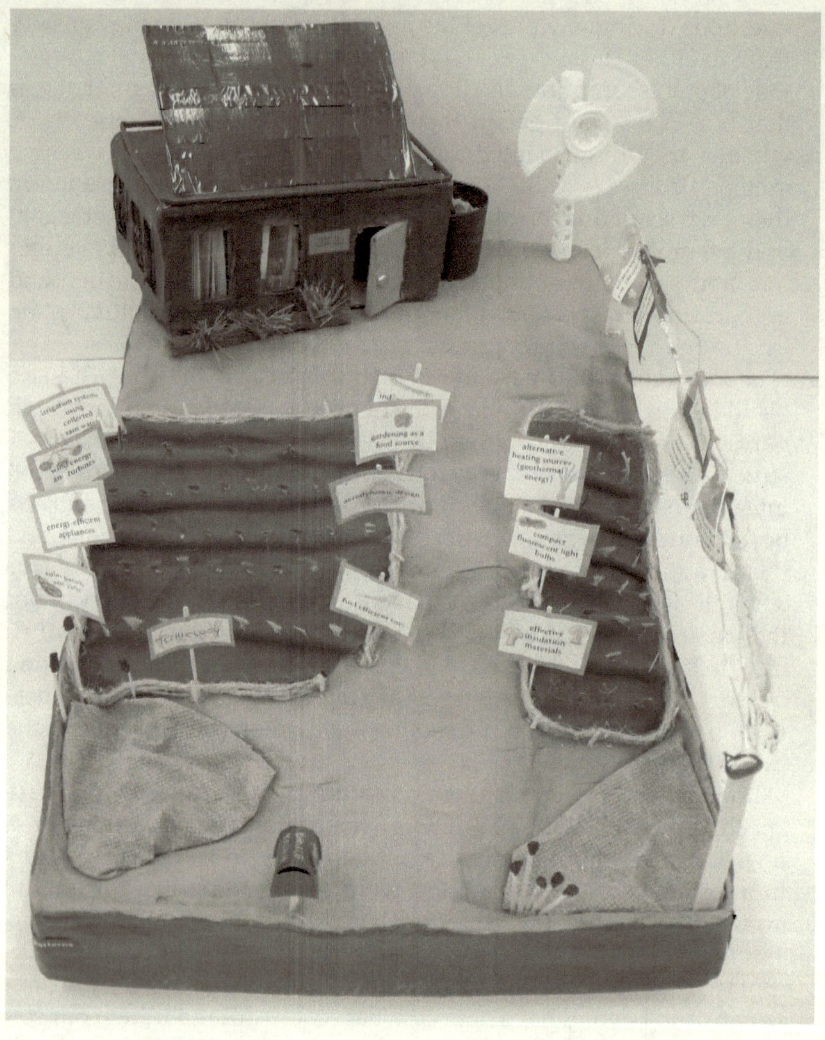

Figure 5.5. Sample student art/science construction. Photo by E. Ashworth.

A: When we created our art/science assignment, we designed the assessment rubric together. It contains expectations for both the science and the art segments of the assignment. We organized them separately within the rubric because the TCs did different parts of the assignment in different classes. In their science education class, they self-selected into groups, chose junior/intermediate division (grades 4 to 10) science topics to examine, and completed visual organizers to display their understanding of STSE expectations related to their topics.

E: About a week later, I introduced them to the art segment of the assignment: design applications, construction expectations, and environmental sustainability considerations – for example, the use of reused, recycled, and repurposed materials. All these elements were included in the rubric, along with a section for assessing the group reflections about the entire project.

A: During both the science and art segments of the assignment we provided feedback to groups and individuals so that the project evolved smoothly. Feedback happened in our own classes, separately.

E: After the art constructions were complete, we marked the subject-specific sections of the rubric individually, but assessed the reflections together, albeit through our own "subject lenses."

A: If, for example, there was a paragraph specifically about the STSE organizer, I would mark that.

E: And if there was one about design elements, I would mark that. But TC reflection comments about the process or benefits of integration were something that we both marked together. Regardless, we both read all the reflections, and each other's comments, in order to assess the assignment through two sets of eyes. That way, the assessment process was both individual and collaborative.

A: Over the lifetime of this integration assignment, we have reflected individually and collaboratively in order to revise our assessment process and the rubric. One of our first revisions was adding specific questions for TCs to use as prompts for their group reflections. This decision came from reading the first sets of reflections; we realized that our TCs needed help with moving from writing assignment descriptions to sharing insightful classroom considerations.

E: A more recent discussion has been around moving from group reflections to individual ones in order to "hear" the voices within the groups.

A: Regardless of whether they are individual or group reflections, they help us to understand not only how learners experience integration, but also how they experience a collaborative assignment.

E: We try to balance our rubric by incorporating sections for science-specific, art-specific, and general integration content.

A: The assessment piece is definitely a component that helps us understand the type of integration that we have created. Recall Drake's (2007) categories for integration: *multidisciplinary, interdisciplinary,* and *transdisciplinary.* Our assessment for the art construction is likely a *multidisciplinary* exercise, since we each mark distinct items. You are looking for elements of design, and I am looking for their understanding of the STSE concepts on which their art construction is based.

E: I see that, but our assessment of their reflection paper seems to me to fall into the *interdisciplinary* category, since we are both looking for their ideas about integration that are not subject specific.

A: Assessment of the assignment is definitely a work in progress for both of us, as we develop a deeper understanding of how different forms of integration might be assessed.

Bringing the Conversation to a Close

A: Liz, we've been talking about the value of the integrative experience for our TCs. As they complete the art/science project, which they might assign to their own students, they are actually thinking about their own learning as teachers who may use integrated curricula in their own classes. I think that such learning spans, and is applicable to, both science and art education. I'm happy that our collaboration enables that kind of learning for them.

E: It has been a positive experience for us, and we've been sharing what we've done and learned with our colleagues in the academic community at large. Although we plan, implement, assess, write, and present together, we've also made presentations separately in which we focus on subject-specific aspects of the integration assignment.

A: I have presented at science conferences where I focus on how the assignment helps learners understand STSE expectations. And you have done presentations at art conferences where you focus on how the art constructions make science concepts visual.

E: We've also presented together, placing a focus on environmental education considerations, including details about the requirement for TCs to use recycled materials to build their constructions. The audiences have seemed very receptive.

Figure 5.6. "Math-art" sample ["8"] from *Take it Outside!* activity. Photo by E. Ashworth.

A: It is worth mentioning that our collaboration quite naturally has evolved into other venues. Recently, we co-planned and implemented a workshop titled "Take it Outside!: Teaching and Learning in Alternative Spaces" (see Figure 5.6).

E: That was fun! We took the TC participants into the bush area adjacent to the university and asked them to work in groups – for example, in their primary/junior (kindergarten to grade 6), junior/intermediate (grades 4 to 10), and intermediate/senior (grades 7 to 12) divisions – to create teaching exemplars from found materials. The TCs used rocks, sticks, leaves, garbage, bark – anything at hand in their "wild" classroom. They had fifteen minutes to plan and create their exemplars, and then each group shared with the rest of us what they had made, including how it could be used as teaching and learning tools.

A: It's good that we can make collaboration and integration happen beyond the formalized courses that we teach.

Table 5.1. Summary of the mine/education metaphor.

Shafts in a Mine	Drifts in a Mine
Holes that reach far down into the earth in vertical columns; each has its separate infrastructures	Horizontal tunnels that may connect the vertical shafts in the mine so that information and materials can travel between the separate shafts and reach laterally into the ore body
Metaphorical Shafts in Education	**Metaphorical Drifts in Education**
Traditional structure of curricula, particularly in secondary schools	Non-traditional curricular structure at the secondary level
Disciplines stand alone, distinct and separated from each other	Disciplines are connected to each other at intersections where disparate knowledge and skills inform teaching and learning through various forms of integration such as *multidisciplinary, interdisciplinary,* and *transdisciplinary* approaches
Teachers work in isolation	Teachers are encouraged to collaborate
Learning is compartmentalized	Learning is recognized as a complex endeavour that draws on knowledge and skills from a variety of disciplines
Subject integration and teacher collaboration are curtailed	Subject integration and teacher collaboration are encouraged and supported
Authentic learning is curtailed	Authentic, contextual learning is encouraged
Students experience disciplines in isolation	Integration increases student success and interest in learning
Students experience discipline-specific thinking	Integration provides rich opportunities for synthesis of ideas from various disciplines
Traditional separate disciplinary learning does not take advantage of the brain's natural inclination to make connections	Integration acknowledges and works with the natural inclinations of brain function through interconnected learning
Timetabling of courses and teacher/student schedules is simplified	Timetabling of courses and teacher/student schedules becomes more complex and problematic
Teacher work is largely traditional	Teacher work requires extra time and workload as required by the organization and implementation of a collaboration
Assessment is largely traditional	Assessment is collaborative, requiring additional planning

A: I'm glad that we took the opportunity to really analyse and summarize our thinking about collaboration and integration – and to connect these thoughts to our mining metaphor (see Table 5.1).

E: I look forward to more collaborative undertakings. They reignite engagement in learning for our TCs and for us. Looking back, I am thankful that a past unsuccessful team teaching experience didn't deter me from collaborating with you a couple of years later. Now that we have developed better understandings of each other's course content and expectations, I would like to move towards team teaching with you.

A: That would be interesting. I have learned quite a bit about art instruction, such as the use of design elements and principles to create art constructions from recycled materials.

E: And I've had a chance to dig into science topics and STSE expectations. I think that we have been able to 'negotiate meaning and construct knowledge" (Kam & Katerattanakul, 2014, p. 2) through reciprocal learning.

A: Kam and Katerattanakul (2014) suggested that 'synchronicity and group awareness promote team-based learning" (p. 1). Although theirs was a study of collaboration among learners, their suggestion may apply to professors as well.

E: I've also learned how to let go of some control within my art program, allowing room for another professor to share planning, implementation, and assessment for an assignment. Our experience supports what Youens et al. (2014) describe as 'reciprocal learning conversations within a genuine learning partnership" (p. 108).

A: Looking back, one of our initial goals for this collaboration was to provide an integration experience for our TCs that had an environmental sustainability piece. That goal was the tenuous common thread that eventually became an important drift between the separate course shafts.

E: We wanted to model for our TCs what a collaboration might look like – another drift!

A: We are also modelling for our colleagues how subject integration might work in higher education. A few have asked about specifics regarding how we work collaboratively to bring our subjects together.

E: We could probably identify some fairly substantive bits that might serve as advice for other educators who are considering collaborations with colleagues around coursework integration. For example, our collaboration works well because we chose to work together, not because we were assigned to each other.

A: There is a level of creativity required of the collaborators to find the connections between courses – these become the drifts that connect ideas between subject areas.

E: I would add that there is also a level of perseverance needed to bring collaborations to fruition. Collaborators need to deal with quite a few logistical problems, such as class scheduling, alignment of assessment, communicating clearly with students to avoid confusing, and possibly contradictory, information and instructions.

A: It can be a juggling act, and it's certainly a lot of work, but the results are perhaps deeper understandings and stronger connections.

E: It has been an enjoyable collaborative journey, and it's not over yet. I think that the intentionality that we imply in our conversation belies the sense of exploration that has really been at the heart of our collaboration.

A: Looking forward to working with you again, Liz.

E: And you, too, Astrid.

REFERENCES

Bruner, J. (1987). Life as narrative. *Social Research*, *54*, 11–32.

Bruner, J. (1991). The narrative construction of reality. *Critical Inquiry*, *18*(1), 1–21. http://dx.doi.org/10.1086/448619

Drake, S. (2007). *Creating standards-based integrated curriculum: Aligning curriculum, content, assessment and instruction* (2nd ed.). Thousand Oaks, CA: Corwin Press.

Drake, S., & Burns, D. (2004). *Meeting standards through integrated curriculum*. Alexandria, VA: Association for Supervision and Curriculum Development.

Ellis, C., & Bochner, A. (2000). Autoethnography, personal narrative, reflexivity: Researcher as subject. In N. Denzin & Y. Lincoln (Eds.), *Handbook of qualitative research* (2nd ed., pp. 733–68). Thousand Oaks, CA: Sage.

Gutiérrez, K. (2008). Developing a sociocritical literacy in the third space. *Reading Research Quarterly*, *43*(2), 148–64. http://dx.doi.org/10.1598/RRQ.43.2.3

Hargreaves, A., Earl, L., Moore, S., & Manning, S. (2001). *Learning to change: Teaching beyond subjects and standards*. San Francisco, CA: Jossey-Bass.

Jensen, E. (2005). *Teaching with the brain in mind* (2nd ed.). Alexandria, VA: Association for Supervision and Curriculum Development.

Kam, H., & Katerattanakul, P. (2014). Structural model of team-based learning using Web 2.0 collaborative software. *Computers & Education*, *76*, 1–12. http://dx.doi.org/10.1016/j.compedu.2014.03.003

Lucas, A.M. (1980). Science and environmental education: Pious hopes, self praise and disciplinary chauvinism. *Studies in Science Education*, *7*(1), 1–26. http://dx.doi.org/10.1080/03057268008559874

McGeehan, J. (2001). Brain compatible learning. *Green Teacher (Toronto), 64*, 7–13.

Ontario Ministry of Education (2007). *Science and technology: The Ontario curriculum grades 1–8, revised.* Toronto, ON: Queen's Printer for Ontario.

Ontario Ministry of Education. (2008a). *Science and technology: The Ontario curriculum grades 9 and 10, revised.* Toronto, ON: Queen's Printer for Ontario.

Ontario Ministry of Education. (2008b). *Science and technology: The Ontario curriculum grades 11 and 12, revised.* Toronto, ON: Queen's Printer for Ontario.

Ontario Ministry of Education (2009). *The arts: The Ontario curriculum grades 1–8, revised.* Toronto, ON: Queen's Printer for Ontario.

Ontario Ministry of Education. (2010). *The arts: The Ontario curriculum grades 9 and 10, revised.* Toronto, ON: Queen's Printer for Ontario.

Richardson, L. (1997). Fields of play: Constructing an academic life. *Qualitative Inquiry*, 2(1), 15–28.

Schroeder, C. (1999). Partnerships: An imperative for enhancing student learning and instructional effectiveness. *New Directions for Student Services, 1999*(87), 5–18. http://dx.doi.org/10.1002/ss.8701

Shacklock, G., & Thorp, L. (2005). Life history and narrative approaches. In B. Somekh & C. Lewin (Eds.), *Research methods in the social sciences* (pp. 156–63). London, UK: Sage.

Shulman, L.S. (1986). Those who understand: Knowledge growth in teaching. *Educational Researcher, 15*(2), 4–14. http://dx.doi.org/10.3102/0013189X015002004

Siskin, L.S. (1994). *Realms of knowledge: Academic departments in secondary schools*. London, UK: Falmer.

Venville, G., Sheffield, R., Rennie, L.J., & Wallace, J. (2008). The writing on the wall: Classroom context, curriculum implementation, and student learning integrated, community-based science projects. *Journal of Research in Science Teaching, 45*(8), 857–80. http://dx.doi.org/10.1002/tea.20245

Venville, G., Wallace, J., Rennie, L.J., & Malone, J.A. (2000). Bridging the boundaries of compartmentalized knowledge: Student learning in an integrated environment. *Research in Science & Technological Education, 18*(1), 23–35. http://dx.doi.org/10.1080/713694958

Venville, G., Wallace, J., Rennie, L.J., & Malone, J.A. (2002). Curriculum integration: Eroding the high ground of science as a school subject? *Studies in Science Education, 37*(1), 43–84. http://dx.doi.org/10.1080/03057260208560177

Wallace, J., Sheffield, R., Rennie, L., & Venville, G. (2007). Looking back, looking forward: Researching the conditions for curriculum integration in the middle years of schooling. *Australian Educational Researcher*, *34*(2), 29–49. http://dx.doi.org/10.1007/BF03216856

Youens, B., Smethem, L., & Sullivan, S. (2014). Promoting collaborative practice and reciprocity in initial teacher education: Realising a "dialogic space" through video capture analysis. *Journal of Education for Teaching*, *40*(2), 101–13. http://dx.doi.org/10.1080/02607476.2013.871163

6 Visual Art and Mathematics Integration: An Interdisciplinary Co-Teaching Experience

ROBERTA LA HAYE AND IRENE NAESTED

Introduction

The authors of this chapter co-developed, co-taught, and conducted research based on the course Visual Art and Mathematics: An Integrated Understanding. Our course integrated mathematics and visual arts for future elementary educators. We come from two different faculties, and our diverse experiences and expertise brought a unique perspective to the co-teaching process. Art educator Dr Irene Naested has extensive expertise in arts integration and co-teaching in both the K–12 and post-secondary levels. Mathematician Dr Roberta La Haye also has interdisciplinary co-teaching experience at the post-secondary level, and had recently expanded her research interests to include the ties between mathematics and art.

Our intention in this chapter is to discuss our co-teaching in the context of the current research regarding co-teaching interdisciplinary courses and co-teaching future educators. Several papers on co-teaching have cited a lack of information on modelling co-teaching for potential team teachers, as well as on planning and delivering collaborative courses (Graziano & Navarrete, 2012; Kluth & Straut, 2003; Letterman & Dugan, 2004). We hope to provide insights into the design and implementation of interdisciplinary and co-taught teacher education courses. We will also address the following questions: Why co-teach? What are the different models of course integration and co-teaching? What are the perceived benefits to students? What were the perceived challenges, and how were they addressed? What were the benefits to us as co-teachers?

The observations, insights, and experiences presented in this chapter were derived through three methods. First, we reviewed the literature on co-teaching interdisciplinary courses and teacher education courses. Second, we drew on our own personal experiences in co-developing and co-teaching both the course discussed here and previous courses. During the piloting of the integrated mathematics and visual art course, we both wrote weekly reflections on our experiences, which have informed our understanding of co-teaching. Third, for the first two iterations of the course, we conducted research and gained permission from students to study their course artefacts and conduct interviews. The purpose of this investigation was to determine if a deliberate attempt to showcase mathematics and visual arts as distinct viewpoints of the world, and to present the two disciplines as equal partners in understanding the world, could make significant changes to pre-service teachers' attitudes towards, and understanding of, mathematics and visual arts and the teaching of these two subjects.

"Interdisciplinary" means combining or involving two or more academic disciplines or fields of study. According to Rhoten and Pfirman (2007), higher education institutions are currently engaged in an "interdisciplinary arms race," expanding interdisciplinary courses, programs, and research opportunities. Holley (2009) maintains that the number of interdisciplinary programs in the United States has more than doubled in three decades to over 2,200 in 2005. She further notes that interdisciplinary education typically involves collaboration between faculty from different fields, so it stands to reason that course co-development and co-teaching has expanded along with interdisciplinary education.

According to Davis (1995), interdisciplinary courses are a necessary response to specialization. He notes that disciplines and professional fields have become more and more specialized, and hence more and more isolated. The isolation hinders discipline scholars from broadening their knowledge outside their field. Discipline specialization also predisposes academics to view the world mainly through the lens of their discipline; as a consequence, they ignore or downplay broader issues and often lack a holistic perspective. One result of this over-specialization can be research of questionable value to the researchers themselves, as it is certainly not dealing with the complex interdisciplinary issues that epitomize the advancement of knowledge in today's world. Another undesirable side effect of specialization is the production of graduates whose personal growth and sense of identity have been stunted by exposure to only a narrow view of one single discipline.

Interdisciplinary co-teaching has an important place in the K–12 level as well. A major motivation for co-teaching in K–12 is the inclusion of students with special needs (Naested, Potvin, & Waldron, 2004). Furthermore, Jones, Lake, and Dagli (2003) noted calls for science, technology, engineering, and mathematics (STEM) integration from various educational organizations, such as the National Council of Teachers of Mathematics (NCTM). STEM education has strong support in primary and secondary education. There is also a significant lobby for arts collaboration to be added to the mix, and the result is called the STEAM model of integrated learning (Sousa & Pilecki, 2013).

While it is certainly beneficial to encourage students to connect knowledge between different disciplines from an early age, interdisciplinary learning in K–12 has other motivations as well. Different educational theories promote the value of interdisciplinary learning (more commonly referred to as integrated learning in this context). The goal of integrated education is to increase students' interest and overall understanding.

A general overview of the entire interdisciplinary co-teaching process has been described by Davis (1995) in the following way. Typically, it starts when at least one person gets an insight and then decides to seek the appropriate team members to carry it out. From this beginning, a team is then formed, the subject is invented, the learning outcomes are determined, and the scope and sequence of the course is planned. Along the way, the team decides on an organizational structure, divides the labour, and chooses potential teaching strategies, which are then used and possibly modified in the classroom. Assessment strategies are chosen and implemented, and at the end of the course, reflections are made and revisions considered.

This simple breakdown of the co-teaching experience belies the complexities involved. Each step has its own challenges, and many researchers have made the following two observations: first, that co-teaching a course is much more time-consuming than teaching alone; and second, that post-secondary institutions typically do not acknowledge or reward co-teaching efforts (Davis, 1995; Naested, 2010). It was our belief in the value of interdisciplinary teaching that convinced us to proceed, even while anticipating the time commitment involved.

The course was the brainchild of Dr Naested and was based on her interest in, as an advocate for, the arts in elementary education and her expertise and experience in both interdisciplinary teaching and co-teaching.

Background: Co-Teaching – One Educator's Story

Having taught for over four decades, my (Naested's) experiences as a K–12 teacher, college instructor, and university professor have convinced me of the value of both interdisciplinary education and co-teaching. These experiences led me to the wonderful opportunity to co-teach an integrated new course of mathematics and art education at a post-secondary institution with Dr La Haye.

My first permanent teaching position was at a challenging junior high school, in which students graduating from grade 9 would typically be the highest educated in their families at that time. Integrated, collaborative, or team teaching was not practiced or encouraged at this school. I was assigned to teach art and social studies. Frustrated with my inability to engage my grade 7 social studies students, I gradually moved the social studies classes into the art room, where I began to develop my own model of an integrated pedagogy. I was able to write and publish a chapter on my teaching theory in 1993. As you can see from the excerpt below, the experience convinced me of the value of integrating other disciplines with the arts:

> I believe it is difficult not only for children, but for all learners, to learn or comprehend, to investigate or question, when the information they are receiving is unrelated to their life and is presented, communicated, and expressed only through word and number. This form of non-inquiry, or forgotten thoughtfulness, does not develop or use the multi-sensory modes of information gathering, perceiving, and expression. (Naested, 1993a, p. 83)

As a first-year teacher in this school, I would have really appreciated the opportunity to co-plan the grade 7 social studies course and expand upon my efforts to integrate social studies with art. Unfortunately, co-teaching was not considered an option at this school.

Around this time, "open-area classrooms" had been designed in some of the new elementary schools being built. The "open-area" movement originated in the British public elementary schools after World War II and was later introduced to the United States and Canada. The theory behind this movement was to focus students on "learning by doing," and to facilitate "teaching teams." The teacher teams were to work collaboratively with one another, rearranging the space as needed from large to small groups of students. However, there was little in the way of professional development for teachers to carry out this pedagogical concept, and within a matter of years many, if not most, open-area schools had constructed interior walls to separate classrooms. This model became another "fad" for co-teaching and learning. In my experience, what is sometimes coined as an "educational innovation," or "reinvention," often becomes merely a short-lived educational fad when ongoing support for professional development for teachers is not provided or encouraged.

I was fortunate to have other wonderful teaching experiences in various settings. By the mid-1980s, I had the opportunity to teach at one of the first "segregated settings" in Calgary, a school for the "gifted and talented" from grades 3 to 9. This school was where I really experienced great teaching that included collaborative, integrated, and co- and team-teaching methods. It was an atmosphere in which (with full support from system and school-based administrators) time, space, and teaching assignments were more flexible, open, and impermanent (and with no bells!). There was a full slate of subject specialists, including drama, music, and art teachers. All were outstanding educators who were subject experts and were excited to take part in collaboration, integration, and co- and team teaching. "Teachers felt that they learned as much as the students. This form of teaching required strong self-concepts on the part of the teacher who is not the 'full-frontal' or 'traditional' teacher" (Naested, 1993b, p. 86). The teachers in this segregated setting realized that students become most engaged in their studies when the topic is something in which they have an interest. The students were guided to ask their own questions regarding study topics. Assessment of students' investigations became a form of exhibition, where students were given the opportunity to demonstrate what they knew and were able to do, rather than be merely a "trial by question" exercise (Naested, 1993b).

In 1990, I was given the position of head of the Department of Fine and Performing Arts at a newly built high school that had the mandate to be a "lighthouse" for high school innovation. The leadership team was hired a year before the school opened to design spaces and pedagogy, school philosophy, and organization. At the time, I had just started my doctoral degree in educational leadership, and the form of teaching and learning taking place at this innovative high school, Lester B. Pearson, gave me great fodder for my studies focusing on educational innovation (Naested, 1993a). I researched the following nine innovative elements that were incorporated into the design and philosophy of the school environment: teacher-advisor program, alternative assessment, team teaching, integration of course disciplines, alternative teaching, elimination of tracking, flexible scheduling, technology in teaching and learning, and school design. The following are three of my findings for team teaching and course integration:

> Team teaching as implemented at Pearson was considered beneficial to both the students and educators with few problems in teaming. Team teaching on an informal basis was more difficult to arrange and in many cases the provision of common planning time was needed ... Integration of courses was considered to be a benefit to both the educators and students. Many features of the design of the school enhanced course integration ... These features included flexible sizes, use, timetable, desks, and seating ... There were barriers which hampered efforts to integrate course disciplines such as the external diploma exams and provincial curriculum guidelines. (Naested, 1993a, p. 273)

One of the final recommendations in my dissertation was this: "In order for educational innovation to become a reality administrative support is needed, together with educators who are willing to take risks and invest time and energy to accomplish shared philosophies" (Naested, 1993a, p. 278). Unfortunately, with a change in administration and teaching staff, the school soon reverted to a "regular" high school. The support for taking risks and "doing things differently" was no longer provided.

In 1995, I was hired to teach and coordinate a two-year educational studies transfer program at a college. I was able to collaboratively teach with many instructors and to collaboratively plan and assess the different sections of the same courses. However, it was difficult to team teach unless it was informally planned, and was without compensation.

The college eventually became a university, and I became chair of the newly formed department and the newly developed degree in education. I continued to research, author, and co-author on the topic of integration and team teaching. These publications included *Art in the Classroom: An Integrated Approach to Teaching Art in Canadian Elementary and Middle Schools* (Naested, 2010), *Understanding the Landscape of Teaching* (Naested, Potvin, & Waldron, 2004), and *Exploring the Math and Art Connection: Teaching and Learning between the Lines* (Jarvis & Naested, 2012).

In the textbook, *Art in the Classroom* (Naested, 2010), I included discussion of discipline integration models and chapters that connected art education with other subject disciplines including mathematics. My main concern was that when art was integrated into the teaching of other subjects, it tended to take on a minor, even detrimental role. Few educators who incorporated art experiences with other subjects understood that visual art is a unique discipline. For example, the use of coloured crayons in a mathematics activity does not make the lesson a valuable art learning experience. The book entitled *Exploring the Math and Art Connection* (Jarvis & Naested, 2012) considers the "bigger picture" of the mathematics and visual art connections to be found in areas such as nature, art, architecture, and human-designed objects. I also decided to pursue the creation of an integrated mathematics and visual arts course, designed mainly for education students (future teachers).

I was very fortunate to have Dr La Haye from the mathematics department agree to co-develop and co-teach with me for the first and second implementation a course we called Visual Art and Mathematics: An Integrated Understanding. La Haye is a fantastic colleague who is not intimidated by what she may not know and secure about what she does know. We share mutual respect and trust.

Co-Planning

Forming a Course Development Team

After the decision was made to pursue the idea for an interdisciplinary course, the next decision was whether or not to form a team to co-develop and potentially co-teach it. Interdisciplinary courses are obvious candidates for co-development and co-teaching due to their innate need for diverse areas of expertise. Co-planning brings together the necessary discipline-based knowledge. It also promotes a balanced approach to course development in which co-developers act as advocates for their own disciplines. As Davis (1995) stated, "The greater the level of integration desired, the higher the level of collaboration required" (p. 45).

Discipline expertise and the goal of a balanced presentation of the disciplines of mathematics and visual art were the primary motivations for Dr Naested to form the co-teaching team. She was interested in inspiring pre-service elementary teachers to integrate visual arts with other disciplines within the elementary classroom. The appropriate balance of the disciplines was of paramount concern.

In the case of the arts integration with other disciplines, researchers have noted (Eisner, 1999; Naested, 2010) that connecting arts to other subjects still does not occur regularly in the elementary classroom. Furthermore, when connections are made with visual arts and other disciplines, the results often fail to advance the students' art education, and/or visual arts play only a minor supporting role. These findings raise concerns that the integrity and value of the arts can potentially be compromised in integrated experiences (Cormack, 1991; Eisner, 1999; Grauer, 1991; Naested, 2010).

Mathematics education can benefit from appropriate integration as well. Mathematics teachers frequently deal with criticisms that school mathematics is not useful, and that mathematics teaching often fails to address the diverse learning styles of students. Alberta's K–9 program of studies for mathematics notes, "[W]hen mathematical ideas are connected to each other or to real-world phenomena, students begin to view mathematics as useful, relevant and integrated" (Education Alberta, 2016, p. 5).

With respect to integrating arts with mathematics, there is also a concern that the mathematics content could become "watered down" to the point of being insignificant (Jarvis & Naested, 2012). As well, many books and Internet sites promoting mathematics and art integrated lessons are authored by non–subject experts. Without involvement from a mathematics educator, the quality of the learning experience is not vetted from a mathematics viewpoint. With the concerns of both visual arts and mathematics in mind, Naested felt that the best way to protect the integrity and value of both art and mathematics was to have discipline experts involved in the planning and teaching processes.

Several other reasons for forming a team to develop interdisciplinary courses also impacted the development of our course. For one thing, in any co-developing experience, people working in groups generate more ideas than they would individually. In addition, co-planning brings together different discipline perspectives (Davis, 1995). In our case, we found the celebration of the different perspectives that mathematics and visual arts bring to the examination of any object or phenomena to be a natural way to engage students in interdisciplinary learning experiences – it became a pivotal teaching strategy in our various mathematics and art learning experiences. Another benefit of co-developed interdisciplinary courses is that students are challenged to build critical thinking skills by synthesizing the multiple perspectives presented to them. The course relates information to a larger framework (Letterman

& Dugan, 2004), which further challenges students. In our course, students were expected to synthesize three main perspectives: art, mathematics, and education.

Once it is established that a team will be recruited to plan a course, the discipline expertise and personal interests of potential participants, as well as perhaps related workplace pressures, will often limit the number of co-teaching teammates. One difference noted by Winn and Messenbeimer-Young (1995) regarding co-teaching at the university level versus the K–12 level is that university team teaching is usually done on a voluntary basis; in K–12 the team teaching is not necessarily voluntary, and team members need not have any experience with one other in advance.

After Naested decided to find a co-planning and co-teaching partner with a mathematical background, the required interests and areas of expertise reduced the number of potential candidates to a very small pool at our university from which to form a team – namely, La Haye. Fortunately, both of us had prior co-teaching and course co-development experience to support the process, and neither of us saw a need for a larger team. Davis (1995), among others, gives characteristics for an effective interdisciplinary team, such as expertise, openness to diverse ways of thinking, flexibility, and the ability to self-reflect. Both of us were aware, from our previous co-developing and co-teaching experiences, that such behaviours were important practices; they were essential criteria that made this partnership viable, pleasant, and exciting. We shared a mutual respect for one another. We had subject expertise that complemented one another. We were willing to compromise and reach a mutual understanding of how we were going to proceed in the planning, teaching, and assessment of the course. We were willing to "do things differently," both of us feeling secure in that our careers were not in jeopardy.

In our case, with only two people on the co-developing team, we did not formally assign either partner as leader. However, it was clear to both of us what expertise each of us brought to this particular project. All decisions were therefore mutual. There were occasions when we agreed to try something in class (content or teaching strategy) that one instructor felt was more promising than the other. In that case, we noted student feedback and used it to inform future course development.

Inventing the Subject

Letterman and Dugan (2004) noted that in the early stages of team collaboration, concept-oriented meetings are quite productive, and that goals and objectives should be clarified during this stage. We found this to be the case as well. Although Naested had started with the concept of a course that integrated mathematics and visual art for pre-service elementary teachers (and had also co-authored a book on integrating mathematics and art education), she was open to considering alternatives. We considered targeting a broader audience with the course, but the opportunity to target pre-service elementary teachers was more viable due to a newly implemented elementary education degree within our institution. We also considered integrating other science disciplines, but it simply was not feasible given the particular expertise of our team. We did incorporate other subjects to a limited extent within a few learning experiences.

Following some discussions, we agreed that the course goals for pre-service teachers would include the following components: showcasing or modelling the value of interdisciplinary teaching – in particular with mathematics and art integration; celebrating connections between mathematics and visual arts; and demonstrating that mathematics and visual art curricular goals from our province's elementary curriculum are attainable through appropriate math-art learning experiences. We felt that we needed to move from the Eurocentric view of teaching to a more ethnocentric approach; in other words, use a real-world approach to understanding both mathematics and visual arts.

We agreed that it was appropriate to target third-year education students, as they would have greater maturity and be able to scaffold their background in educational theory, mathematics, and visual arts. We quickly agreed on the fundamental concept of balance between disciplines. We decided to treat our pre-service elementary teachers as if they were teachers in professional development workshops and lead them through what we considered to be balanced and natural integrated mathematics and visual arts learning experiences.

The integration of subject models is certainly not a new idea. Over seventy-five years ago, Dewey (1938) wrote: "[T]he subject-matter of education consists of bodies of information and of skills that have been worked out in the past; therefore the chief business of the school is to transmit them to the new generation" (p. 17). He did not believe that the *subject-matter model* would assist the students for a future in "a changing world" (p. 20). Greene (1971) echoed this idea when he stated:

> Curriculum, from the learner's standpoint, ordinarily represents little more than an arrangement of subjects, a structure of socially prescribed

> knowledge, or a complex system of meanings which may or may not fall within his [the student's] grasp. Rarely does it signify possibility for him [the student] as an existing person, mainly concerned with making sense of his own life-world. (p. 254)

Developing this thread further, Fogarty (1991) wrote a summary of the ten ways or models for integrating curriculum. She separated the ten models into specific categories: within single disciplines, across several disciplines, and within and across learners. The "within single disciplines" category included fragmented, connected, and nested models. In the "across several disciplines" category, Fogarty listed five models: the *sequenced model* (taught separately but connected by a common topic); the *shared model* (shared planning or teaching in two disciplines); the *webbed model* (using overlapping concepts as organizers; cross-discipline theme, for example, inventions); the *threaded model* (big ideas, superseding discipline content); and the *integrated model* (interdisciplinary topic rearranged around overlapping concepts). In the "within/across learners" category, Fogarty placed the *immersed model* (within learners funnelled through an area of intense interest) and the *networked model* (learner-directed integration). Fogarty concluded, "These models are just beginnings. Teachers should go on to invent their own designs for integrating the curriculum. The process itself never ends" (p. 65).

Since Fogarty's article was published, many educational planners have indeed gone on to invent further designs for integrating curriculum and have expanded on further motivations for integrated learning. These include models such as project-based, inquiry-based, site-based, and problem-based learning; constructivist approaches; multiple intelligence teaching; twenty-first century learning and teaching; STEM, and the more recent adaptation including the arts – STEAM-based teaching.

While we were aware of all this research on integrated learning, we believed that we had a "game changer" with respect to integrating visual art and mathematics. "Game changer" is defined as a newly introduced element or factor that changes an existing situation or activity in a significant way. Our early conceptual decisions on the course, especially the demand for balance and relevance in our learning experiences and our intention to team teach it, would make our course drastically different from courses we had seen at other universities that connected art with mathematics. Our conceptual decisions would also make our math-art learning experiences markedly different from the K–8 math-art learning experiences that we had both previously encountered.

One integration concept that resonated with our course development ideas was the newly defined ethno-mathematics idea of *mutual interrogation*. Mutual interrogation is defined as "the process of setting up two systems of knowledge in parallel to each other in order to illuminate their similarities and differences, and explore the potential of enhancing and transforming each other" (Adam, Alangui, & Barton, 2010, p. 86). This concept played a large role in the co-planning and co-teaching of the second iteration of our integrated course.

Scope and Sequence of the Course

We were cognizant of our planned learning outcomes for the course at the earliest stages of development. We wanted students to gain an understanding of the motivations for, and challenges of, integrated learning. We wanted our pre-service teachers to become sufficiently comfortable with math-art integrated learning so that they would be able to critically assess integrated learning experiences and create rich integrated learning experiences of their own.

After we mutually agreed on the above conceptual decisions regarding the course, we then were able to develop specific mathematics and art learning experiences that were to form the "backbone" of the course. The mutually agreed upon course goals and learning outcomes helped us avoid slipping back into the traditional content approaches of our respective disciplines.

Since our course was new, it was required to go through a curriculum submission process, which had our course (including calendar description and course outline) vetted by a university-wide committee. We met once weekly for two to three hours in order to make conceptual decisions, put together the submission, and develop the course outline. We agreed to schedule the course as a three-hour lecture, meeting once per week. This was a natural schedule, given our decision to treat the students similar to teachers experiencing professional development sessions, and we anticipated the math-art learning experiences to be lengthy.

We had the Alberta mathematics and art program of studies resources for the course to support our intention to actively demonstrate to the students how integrated learning experiences could address the curriculum. In addition, La Haye, in particular, was keen to have a textbook for the course, if possible. We considered various possibilities but felt that the available books were either too math-oriented or too art-oriented. We decided to use the book that Naested had previously co-authored, *Exploring the Math and Art Connection: Learning between the Lines* (Jarvis & Naested, 2012). The book was intended as a teacher resource rather than a course textbook, but it was the only book we found with the balanced perspective so integral to our course. The sections in the math and art book are categorized under the themes of flora, fauna, the human body, designed objects, and the designed world. This atypical organization helped discourage either discipline from dominating the other. Further, it predicates every math-art lesson idea on observing and understanding the natural and human-made world around us.

We decided to use the book's organizational structure for the course, taking many of our lesson themes from it. Nevertheless, a great deal of work was required to further develop math-art connection ideas (textbook-based or otherwise) into rich, meaningful math-art learning experiences attaining specified curriculum outcomes. Naested was often impressed at the mathematics connections that La Haye was able to envision when developing the mathematics parts of the experiences.

Following the acceptance of our course submission, we continued to meet for roughly the same amount of time each week and planned the scope of the course and the draft for each class session. As the course start date approached, we increased the frequency of the meetings to twice per week. The first meeting early in the week was to confirm plans for a particular session, to propose math-art learning experiences in general terms, and to delegate the discipline-based expert who would "flesh out" specific content and teaching strategies. The second meeting was to unite the draft plans into a cohesive teaching and learning experience for students (and for us). After the course began, we also used the first weekly meeting to reflect on the previous week's session.

In the first few lectures, we discussed with our students what integrated learning was and the pedagogical motivations for it. Classes thereafter typically started with a general theme, such as fauna, and what we agreed to was one or more substantial math-art connections relating to that theme, and included an idea of the appropriate elementary grade level/s. Each co-teacher considered how the experience could be adapted with respect to her discipline in order to meet the elementary curriculum learning objectives in each subject area. The planning of the lesson included the discipline-specific content/learning objectives and the pedagogical approach capitalizing on individual expertise. We realized that each discipline expert had to completely understand both the art and the mathematics involved, including the creation of the artefact in advance of the lesson. This was an important step in the interdisciplinary team teaching process, as we did not want to give contradictory directions, fail to anticipate potential problems, or miss opportunities for enlightenment.

Developing and teaching the course represented a steep learning curve for us as the teachers, especially for La Haye, who had less experience with education students and with integrated learning. Not only did we expand our knowledge of each other's disciplines, but we also revised our understanding of our own disciplines. For example, La Haye, as a mathematician, quickly discovered that many of the alleged math-art learning experiences with which she was familiar she would now consider to be merely *math crafts*, since they did nothing to teach or reinforce the principles and values of visual art. It is not uncommon to find the construction of cubes and pyramids from nets and string art, and so forth, labelled as math-art connections, but in each case there is rarely any personal choice or creativity involved. The student simply follows an algorithm to end up with an interesting visual drawing or construction.

As non-experts in each other's disciplines, we could usually see math-art connections in various situations, but we were not always able to gauge the value of the connection from the educational standpoint of the other discipline. This observation reinforces the value of co-planning in our particular case. With intensive planning, where different ideas for learning experiences were vetted, we each became more adept at evaluating the connections to one another's discipline. We also realized that even discipline experts could miss opportunities to connect to their own discipline, because they are overly accustomed to the typical, traditional delivery of curriculum. Our ability to exploit connections became better through experience in integrated lesson planning. Wilson and Martin (1998) also report being better able to recognize areas of integration as their co-teaching relationship matured.

As an example, one learning experience that we co-developed for our course involved studying the human figure and facial features, and how visual arts and mathematics can help us more accurately depict the human body and do portrait drawing using sight measurements. We discussed the question that we brought in from the viewpoints of both disciplines, including body measurement, data collection, and proportions through the lens of mathematics. We noted how art used this mathematical analysis to inform figure drawing and sight measuring. The art concept of sight measurement was then applied to a mathematical problem, namely estimating the heights of objects based on the known heights of others and a proportional relationship determined by sight measurement. Many artists, such as the ancient Egyptians, Vitruvius, da Vinci, and Dürer, have studied the proportions of the human body mathematically as part of their artistic process, and we discussed some of their different ideas and ideals. We also discussed how the experience could fulfil the mathematics and art elementary curriculum objectives, and pointed out how the line $y = x$ was a suitable mathematical model for height versus arm-span data.

The students in the course were pre-service teachers, so as the professors of the integrated course, we felt the need to demonstrate where key terms and understanding in both visual arts and mathematics could be found in our jurisdiction's program of study teacher manuals and the grades 1 to 6 textbooks. In this, we were consistent with Krometis, Clark, Gonzalez, and Leslie (2011), who recommend that co-teachers have a basic understanding of the vocabulary and fundamentals of each other's discipline. Further, an appendix of the selected textbook featured key terms from visual art and mathematics.

Many of the math-art learning experiences in the course were motivated by real-life interdisciplinary examples. Historically, artists like Vitruvius and da Vinci took measurements and collected data on a sample of people (living and otherwise) to better understand human proportions well before the mathematical branches of statistics and data management were popularized. Artists were the first to use grids in drawing and painting before René Descartes (b. 1596) added numbers to them and created the Cartesian coordinate system. Platonic solids and other three-dimensional figures fascinated mathematicians and artists, but it was the artist Dürer who came up with the idea of nets as a method of constructing them (Wilson & Fasanelli, 2000). More recently, the late artist M.C. Escher owed much of his success to how he used mathematicians' studies of symmetry to inform his art. Ironically, mathematicians subsequently used his artistic ideas to extend their mathematical understanding of symmetry (Ernst, 1978/2007).

Co-Teaching

Co-Teaching Models and Teaching Strategies

As Davis (1995) points out, the team that develops an integrated course need not be the team that teaches the course. We agreed when our team was formed that we would both co-develop and co-teach the course, as our discipline expertise would be of value and our desire for a balance between mathematics and visual art would be more attainable with both discipline advocates teaching together.

Co-teaching encompasses many possible models: one instructor teaches, one instructor observes; one instructor teaches, one instructor "drifts"; station teaching; parallel teaching; alternative teaching; and team teaching. Another approach to this is "tag team," a more traditional method of team teaching, where each co-teacher meets the class alone to "cover" a segment of the material. "Tag-team teaching has its benefits, but it misses out on the benefits of dialogue and the give-and-take engaged in by the team of instructors" (Vanderbilt University, 2017).

In terms of the co-teaching models just mentioned, we would describe our co-teaching as the team teaching model. For every class, both instructors were present and involved in that day's session. Expertise was the main factor in determining who led various parts of the class, but we had planned sufficiently so that we were both comfortable interjecting comments and posing and answering questions as needed.

Co-teaching, like co-planning, has its own benefits for interdisciplinary courses and courses for pre-service teachers. However, the discipline perspectives that are shared in the course co-development are more obvious to students and are more likely to become evident if the discipline experts deliberately model them.

Co-teachers can model strategies that they desire students to adopt in their future careers. An interdisciplinary course can provide students with an example of interdisciplinary team work in action (Davis, 1995). We felt it would be of value for students to see the sharing of our discipline viewpoints, as well as to note how we worked together to achieve a balance between mathematics and visual art within any particular learning experience. Similarly, co-teaching a course also demonstrates co-teaching to pre-service teachers who may one day be expected to co-teach in their own respective practices. Further, it is also an opportunity to examine individual teaching styles and strategies.

Graziano and Navarrete (2012) note that the team approach to co-teaching provides opportunities to vary content presentation. Even at the developmental stages in a course, co-teaching partners will bring together different teaching philosophies and different teaching strategies. Some of these differences may be discipline related, and so these differences should be considered within the context of co-planning and developing a range of teaching strategies.

We found that, similar to the co-development process of curriculum, co-teaching takes significantly longer than individual teaching. Roughly half our weekly co-planning meeting for the next week's session was devoted to reflection on the previous week's teaching, the remaining time being used to go over teaching strategies, synchronize the presentation, plan interjection strategies, and anticipate possible challenges. In addition to this shared reflection/planning time, we were also individually spending time planning our own designated parts of each lesson.

Revising Our Teaching Strategies

Krometis, Clark, Gonzalez, and Leslie (2011) conclude that the revising of the original team-developed course is an important part of the process and can result in substantial improvements. As we noted earlier, one of the benefits of co-developed interdisciplinary courses is that students are challenged to build critical thinking skills by synthesizing the multiple perspectives presented to them. We realized that, in our integrated course, this benefit also brought with it certain challenges.

We encountered a surprising level of resistance in our pilot offering of the course, although we had a sense that by the end of the course students appreciated what we were doing. We wanted to hear the student perceptions of our co-teaching and try to ascertain the cause of the resistance we had perceived. We acquired an ethics approval to interview the students upon completion of the course and to document course artefacts. We had three main guiding questions for the study: (1) How does students' experience contribute to their individual understanding of both art and mathematics? (2) Did the students develop a greater appreciation of the value of the integration of the two disciplines? (3) Did the course decrease students' math and/or art phobia? Upon completion of the course, students were interviewed with scripted questions, and their responses were transcribed. A comparative approach was used to identify themes that emerged from the data (Patton, 1990). Student participants indicated that by the end of the course they had a greater understanding of both art and mathematics, that they further appreciated the value of the integration of the two disciplines, and that, in some cases, they found that the course did decrease their perceived math and/or art phobia (La Haye & Naested, 2013).

We concluded that a major reason for the resistance we experienced when we piloted our integrated course was the challenge many students face in synthesizing the mathematics, visual arts, and education perspectives (Naested & La Haye, 2014). This difficulty is aggravated by the fact that many of our pre-service teachers only had experiences as students in more traditional methods of curriculum integration. As one interviewed student noted, "It is difficult to change one's mindset." Before taking our course, teacher candidates had each experienced over a decade of education in which the traditional disciplines were kept isolated as separate subjects in their K–12 schooling.

Further aggravating the resistance was the unfortunate reality that, with both visual arts and mathematics, there is the added temptation to take the easy way out (crafts in the case of art, and adherence to rote learning in the case of mathematics). Our experience with resistance was not unique. For example, Colley (2012) noted that initially some pre-service teachers in their study (which integrated sociology with theatre arts) complained about the amount of work involved, and initially voiced a preference for more stereotypical, craft-based activities to connect art with sociology. With respect to mathematics, Friesen (2008) explains that mathematics lends itself to procedural recipes and teaching practices. What commonly flows from this procedural view is demonstration, repetition, and individual practice. This traditional method of teaching is more familiar and typically easier to implement than reform-based methods involving problem solving, communication, and critical thinking.

Research (Bloomfield, 2000; Fiore, 1999; Thames & Ball, 2010) indicates that teachers with mathematics anxiety are more likely to depend on rote learning and worksheets at the expense of problem solving and understanding. Similarly, teachers with an art phobia are more likely to use the step-by-step craft techniques (Edwards, 1999; Hoffer, 1977; Naested, 2010). This finding creates an unfortunate scenario in which pre-service teachers might cling to traditional methods, because either they themselves had no trouble achieving in such a system or they themselves have anxiety and see the traditional methods as the *easier way out*.

We revised the second implementation of the course to increase the emphasis on, and appreciation of, the different discipline perspectives that come into play when considering any of our learning experience topics. We referred to this as a mutual interrogation of mathematics and art. We found that resistance during the course dissipated when students better understood the educational value of considering the different discipline perspectives. The students felt that they had gained a greater understanding of visual arts and mathematics, and the connection between the two, and had also developed an overall greater self-confidence in their teaching of math-art (Naested & La Haye, 2014).

Co-Assessment

Assessment Strategy Selection

If the co-development team has been thorough in course development in their planning, then, as Davis (1995) points out, the assessment options are much easier to choose. Two areas for potential mistakes with interdisciplinary courses are as follows: (1) using too narrow a range of artefacts to determine grades (often things like tests and research papers); and (2) considering only traditional grading options. In an interdisciplinary course, the instructors are creatively combining curriculum expectations, and, as a consequence, alternative grading options also deserve consideration. Davis further urges interdisciplinary course developers to emphasize assessment of the "higher-order skills" such as application, analysis, synthesis, and evaluation.

As a co-developing team, we felt confident enough in our organization of the course to know *what* we wanted to assess – the question became *how*? La Haye, the mathematician, understood from the moment that we created the learning goals and outcomes that standard assessments would not be adequate, but she had little knowledge of, or experience with, alternative methods. Fortunately, Naested's expertise in integrated learning and education brought the needed insight, as she was familiar with many alternate assessment options. Assessment of students' learning can and should use a variety of strategies and tools, which might include reflective journals, peer-teaching, performance-based achievement, portfolios, peer assessments, debates, self-assessments, student-led conferences, displays, sharing circles, discussion and questioning, critiques, checklists, rubrics, higher-order questioning, critical thinking questions, and so forth (Naested, 2010).

Naested proposed the following considerations for informing the selection of assessment tools:

- How can students transform information into understanding and then show what they know?
- How might students and teachers be involved in the presentation of learning?

- What ways will the learning experience be evaluated?
- What ways can be used to assess the quality of student work?
- Do the products reflect the individuality of the creator?
- Does the evaluation tool give students informative feedback? (Naested, 2010, p. 76)

Naested was also aware of the ramifications of the choice of assessment tools. She had researched the alternative assessments that were developed and used at Pearson, "the lighthouse" high school of 1991, including portfolios. In that particular context, the following was concluded:

> Alternative assessments have the potential to evaluate students with greater breadth and depth over traditional methods, but they require a greater investment of the educator's time and energy. Further, professional development and allocation of time is needed in researching and instituting the assessment, and reporting to parents. Potential conflicts arise in the use of alternative assessment devices if the final measurement of success is related only to achievement on standardized tests. (Naested, 1993a, p. 272)

A major portion of the students' assessment in our course, Visual Art and Mathematics: An Integrated Understanding, was based on the learning log/portfolio, as well as on lesson planning and teaching. We decided that each math-art learning experience would involve the creation of an artefact, a detailed discussion of the potential art and mathematics connections (and if appropriate, ties to other disciplines), and further discussion on how it could be tailored to fit the local curriculum. We required our students to keep a learning log/portfolio documenting each learning experience, the created artefact, and their reflections (as student and teacher) on the experience. Reflections were to include considering the mathematics learning and visual art learning within the experience, and its further potential. This learning log/portfolio had to be handed in three times throughout the course for assessment.

In addition, students had to find and critically evaluate two Internet-based lesson plans that claimed to integrate mathematics and visual arts. Some of the points they needed to consider were whether or not the lessons positively exploited natural connections between the disciplines, addressed the curriculum related to both disciplines, and were perceived as balanced in terms of the discipline perspectives. Students had to submit an evaluation of one good lesson plan and one poor lesson plan. For the poor lesson plan, they were to revise it into an appropriate math-art learning experience. Students were also assigned to lead a math-art integrated learning experience with a class of elementary students and, working in teams, lead a math-art integrated learning experience with their peers.

Assessment Strategy Implementation

Various researchers warn that assessment can be a source of tension and dissatisfaction for students in a co-taught course. They further note issues can arise because of student uncertainty as to how the assessment will be implemented, and because students fear the possibility of inconsistent grading (Davis, 1995; Graziano & Navarrete, 2012; Robinson & Schaible, 1995; Winn & Messenbeimer-Young, 1995). Suggested solutions include making expectations clear for all assignments, ensuring a common grading scheme is implemented, and alternating the assessor on assignments (so that there is only one instructor marking each assignment).

We would like to add that because interdisciplinary courses and co-teaching are often associated with non-standard assessments, it is even more vital that expectations be made clear for all assessments. We found it very valuable to give students assessment information in advance and to discuss with them the rubric that we would be using to assess their work. Table 6.1 shows the rubric that we used for all three learning log/teaching portfolio submissions during the course.

With respect to co-assessment, we tried several options within our course. For the portfolios, we agreed upon a common grading scheme and then literally sat together and each assessed a different set of student portfolios. Any questions or concerns could then immediately be brought up with the other instructor. We also reflected on a sample of each other's marked portfolios to try and ensure that we were being consistent. We found this method convenient because it prevented procrastination, and our schedules were flexible enough that we were able to easily schedule the required co-assessment time together. We were fortunate to have a large, private, and comfortable space in which to sit together, and our class sizes were relatively small. We recognized that this approach would be more efficient than any other option for preserving consistency in assessment.

We also tried alternating grading, with La Haye marking all the Internet lesson plans and Naested marking all the school lesson plans. The in-class peer presentations proved the least difficult to assess, as both instructors were present for all peer lessons. All students wrote a

Table 6.1. Rubric for EDUC 3201/MATH 3201 learning log and teaching portfolio.

Excellent: 85% or more
- Demonstrates a ***complete understanding*** of key mathematical and art concepts/terms encountered in the course
- Communicates in a ***clear*** and insightful manner; ***well organized***
- Fulfils task completely and moves beyond in some way that shows higher-level thinking and novel responses/reflection

Proficient: 70% to 85%
- Shows an understanding of key mathematical and art concepts/terms encountered in the course
- Communicates clearly and generally well organized
- Demonstrates perseverance in the task to show what the student knows and understands about math and art

Adequate: 55% to 70%
- Demonstrates basic understanding of most mathematical and art concepts/terms encountered in the course
- Communicates in a restricted or unorganized manner
- Shows basic understanding of concepts/key terms

Limited: below 55%
- Demonstrates an understanding of some mathematical and art concepts/terms encountered in the course but with evidence of gaps in understanding
- Shows minimal completeness of task or unorganized
- Chooses some appropriate and some inappropriate tools or techniques

peer- and self-assessment for both lessons and submitted additional supportive research materials. Following a brief discussion in private, La Haye and Naested mutually decided on the student grades and the content of the related comments for the collaborative peer-teaching lessons.

We note that the time it took to assess student work was significant – much more than if it were a standard discipline-based course or involved only traditional assessment methods. In both instances when we team taught the course, we had approximately twenty students. We spent roughly forty-five minutes on each student's portfolio, and did these assessments three times during the term.

We recommend that instructors make the assessment criteria as clear as possible to students; if it has been decided that one instructor will do all the assessment for any one assignment, that instructor would (preferably) discuss the related assessment and marking criteria with students.

Conclusion

Interdisciplinary co-teaching involves the combining of two or more academic disciplines or fields of study with at least two teachers.

Dr Roberta La Haye and Dr Irene Naested came from two different faculties and brought with them their own diverse, unique experiences and expertise to the co-teaching process.

In this chapter we have addressed the following questions, based on our own teaching experiences and research findings: Why co-teach? What are the different models of course integration and co-teaching? What are the perceived benefits to students? What were the perceived challenges and how were they addressed?

One of the main reasons that we co-planned and co-taught this unique course was to clearly showcase the value of integrated learning in education. There are many models for course integration and co-teaching. Course goals and outcomes will help course developers to choose the appropriate model(s). We agree with Davis (1995) that the only way to achieve a significant level of integration is to work closely with an individual or team of experts from the disciplines involved. Deciding on goals and learning outcomes early in the co-development process discourages a slipping back into more traditional pedagogy and may also reduce conflicts that may arise, such as "discipline turf wars."

For us, co-teaching was vital in achieving the balanced integration of disciplines that we wanted to demonstrate for our teacher candidates. It was necessary to team teach (together, in the same room at the same time) in order to share our discipline perspectives with students and to exemplify the mutual interrogation model that we felt best captured the balanced presentation of discipline perspectives. It was not easy for students to see beyond the traditional or stereotypical methods of teaching mathematics and visual arts, especially given the ease and security of implementing those methods, but we were able to expand students' pedagogical perspectives by personally modelling this approach. We challenged the students to build critical thinking skills by synthesizing the art, mathematics, and education perspectives that were presented to them. They gained an understanding of alternative pedagogy through the modelling of interdisciplinary co-teaching, including teaching styles and alternative assessment methods.

Our research following the class indicated that we were able to improve students' understanding and appreciation of both mathematics and visual art, and to motivate them, in some measure, to consider integrating subjects in their future educational careers. Through this experience, we believe our students became more comfortable with art and mathematics integrated learning and teaching. We also feel that they will be better able to critically assess integrated learning experiences and to create valuable curriculum experiences for their future students. Our modelling of co-teaching to pre-service teachers may assist them should they one day be able or expected to co-teach within their own practice.

To meet the challenges of co-teaching, it is paramount that the teaching team have mutual respect and trust. All team members need to be self-assured enough to realize they do not know everything, yet confident that "trying things differently" is worthwhile. Trying things differently includes developing alternative assessment beyond the traditional methods of assessment often expected from the institution. Co-teaching team members need to be prepared to invest a considerable amount of time in this process – every stage (co-development, co-teaching, and co-assessment) requires more time than when an individual works alone.

A major further consideration for potential co-instructors is that institutional support for the efforts of the co-teaching team members is often lacking, and university structures tend to prevent cross-disciplinary collaboration. Graziano and Navarrete (2012) go so far as to say that the largest barriers to co-teaching are the policies and practices for tenure and promotion at post-secondary institutions. We believe that this issue is a serious concern. As Naested noted earlier in her career, teaching innovations without support will not flourish, and will become short-term "educational fads."

An important question that we have not yet addressed is, What are the benefits to the co-teachers themselves? Fortunately, the benefits to the teachers involved in interdisciplinary co-teaching are many. Co-teaching can be an outstanding form of professional development. Co-teaching encourages one to be more flexible and cognizant of the teaching process, including planning and assessment (Davis, 1995; Kluth & Straut, 2003; Wilson & Martin, 1998). Nevin, Thousand, and Villa (2009) point out that co-teaching can also lead to insights about the co-teachers' respective disciplines. Further, Letterman and Dugan (2004) note that collaboration can alleviate the isolation that academics often feel in their respective disciplines.

We experienced all of these benefits during our collaboration efforts. Although we had both co-taught previously, neither of us had collaborated to the same extent as we did in the development and implementation of this particular course. Furthermore, our diversity of backgrounds was more extreme than it had been in our previous co-teaching experiences, forcing us to be even more flexible than we had been in previous co-teaching contexts. We were both impressed with the new perspectives that we gained relating to our own disciplines, as well as to each other's. As our co-teaching relationship matured, we were better able to recognize rich areas of integration. Finally, our collaboration helped to facilitate the development of more connections between our respective departments. We further used this opportunity to conduct meaningful research on integrated learning, co-teaching models, and alternative assessment methods.

REFERENCES

Adam, A., Alangui, W., & Barton, B. (2010). Bright lights and questions: Using mutual interrogation. *For the Learning of Mathematics, 30*(3), 10–16.

Bloomfield, S. (2000). Math phobia can be beaten! *Ontario Mathematics Gazette, 38*(3), 5–7.

Colley, B. (2012). Teaching social studies through the performing arts. *Educational Forum, 76*(1), 4–12. http://dx.doi.org/10.1080/00131725.2011.627986

Cormack, W. (1991). On the struggle for school-based arts. *Design for Arts in Education, 92*(3), 40–5. http://dx.doi.org/10.1080/07320973.1991.9935582

Davis, J. (1995). *Interdisciplinary courses and team teaching: New arrangements for learning*. Phoenix, AZ: American Council on Education.

Dewey, J. (1938). *Experience and education*. New York, NY: Collier Books.

Education Alberta. (2016). Mathematics kindergarten to grade 9 program of studies. Retrieved from https://education.alberta.ca/mathematics-K-6

Edwards, B. (1999). *The new drawing on the right side of the brain*. New York, NY: Penguin Putnam.

Eisner, E. (1999). Does experience in the arts boost academic achievement? *Clearing House: A Journal of Educational Strategies, Issues and Ideas, 72*(3), 143–9. http://dx.doi.org/10.1080/00098659909599615

Ernst, B. (1978/2007). *The magic mirror of M. C. Escher*. Cologne, DE: Taschen.

Fiore, G. (1999). Math-abused students: Are we prepared to teach them? *Mathematics Teacher, 92*(5), 402–5.

Fogarty, R. (1991). Ten ways to integrate curriculum. *Educational Leadership, 49*(2), 61–5.

Friesen, S. (2008). Raising the floor and lifting the ceiling: Math for all. *Education Canada, 48*(5), 50–4.

Grauer, K. (1991). Integrating art. *British Columbia Art Teachers' Association Journal for Art Teachers, 31*(1), 23–7.

Graziano, K., & Navarrete, L. (2012). Co-teaching in a teacher education classroom: Collaboration, compromise, and creativity. *Issues in Teacher Education, 21*(1), 109–25.

Greene, M. (1971). Curriculum and consciousness. *Teachers College Record, 73*(2), 253–69.

Hoffer, A. (1977). *Geometry and visualization: Mathematics Resources Project*. Palo Alto, OR: Creative Publication.

Holley, K. (2009). *Understanding interdisciplinary challenges and opportunities in higher education*. Hoboken, NJ: Wiley.

Jarvis, D.H., & Naested, I. (2012). *Exploring the math and art connection: Teaching and learning between the lines*. Calgary, AB: Brush Education.

Jones, I., Lake, V., & Dagli, U. (2003). Integrating mathematics and science in undergraduate early childhood teacher education programs. *Journal of Early Childhood Teacher Education, 24*(1), 3–8. http://dx.doi.org/10.1080/1090102030240103

Kluth, P., & Straut, D. (2003). Do as we say and as we do: Teaching and modeling collaborative practice in the university classroom. *Journal of Teacher Education, 54*(3), 228–40. http://dx.doi.org/10.1177/0022487103054003005

Krometis, L., Clark, E., Gonzalez, V., & Leslie, M. (2011). The "death" of the disciplines: Development of a team-taught course to provide an interdisciplinary perspective for first-year students. *College Teaching, 59*(2), 73–8. http://dx.doi.org/10.1080/87567555.2010.538765

La Haye, R., & Naested, I. (2013). Cross-curricular experiences in visual art and mathematics. *BCATA Journal for Art Teachers, 55*(2), 9–15.

Letterman, M., & Dugan, K. (2004). Team teaching a cross-disciplinary honors course: Preparation and development. *College Teaching, 52*(2), 76–9.

Naested, I. (1993a). *Educational innovations at Lester B. Pearson High School in Calgary, Alberta, Canada*. Doctoral dissertation, Brigham Young University, Provo, UT.

Naested, I. (1993b). Toward the forgotten thoughtfulness. In R. Shute & S. Gibb (Eds.), *Students of thought: Personal journeys* (pp. 75–88). Calgary, AB: Detselig.

Naested, I. (2010). *Art in the classroom: An integrated approach to teaching art in Canadian elementary and middle schools*. Toronto, ON: Nelson Education.

Naested, I., & LaHaye, R. (2014). Arts integration: A celebration of alternative perspectives. *Canadian Review of Art Education: Research and Issues, 41*(2), 185–201.

Naested, I., Potvin, B., & Waldron, P. (2004). *Understanding the landscape of teaching*. Toronto, ON: Pearson Education Canada.

Nevin, A., Thousand, J., & Villa, R. (2009). Collaborative teaching for teacher educators: What does the research say? *Teaching and Teacher Education, 25*(4), 569–74. http://dx.doi.org/10.1016/j.tate.2009.02.009

Patton, M.Q. (1990). *Qualitative evaluation and research methods* (2nd ed.). Newbury Park, CA: Sage.

Rhoten, D., & Pfirman, S. (2007). Women in interdisciplinary science: Exploring preferences and consequences. *Research Policy, 36*(1), 56–75. http://dx.doi.org/10.1016/j.respol.2006.08.001

Robinson, B., & Schaible, R. (1995). Collaborative teaching: Reaping the benefits. *College Teaching, 43*(2), 57–9. http://dx.doi.org/10.1080/87567555.1995.9925515

Sousa, D., & Pilecki, T. (2013). *From STEM to STEAM: Using brain-compatible strategies to integrate the arts.* Thousand Oaks, CA: Corwin.

Thames, M.H., & Ball, D.L. (2010). What math knowledge does teaching require? *Teaching Children Mathematics, 17*(4), 220–9.

Vanderbilt University, Centre for Teaching. (2017). Team/collaborative teaching. Retrieved from http://cft.vanderbilt.edu/guides-sub-pages/teamcollaborative-teaching/#constructing

Wilson, R., & Fasanelli, F. (2000). Mathematics and art II: Albrecht Dürer. *Mathematical Intelligencer, 22*(2), 80. http://dx.doi.org/10.1007/BF03025382

Wilson, V., & Martin, K. (1998, February 13–17). *Practicing what we preach: Team teaching at the college level.* Paper presented at the Annual Meeting of the Association of Teacher Educators,Dallas, TX.

Winn, J., & Messenbeimer-Young, T. (1995). Team teaching at the university level: What we have learned. *Teacher Education and Special Education, 18*(4), 223–9. http://dx.doi.org/10.1177/088840649501800402

7 Co-Teaching in Undergraduate Education: Capacity Building for Multiple Stakeholders

JENNIFER C. WILSON AND JACQUELINE FERGUSON

Introduction

The act of co-teaching, its history as well as its progression, dates back to the 1960s era when "progressive education" was made fashionable (Nevin, Villa, & Thousand, 2004). During the 1970s, legislated school reforms were a catalyst in advancing the need to co-teach as teachers found themselves modifying their instruction in order to service a "more diverse student population" (Nevin et al., 2004; Walther-Thomas, 1997). This diversity is even more pronounced today: in the United States, for example, over 4.4 million students, or about 9.4 per cent of the school-aged population, are English language learners (ELL). In states such as Texas and California, the percentage of ELL students is as high as 23 per cent, and over 50 per cent of students are non-Caucasian, with 13 per cent of the total population in schools classified as Special Education (U.S. Department of Education, 2017). Similar statistics are reflected in current college-aged student populations. Engaging in practices that benefit all students, yet are differentiated for their needs, is a practice that more institutions of higher education need to consider; co-teaching is one such strategy.

Co-teaching throughout the years has taken a variety of forms in the classroom and has also been defined in many ways. Cook and Friend (as quoted in Bacharach, Heck, & Dahlberg, 2008) describe co-teaching as "two or more professionals delivering substantive instruction to a diverse, or blended group of students in a single physical space" (p. 43). Wenzlaff et al. (2002) define co-teaching as two or more individuals who come together in a collaborative relationship for the purpose of shared work in order to achieve what none could have done alone. Many of the institutions who currently utilize co-teaching at the college or university level may identify with the definition that co-teaching is characterized as "two teachers working together with groups of students and sharing the planning, organization, delivery, and assessment of instruction, as well as the physical space" (Bacharach et al., 2008, p. 9).

Co-teaching is most often offered as a solution for general educators, primarily at the elementary or secondary levels, working hand in hand with special educators in order to service students with special needs who have been mainstreamed into general education classrooms so that they feel included (Bauwens & Hourcade, 1991; Cook & Friend, 1995; Platt, Walker-Knight, Lee, & Hewitt, 2001; Vaughn, Schumm, & Arguelles, 1997). Since co-teaching has often led to encouraging results, it is little wonder that students, parents, teachers, and administrators have learned to appreciate and trust its methods (Nevin et al., 2004; Walther-Thomas, 1997). Co-teaching allows more individualized instruction and increases access to expertise, collaboration, and accountability for a teacher's practice. As Scruggs, Mastropieri, and McDuffie (2007) discussed in their qualitative meta-analysis, co-teaching in its ideal form creates space for critical analysis of an individual teacher's practice and for an increase in knowledge concerning the other co-teacher's area of expertise. Participants in the study noted that co-teaching also serves as a role model for collaboration, explaining that it isn't often in the working world that people really work well together.

Co-teaching and co-learning has been discussed as a necessity for the twenty-first century by proponents in industry, healthcare, social science, and, perhaps most rigorously, education. As Friend (2014) explained, "Working together is not just rhetoric – it is essential in order to address the increasingly diverse and sometimes daunting needs of students, students with IEPs, students for whom English is not their first language, students whose lives outside school may be chaotic and unsafe, students who need structure and stability" (para. 5). This diversity aptly describes today's classrooms, and, by extension, the post-secondary context is no exception.

Despite the positive results, however, "co-teaching at the university level has been much less prevalent and very loosely studied" (Bacharach et al., 2008, p. 9). It has been discussed as most ideal when administration supports the undertaking and teachers choose their collaborative partners, are trained in collaborative techniques, and are given time to plan and discuss content and activities to be used in the classroom (Scruggs, Mastropieri, & McDuffie, 2007). While these notions are supported in the following research, there are very few contexts wherein the above conditions are fully met. By far the method of co-teaching most often used is the model in which one instructor teaches and another assists (National Dissemination Center for Children with Disabilities, 2011; Scruggs, Mastropieri, & McDuffie, 2007).

This chapter presents a look at an undergraduate reading education program involving co-teaching as a means to model good practice, collegial collaboration, and reflection. It will highlight the details as to how such a course was planned, structured, taught, and assessed at the post-secondary level.

Co-Planning: The *Before* Stage

The most difficult part of co-teaching just might be the planning. When done well, planning changes praxis for both the professors and the students in significant ways. However, when a co-taught class is underplanned or sporadically planned, the lessons and their subsequent utility for students and professors are often lost. When planning in the higher education classroom, commodities such as time for planning are hard to come by; for example, schedules in higher educational settings are such that different professors are often not on campus at the same time, as their teaching times are negotiated individually and can vary accordingly.

In colleges and universities, as in all educational settings, management of time and utility of instruction are high priority. As such, co-teaching, while serving as professional development for both the professor and the student, takes a great deal of time and energy (Ferguson & Wilson, 2010). For higher educators, this energy and time can have seemingly little return on the investment with regards to tenure and promotion. Most colleges and universities do not favour two professors in one classroom, citing arguments such as, Who actually gets paid, and how much? (For example, is each professor only paid for 50 per cent of a regular course amount?) Sometimes in co-teaching arrangements, class size is also increased, making it appear even less worthwhile for instructors because of the associated stress. As a result, co-teaching is not often seen in higher education contexts, regardless of its benefits for classroom instruction, retention, and connection to a diverse range of students. When professors work together, however, time is a negotiated pattern in which planning occurs. Thus, it is often the case that co-teaching professors must arrange planning times that honour each other's work and life schedules. This consideration is especially important if the school is not supporting the vision of co-teaching through pay, scheduling, and/or student experience.

Planning should be done both *vertically* and *horizontally*. The course syllabus needs to represent the course over the entire semester, with both teachers involved in the project and topic creation (horizontal planning). The course must also be situated within the varied and changing needs of students, and within the department as a whole, so that the knowledge base and learning experiences are implemented in a logical fashion (vertical planning). Professors engaging in co-teaching should ask the following questions: Is co-teaching in this particular course beneficial to me and to the students? If so, why, and in what specific ways? Such metacognitive planning for the semester sets up a series of learning experiences that are highly engaging for both students and the co-teachers. Answers to the above questions then serve to guide the process of course planning and implementation.

In our experience, time for co-planning represents a challenge, an investment, and a necessity for effective and efficient co-teaching. The amount of time it takes to work in collaboration, and through negotiation, is often considerably greater than that of teaching a course alone. When teaching solo, professors are able to design an activity and implement it as they see fit. In a co-taught classroom, where both professors come to the table with ideas and knowledge, it takes time to reconfigure what each activity will look like, who will implement it, and what support from the other co-teacher may be required. Such compromise of pedagogy and knowledge often does not come quickly or intuitively. As Jenny explained in her journal during our first co-taught semester in 2011 (see Ferguson & Wilson, 2011), "Planning takes an inordinate amount of time as we sit, discuss, and make decisions concerning our class. This notion of 'our' is something that is hard to understand right now." As the "our" is further explored over time and through discussion, a partnership occurs in which both teachers become co-participants. In our experience, time needed to prepare for a class increased from an average of 1.5 hours (for a class taught alone) to an average of 3.5 hours for a co-taught class (1.5 hours for co-planning and 2 hours for individual preparation) throughout the semester. The time-on-task in direct preparation for teaching also increased when compared with single teacher teaching. Extra time is needed to negotiate the curriculum and each other's expectation for the content, and to bring to fruition the discussion of "our" class through planning in real time, especially in the initial teaching of a co-taught course.

As our course progressed and we, the professors, learned how to collaborate effectively with one another, certain benefits to the time invested in a co-taught course became evident. Much of the front-end planning and negotiating ultimately saved us time when we taught a different section of the class independently and/or taught the same class a second time together. Time was also saved when it came to grading assignments. Of course, a schedule of who would grade what, and when, had to be established from the beginning, as well as the rubrics that would be used to assess students' learning. In addition, if one of us planned to be absent, perhaps for a conference or some other event, classes did not need to be cancelled or rescheduled, and thus quality educational time for students was not lost. As we learned from each other and engaged in the process of co-teaching, we were able to be flexible with one another, allowing us to build on each other's strengths and to capitalize on shared resources.

Key Points for Co-Planning

1. Create a Collaboration Schedule

A collaboration schedule is especially important due to the time and energy required when working with another individual. We use the term "collaboration schedule" because of the specificity involved when planning a class and/or session. Working together, and not the mere meeting of two individuals, is of utmost importance. Focusing on each co-teaching partner's goals, areas of expertise, and the planned amount of shared classroom leadership are all paramount. Collaboration meetings are well served when the partnership is clearly evident in both the discussion and its subsequent outcomes for both parties. In other words, both members must feel that they have been adequately heard, their opinions have been included in decisions, and the ensuing lessons will be better as a result of the meeting. Scheduling and adherence to the meeting times, with as little adjustment as possible, allows for clearer expectations regarding both team members. It should be noted that when meeting times are continually changed, participating co-teachers may become more lackadaisical in terms of their commitment to planned meetings.

Our collaborative sessions included initial meetings for the planning of the larger scope-and-sequence of the course syllabus overview, as well as weekly meetings during which the individualized sessions were prepared. Lastly, short debriefing sessions immediately following co-teaching experiences were helpful for recording shared memories of classroom activities, comments, and personal reflections. This form of co-reflection also helped us to revisit and refine plans for future lessons. Weekly planning meetings lasted longer if, as often happened, we took time to discuss our individual reflections, and both parties shared details from their observations of the teaching experiences.

As time progresses, professors may decide that they do not need such a regimented schedule for their co-teaching, depending on their professional relationship, experience, and course knowledge. However, it is recommended that a detailed schedule be used at the beginning to aid in establishing collaborative processes and efficient communication.

2. Determine Each Professor's Primary Responsibilities

Responsibility in the co-taught classroom is a shared experience. However, it is helpful to have one person, perhaps even on a rotating schedule, take charge of particular aspects of classroom structure. Small tasks such as taking attendance, posting course materials, answering student email, and obtaining course materials all take time. The goal is to share such responsibilities and to ensure that students receive what is needed in terms of both course content and context. While answering emails might sound simple, students need consistency and continuity. Multiple (that is, differing) perspectives shared by co-instructors can sometimes be confusing and time-consuming for students *and* for the co-teachers. Decisions that affect weekly activities or course assignments must be jointly made by the co-teaching team and be clearly communicated to students throughout the course.

Taking time to determine each professor's responsibilities, or creating a schedule for rotating responsibilities, will save time logistically while allowing students and faculty direct access to clear, updated information. Again, as the collaborative relationship is established, such regimentation may not be needed, but it is still very helpful to those outside the co-teaching relationship to know who to contact, when, and how regarding any concerns or questions that they may have during the course.

3. Determine a Grading Criteria with a Timeline for Feedback and Reporting

Most classrooms use a hundred-point scale for assessment (percentage final grades); however, the description and negotiation of due dates, assignment criteria, and instructor expectations are also important parts of the co-taught experience. Professors should pre-determine how they will use the grading criteria and provide related instructions to students beforehand. A question such as, Do we check off the rubric and write comments on the paper? represents the kind of issue that needs to be discussed within co-planning meetings, because each teacher has personal past experiences, preferences, and assessment expertise relating to the running of the classroom and subsequent evaluation and reporting.

With regard to assessment, it might also be helpful to discuss *turn-taking* assessment, in which each co-teacher is responsible for grading half the assignments; *collaborative grading*, in which assessment of assignments is done together; or some combination of the preceding two methods. We strongly recommend that the co-teaching team engage in the creation of expectations and rubrics for use with the course assignments. Joint development of evaluation criteria is critical: just as student ideas and abilities vary inside a classroom, so professors' grading criteria and expectations might also vary. Variation in expectations and evaluation rubrics can be (or could lead to) a problem in the classroom. When students experience two professors' ideas that are not in alignment, they will often focus on the one that most fits their own understanding. We refer to this phenomenon as the "ask the other" notion of co-teaching. If the answer from one professor is not making sense to a student, he or she should also ask the other professor, expecting to hear a matching answer or explanation. When communication has been clear between professors and with students, and rubrics and scales for grading have been clearly presented and explained – specifically by both co-teachers to the class – then working within the defined criteria is easier for all involved. Letting students know who is in charge of grading or if both professors will be grading will drastically improve the experience of the students and co-teachers within the co-taught classroom.

Finally, deadlines for completed assignment feedback, posted grades, and returned work should be consistent and, of course, negotiated between the co-teaching instructors. A student-accessible calendar with significant dates, as well as assignment rubrics, is a definite requirement. Participation in regular co-teacher collaborative meetings to prepare for each week and to discuss and make necessary adjustments to the calendar, syllabus, responsibilities, and expectations is also strongly recommended.

Co-Teaching: The *During* Stage

Negotiations regarding time also include time to be spent in front of the students to guide a class or activity. We have found that discussion of specific roles is essential for the co-taught classroom. While co-teaching can take many forms, including small groups led by the different teachers, situations where one teacher leads and the other acts as an assistant, or occasions when both professors team teach, the question of who is ultimately in charge of each class is one that should not be taken lightly. While trying not to sound pretentious concerning our content knowledge areas, we, as academics, often unassumingly default to our own knowledge of pedagogy and content; after all, we are specialists and thus feel that we are masters of our own subject area(s). While such a statement might seem overly aggrandizing, professors, like any other professionals, do indeed possess many accumulated ideas and experiences from previous practice, and therefore are often overflowing with new and old understandings that they want (perhaps even need) to share with each other. Trying to decide whose knowledge and/or skills are better suited to a particular lecture or learning experience, and thus who should facilitate or teach which session, obviously represents an arduous task. As Jackie explained in one of our discussions, "I have taught before and was in charge, so I think I default to 'the leader' as a way to manage classroom structures, and so working with someone else threatens my control."

Because of the nature of a co-taught classroom, both professors must have occasion to be in front of, and seemingly in charge of, the students' learning. While both professors imagine themselves as equally important within the classroom, student perception must also be taken into consideration. Students might equate the name appearing on the course schedule, or the teacher who speaks the most in class, or even the one who stands at the front of the classroom most often as the one *in charge*, that is, the one with the power. Therefore, negotiation of power is an important aspect of the co-taught classroom.

As we explained in the article "The Co-Taught Professorship" (Ferguson & Wilson, 2011), the balance of power is one that the students often define, and yet it is one that we both also felt while co-planning. Whether it was Jackie writing, "Planning is so full of ideas, especially hers, so we need to get her [Jenny's] name on the books too," or Jenny explaining, "I keep having to remind myself that it is her class AND my class. I have to listen while in the classroom and not just take the stage," it was clear that co-teaching sometimes involves inherent power struggles for the co-teachers. Both of us, over time, wrote in journals chronicling our thoughts and discussions regarding authority and power, while also admitting that there were few adequate or deep discussions about its importance and manifestations in our co-taught experience. Currently, we both agree that there needs to be frank, open discussion about feelings concerning power and placement of each other in the role of *knowledgeable other* in ways that help students to discover the true meaning of collaboration and cooperation.

While in planning meetings, we were perfectly able and willing to discuss our expertise, knowing that both of us come from different teaching backgrounds. We were aware of the attempted equality of power and wanted to make the classroom a place of leadership equality, where there is not one leader or facilitator, but rather a shared dynamic. While educators often want to act as facilitators, co-teaching forces a necessary release of power, to a certain extent, and the relinquishing of this power is modelled for the students in both the details of the course outline/expectations and within the actual class sessions. As a student described in a focus group interview, "Do teachers ever let go of being in front of the classroom? I mean, even in this class, they take turns being in charge." This statement touches on the angst regarding perceived power among teachers. Yet, negotiated power is the best kind, one in which experiences are shared in ways that lead all those involved to question power dynamics. We were able to guide ourselves through this experience, but also realized that it may have been partially due to just blind luck that we got along so well. Mahon's (2009) research on conflict and teachers illustrates our need to engage in collaborative problem solving as a twenty-first century skill and to have this process serve as a model for our students. Knowing the foundational skills of collaboration and conflict resolution (Jones & Brinker, 2008), such as active listening and interest-based negotiations, becomes a valuable resource when engaging in co-teaching practice.

For students, power was also a significant issue as they engaged with both professors. It was something that they felt the need to both comment on and question. On anonymous feedback forms, students mentioned thoughts such as, "[T]he hardest part about co-teaching was having different teachers, different ideas about things. I wonder how much they really are communicating." Students' intent was honest as they wondered, given their limited experience with multiple teachers in the same classroom, if they could trust both professors to be on the same page and judging the effectiveness and intricacies of their knowledge in the same ways. Another comment read, "Is this going to be fair?" Students' prior experiences often define teaching in one particular way – that there is only one person in charge of the class and this single teacher is responsible for making decisions about course content and grading. There is one chief executive officer, one manager on duty, one president, one single "*jefe*," and so the question for many students in a co-taught context seems to be, Which professor is truly *in charge*? In the classrooms where we have co-taught, students spent much time discussing this question. However, as we repeated our co-teaching experiences, our expectations of each other, of the learning objectives, and of the students became clearer through reflective refinement and negotiation. While at the beginning of each course, the questions of cohesion and shared responsibility would certainly exist, these issues became resolved more quickly each time we refined our practice. This modelling of shared leadership and collaboration is vital to professors' success as teachers in the twenty-first century (Wagner, 2008); education can no longer be an act of isolation, but rather must become one of collaborative facilitation in order to increase overall effectiveness and student achievement (Hargreaves & Fullan, 2012; Rosenholtz, 1989).

One solution to our power struggle was to identify exactly which student learning objective, activity, or discussion question we'd each be responsible for. We also began to learn each other's strengths and to use them in the logistics and pedagogy of the class. For example, Jackie was responsible for posting our learning objectives and the agenda for each day, while Jenny would create open-ended discussion questions to probe students' understanding. Throughout the course, there were days when we both wondered if the two of us, eager to share our insight and experiences, had monopolized the conversation from our students. When students responded within a focus group interview, however, they mentioned that the course was actually much more engaging than one taught by a single professor.

Those seeking to engage in co-teaching should also be aware that there will be conflict. There was an incident where we had a misunderstanding about who was preparing which activities for a station-based learning session. As professionals, we realized that we had overprepared, quickly selected what we would use, and began our class session. The students were engaged during the class session, but we, as instructors, were still experiencing frustration based on our individual preparation. While, overall, the course objectives were met that day and we managed (from our perspectives) to maintain our professionalism, many students made comments such as the following statement in their exit surveys: "This one day, they didn't seem to be getting along. They didn't say or do anything exactly, but there was definitely tension in the classroom." The students never did ask us directly about that day, and such an incident was not repeated, especially as we continued to co-teach and build our collaborative relationship. Based on the conversation we had during our reflection session that day, we were able to learn how to communicate more clearly with each other and to be more forgiving when miscommunications arose. The bottom line is that while maintaining professionalism through mutual respect, we did need to openly discuss our perceptions and expectations in order to strengthen the shared leadership of the classroom. The art of co-teaching is not in avoiding conflict, but in learning from the conflict and becoming stronger as a result of this process.

We used several co-teaching formats when implementing our reading course. Over time, we were able to discover which models we preferred, but more importantly, which models best met the students' needs with regard to particular learning objectives. The first model that we attempted was having both teachers present in one class. In this model, we divided the lesson and took turns leading in front of the class. Eventually, we became comfortable with one another and would spontaneously begin a relaxed dialogue or trade-off between the two of us. We had to be careful with this model, however, to ensure that it didn't become the "Jenny and Jackie Show" and that there was sufficient student involvement in the lesson. The other model that we attempted early in the semester was having one teacher lead the session and the other serve more as a teaching assistant. Here, one of us was responsible for the primary instructional delivery, and the other provided various forms of support throughout the classroom. This model was helpful when one of us felt very confident, in terms of expertise, with a particular student learning objective or area of research. This model, though, risks that students may perceive the professor serving as the assistant to be less knowledgeable or engaged. Thus, we recommend that if this model is used, each professor should, over time, have an opportunity to serve both in the teacher and the teaching assistant roles.

Another model, station-based learning, allowed us to meet with students in small groups. This model was beneficial when we had a number of learning objectives or perspectives to address in one class period. We would set up different stations for the students to engage in, and while they rotated through these student-directed learning opportunities, we were able to scaffold students' understanding of the topics through direct questioning and dialogue. Yet another co-teaching model, small group teaching, also allowed for small group instruction. Here we would divide the class, teach our designated small group, and then switch student groups. This practice allowed us, the professors, to focus on planning for one specific learning objective and the students to participate in small group discussion for increased engagement. Finally, we also used the parallel teaching model. In parallel teaching, each professor instructs the same learning objective, but only to half the class. This model allowed us to match the instruction of the objective to students' learning styles, since our delivery methods of the same content could be different. Parallel teaching, along with small group and station-based teaching, led to increased student engagement and immediate feedback. Overall, we learned to match the co-teaching model with our learning objectives, students' needs, and our own areas of expertise so that we were delivering high quality, engaging, differentiated instruction.

Key Points for Co-Teaching

- Determine the co-teaching model to be used for each class session so that it aligns with the learning objective(s) and the professors' teaching strengths. Knowing the models to be used for instruction will aid in focusing the collaborative planning of the class sessions.
- Make decisions based on students' needs, rather than teacher preferences, whenever possible.
- Have a plan for collaboration and conflict. This plan should include the following elements: how to establish and follow agendas for meeting and instruction; ground rules for collaboration meetings, discussions, and classroom instruction; an understanding of, and emphasis on, active listening and the asking of questions during planning/implementation; an acknowledgment of each professor's interest and investment in the co-teaching framework; a plan of how decisions will be made regarding differing priorities; and a method of addressing miscommunication or missed deadlines.

Co-Teaching: The *After* and *Before* (Recursive) Stages

Many educators ask the question, Why co-teach, since it appears to require more investment than there is benefit? We have found this statement to be unfounded. In fact, there are four immediate benefits to the co-taught classroom. The first is the *refinement and modelling of the art of teaching*. As current research states, "Rather like the best jazz music, the best teaching requires self-expression but demands mutual collaboration" (Brundrett, 2010, p. 101). We are preparing students to be active participants in a twenty-first century world that demands collaboration and effective communication. Co-teaching allows professors to model this practice for future teachers, since our future teachers must teach differently. Individualist teaching may indeed limit student achievement, reduce self-confidence, and restrict professional learning (Rosenholtz, 1989). A school can never exceed the quality of its teachers. Good teaching requires high levels of education and training, is perfected through continuous improvement, and is a collective accomplishment and responsibility (Hargreaves & Fullan, 2012).

The second benefit is the *embedded professional development* that comes from having "iron sharpen iron" when two experts engage in collaboration. As co-teachers, we live out the motto of life-long learning. We show future teachers that there is power in numbers and that we are no longer the only source of knowledge. Our students are "digital natives" who regularly use Google or YouTube to find what they need or wish to learn about. Our new role is to facilitate learning from each other, to evaluate information, and to use information to solve problems. We can no longer survive as autonomous distributors of knowledge. Instead, we must embrace the fact that we are all learners and model how to collaborate and engage in social learning. What better source from which to gain not only new knowledge but also new forms of pedagogy than other experts modelling this process. We all have something to offer to, and receive from, those in the offices located next to us. Co-teaching allows us to see that knowledge in action, to engage in that type of practice, and to refine our understandings. Co-teaching also allows us to take risks with new pedagogy that we might not be willing to attempt alone. The regular habit of reflection is beneficial to our professional development, and is underscored within the accountability framework that is naturally part of the co-teaching process.

The third benefit is the *increased synergy* created in the classroom. Having two experts present with whom students can brainstorm and engage in discussion creates a learning environment that allows individuals to feel eager to take risks. Jackie wrote in her journal, "The quality of instruction will be high … My focus will be to always give my best." Jenny mentioned the value of having someone she trusted to bounce ideas off of when planning – the proverbial "two heads being better than one." When working collaboratively, there is an increased excitement and diligence regarding the successful completion of tasks and the advantage of having a trusted colleague who can offer constructive feedback.

Finally, the fourth benefit, *increased individual student achievement*, speaks for itself. Having two experts in the room allows students twice the access to have their questions about the learning objectives, assignments, and expectations answered. Co-teaching also allows for multiple student learning styles to be met and provides increased small group instructional experiences, depending on the co-teaching models that are implemented. All of which, taken together, can allow for more individualized instruction for students, and often leads to increased student engagement and hence achievement.

Key Points for Co-Reflection and the Co-Planning Cycle

- Assess your attainment of the desired goals and student learning objectives.
- Elicit constructive student feedback.
- Practice reflection, both individually and collaboratively.
- Celebrate the success of your students and of yourselves.
- Determine your next attempt and a specific goal(s) to extend your learning and practice.

Discussion

Adopting a stance that focuses on practice within the confines of higher education allows participants (students as well as instructors) to pay careful attention to the crafting of a course from varied positions, yet with similar goals. Both parties want to create a space for learning, to assess their understandings, and to invite participation in the world of their content knowledge and expertise. Co-teaching allows two professors to work with one another towards such ends, using combined knowledge sets, prior experiences, and foundational understandings in order to develop and implement a rich course based on the perceived needs of the students involved. For students, a co-taught class allows for the unique experience of seeing multiple experts share their knowledge and skills in real time.

Co-teaching's most powerful benefit may actually be the opportunities it creates for building capacity among pre-service teachers, as well as among professors, through practice-based professional development. Such affordances occur when we are open to making mistakes (a learning orientation); to letting each other take risks we might otherwise not understand, or be willing to engage in; and to reflecting in substantive ways on our thinking, experiences (both individually and within the dyad), and progression. All this must be done with a positive mentality in spite of the challenges and inherent angst that may be associated with this kind of teamwork. Our own experiences confirm that "pushing through the tough spots," recognizing differences in opinion, and respectfully disagreeing with one another can be tremendously empowering for a co-teaching team. Working with a colleague who also possesses expert knowledge in one's own field serves to change one's perception of self and position in positive ways. The co-teacher represents a knowledgeable other, full of expertise and accumulated experiences, with whom one can dare to implement new instructional paradigms in ever-deepening ways. Co-teaching at the university level also provides the opportunity to minimize the stereotypically stressful, judgmental, and competitive nature of post-secondary teaching. Allowing for multiple perspectives, co-teaching encourages the taking of calculated risks with another trusted risk-taker.

Conclusion

While it is said that co-teaching has the potential to change praxis at all levels of education (Roth & Tobin, 2004), we found it to be especially true within our higher education classroom. Exceptional teaching and learning was regularly modelled and observed, respectively, in class sessions, which led to the intellectual growth of students, as expected in a college class, and also of the co-instructors. One can accurately conclude that for students negotiating the world of a co-taught classroom at times represented a difficult task; likewise, the same could be said for the co-teaching professors involved. Yet, it is also true that the professors involved learned more about their own beliefs, values, and collaboration skills regarding outcomes within a specific content area than they ever had before. Using a co-teaching format at the university level allows future teachers to experience the real strengths and challenges of working collaboratively. Co-teaching allows professors to continue to grow, reflect, and change, while also providing students with a variety of effective instructional methods and a framework in which to reflect on their own teaching beliefs and preferences. Further, in promoting critical thinking, problem solving, and collaboration among students, co-teaching experiences serve to model the kind of complex skills that characterize the contemporary workplace, regardless of one's chosen field.

REFERENCES

Bacharach, N., Heck, T., & Dahlberg, K. (2008). What makes co-teaching work? Identifying the essential elements. *College Teaching Methods & Styles Journal, 4*(3), 43–8. http://dx.doi.org/10.19030/ctms.v4i3.5534

Bauwens, J., & Hourcade, J. (1991). Making co-teaching a mainstreaming strategy. *Preventing School Failure, 35*(4), 19–24. http://dx.doi.org/10.1080/1045988X.1991.9944254

Brundrett, M. (2010). Developing your leadership team. In B. Davies & M. Brundrett (Eds.), *Developing successful leadership* (pp. 99–114). London, UK: Springer.

Cook, L., & Friend, M. (1995). Co-teaching: Guidelines for creating effective practices. *Focus on Exceptional Children, 28*(3), 1–16.

Ferguson, J., & Wilson, J.C. (2010). Co-teaching in higher education. *Scholar-Practitioner Quarterly, 4*(9), 134–60.

Ferguson, J., & Wilson, J.C. (2011). *The co-taught professorship.* Paper presented at the annual meeting of the American Educational Research Association, New Orleans, LA.

Friend, M. (2014). Thoughts on collaboration for 21st century professionals: Moving forward or lost in space? [SERC blog post]. Retrieved from http://www.ctserc.org/index.php/co-teaching/item/52-thoughts-on-collaboration-for-21st-century-school-professionals

Hargreaves, A., & Fullan, M. (2012). *Professional capital: Transforming teaching in every school.* New York, NY: Teachers College Press.

Jones, T.S., & Brinker, R. (2008). *Conflict coaching: Conflict management strategies and skills for the individual.* Thousand Oaks, CA: Sage.

Mahon, J. (2009). Conflict style and cultural understanding among teachers in the western United States: Exploring relationships. *International Journal of Intercultural Relations, 33*(1), 46–56. http://dx.doi.org/10.1016/j.ijintrel.2008.12.002

National Dissemination Center for Children with Disabilities. (2011). *Co-teaching in inclusive classrooms: A metasynthesis of qualitative research.* Newark, NJ: Author.

Nevin, A., Villa, R., & Thousand, J. (2004). *A guide to co-teaching with paraeducators: Practical tips for K-12 educators*. Thousand Oaks, CA: Corwin Press.

Platt, J., Walker-Knight, D., Lee, T., & Hewitt, R. (2001). *Shaping future teacher education practices through collaboration and co-teaching*. Paper presented at the annual meeting of the American Association for Colleges of Teacher Education, Dallas, TX.

Rosenholtz, S.J. (1989). *Teachers' workplace: The social organization of schools*. New York, NY: Teachers College Press.

Roth, W.M., & Tobin, K.G. (2004). Coteaching: From praxis to theory. *Teachers and Teaching: Theory and Practice*, *10*(2), 161–80.

Scruggs, T.E., Mastropieri, M.A., & McDuffie, K.A. (2007). Co-teaching in inclusive classrooms: A metasynthesis of qualitative research. *Exceptional Children*, *73*(4), 392–416. http://dx.doi.org/10.1177/001440290707300401

U.S. Department of Education, National Center for Education Statistics. (2017). *The condition of education, 2017*. NCES 2017-144. Retrieved from https://nces.ed.gov/pubs2017/2017144.pdf

Vaughn, S., Schumm, J., & Arguelles, M. (1997). The ABCDEs of co-teaching. *Teaching Exceptional Children*, *30*(2), 4–10. http://dx.doi.org/10.1177/004005999703000201

Wagner, T. (2008). Rigor redefined. *Educational Leadership*, *66*(2), 20–5.

Walther-Thomas, C.S. (1997). Co-teaching experiences: The benefits and problems that teachers and principals report over time. *Journal of Learning Disabilities*, *30*(4), 395–407. http://dx.doi.org/10.1177/002221949703000406

Wenzlaff, T., Berak, L., Wieseman, K., Monroe-Baillargeon, A., Bacharach, N., & Bradfield-Kreider, P. (2002). Walking our talk as educators: Teaming as a best practice. In E. Guyton & J. Ranier (Eds.), *Research on meeting and using standards in the preparation of teachers* (pp. 11–24). Dubuque, IA: Kendall-Hunt.

8 Co-Teaching and Co-Assessment in a Geometry Course for In-Service Teachers

DORIT PATKIN AND ILANA LEVENBERG

The Teaching Profession

Teaching is a very complex, demanding, and extremely challenging profession. As Shulman (1986) stated: "The person who presumes to teach a subject matter to children must demonstrate knowledge of that subject matter as a prerequisite of teaching" (p. 5). Nevertheless, subject expertise is insufficient. Teachers also need to possess a range of skills and various types of knowledge and abilities such as pedagogical knowledge concerning available teaching materials and methods; ability to adapt teaching approaches to specific subjects, along with a rationale for these adaptations; knowledge and ability to design lessons, ask questions, and present problems; knowledge and abilities relating to students, such as understanding the difficulties, mistakes, and misconceptions that students have, the ways students construct their knowledge, and how to communicate with students; and knowledge and ability to reflect on practice, analysing classroom experiences to improve their practice (Danielson, 2001; Shulman, 1987).

Co-Teaching: Patterns and Advantages

Co-teaching was conceived in the United States as a function of special education pupils' inclusion in mainstream classes (Murawski & Swanson, 2001). Bauwens, Hourcade, and Friend (1989) co-authored a paper on this issue, in which they coined the term "cooperative teaching," describing a pragmatic integration of mainstream and special education practitioners' work. The term was designed to represent the interdisciplinary relations of teachers in both types of education. Cook and

Friend (1995) subsequently shortened the term to "co-teaching." They defined co-teaching as "two or more professionals, engaging in independent and collaborative teaching of heterogeneous students group in one physical place" (p. 2). Since publication of the Bauwens et al. (1989) paper, the educational literature has extensively described experiences of co-teaching, as well as presented proposals for implementing teaching situations according to this model (Cook & Friend, 1995; Reinbiller, 1996). Today, there is a growing trend of co-teaching, mainly with regard to pupils with special needs who are included in mainstream education (Mastropieri, Scruggs, Graetz, Norland et al., 2005). At the same time, this type of teaching can also be found in higher education institutions (Duchardt et al., 1999; Wolffensperger & Patkin, 2013b).

The expression "two heads are better than one" embodies the main rationale underlying the development of the co-teaching model. That is, one single teacher cannot meet all the educational learning needs of his or her pupils. The literature dealing with co-teaching presents other reasons for the importance of this teaching model, namely the aspects of examination, comprehension, and conceptualization of teaching. Roth, Lawless, and Tobin (2000) perceive co-teaching as a way for conceptualizing teaching as well as assessing it. As Wolffensperger and Patkin (2013a) noted:

> The experience of "being together" shows that each partner can distance him/herself from the "togetherness" of teaching alternately and, thus, objectify the assessed teacher's experience. Objectification facilitates assessment and conceptualization of teaching, while the assessed teacher continues it in practice. (p. 146)

Roth et al. (2000) stipulate that the co-teaching model provides fertile soil for the development of a praxeology relating to practice. Teachers engaging in co-teaching process and assess their experiences through the developing praxeology and, thus, promote the understanding of their own teaching.

Co-Teaching and Care in Teaching

Papers about co-teaching present evidence relating to the relation between co-teaching and the concept of caring in teaching. Noddings (1986) claimed that teachers' education focusing on the development of pedagogical beliefs and activities should, at its very core, feature the

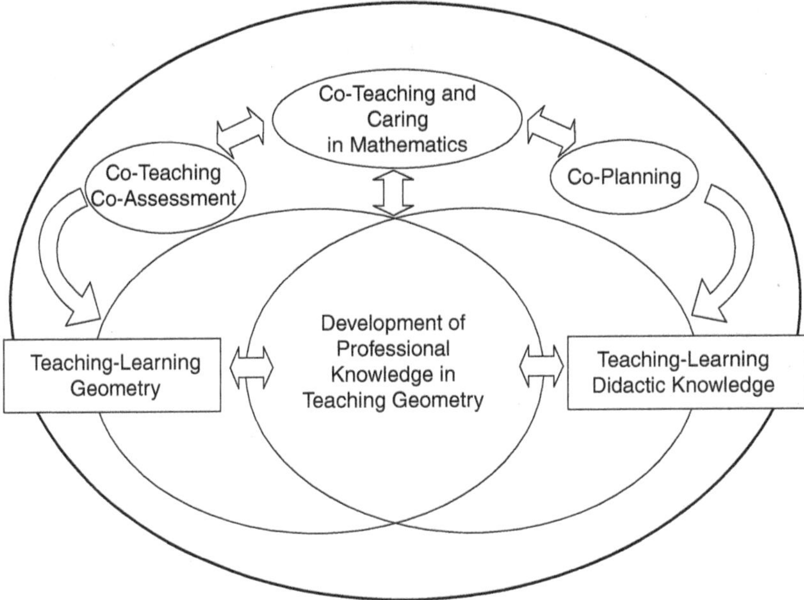

Figure 8.1. The contribution of caring co-teaching and co-assessment. Adapted from Yochi Wolffensperger and Dorit Patkin (2013a).

notion of an ethics of care. She also argued that we should educate caring teachers by being an example. Lake, Jones, and Dagli (2004) conducted a study of co-teaching with two college lecturers who taught methodological courses for mathematics and science pedagogy. The research findings showed that teachers grounded their co-teaching in materialization of the ethics of care theory, developed by Noddings (1986). The lecturers applied this pedagogy with the purpose of addressing students' anxiety within these specific disciplines. All these findings are summed up in the model shown in Figure 8.1, adapted from Wolffensperger & Patkin, 2013a.

Co-Teaching in Teacher Education

In recent years, co-teaching has also become more and more prevalent in teacher education and in-service training programs (Duchardt et al., 1999; Wolffensperger & Patkin, 2013a). This trend is growing, even though the implementation of this type of teaching is often not conducive to the structure of higher and teacher education institutions (Dochy, Segers & Sluijsmans, 1999). Duchardt et al. (1999) argue that there are different variations of co-teaching, some of which also include co-planning within the framework of co-teaching. Co-teaching has been introduced into mathematics teaching as well (Lake, Jones, & Dagli, 2004; Wolffensperger & Patkin, 2013a). Moreover, Duchardt et al. (1999) have found that higher education teachers acknowledge more and more the advantages of this teaching model. Consequently, they attribute importance to the development of the co-teaching model in the field of teacher education and to its empowerment among teaching practitioners in general.

The study conducted by Duchardt et al. (1999) illustrated several findings that focused on three main areas. In the area of *daily practice*, trust was established between the collaborating entities, flexibility and collegiality were developed, collaboration in the teaching itself was formed, collaboration in planning the teaching was evident, and a framework for problem solution was implemented. In the area of *professional knowledge*, knowledge and development were challenged through co-teaching. Concerning the third area, *students*, co-teaching was shown to enhance the addressing of their various needs. The findings of another co-teaching research study by Mastropieri et al. (2005) indicated that the variables with the most significant contribution to the success of co-teaching were knowledge in the discipline and compatibility between the collaborating entities.

Self-Assessment and Co-Assessment

Self-assessment is considered one of the essential competencies required for effective learning and professional development (Taras, 2001). This type of assessment requires that teachers make a long-term commitment to staying current regarding new knowledge in their field of expertise. It also represents a form of assessment that must be regularly modelled for students, who are, in turn, being encouraged to develop habits of self-oriented learning (Boud, 1995; Wolffensperger & Patkin, 2013b).

Self-assessment has been prevalent for a long time, but the regular use of it in an individual practice, according to the professional literature, is still relatively rare in higher education (Taras, 2001). Self-assessment is perceived in the literature as a way of developing self-regulated learning, increasing responsibility for the learning, and achieving independent learning. This perception has come about because self-assessment is based on developing self-awareness in learning through critical reflection on the learning (Boud & Falchikov, 1989; Dochy et al., 1999; Taras, 2001). These activities promote the learners' ability to realistically assess their strengths and weaknesses, as well as their ability to regulate their learning in a productive way (Schon, 1987).

In the process of learning-oriented assessment, assessment constitutes an integral part of the learning and aims to provide constructive feedback to learners (Mok et al., 2006; Noddings, 1986, 2003). Assessment can take a variety of forms such as self-assessment of the learners; peer-assessment, whereby teachers assess the learning products of their colleagues; and co-assessment conducted by lecturers and teacher candidates in the teacher in-service training program. In addition, summative assessment focuses on procedural-formative assessment that is based on a continuous dialogue between the lecturers and participants in the program, as well as on the writing of learning diaries (Boud & Falchikov, 1989; Leathwood, 2005). Integration of these assessment types results in an impactful and deeper approach to learning (Dochy et al., 1999).

Self-assessment also involves aspects of validity and reliability. Review of studies in the field illustrates that methods of self-assessment and co-assessment are usually valid and reliable (Topping, as cited in Dochy et al., 1999). A study conducted by Stefani (1994) shows that learners' self-assessment can be as reliable as the lecturers' assessment of the learners' class work and participation. Moreover, her research findings refuted the argument that students with high achievement assess themselves too low, whereas students with low achievement assess themselves too high.

Taras (2001) argued that students should be involved in the discussion about assessment criteria, in terms of their identification, comprehension, and shaping. Similarly, Hall (as cited in Dochy et al., 1999) reported that students and lecturers collaborate in clarifying the objectives of the learning and assessment, as well as in elucidating the assessment criteria when self-assessing their own learning. The goal of criteria-dependent self-assessment is to enhance the transparency of the process, because, although this type of assessment embodies many advantages, it may lead to superficial assessment (Leathwood, 2005). Moreover, Smith (as cited in Wolffensperger & Patkin, 2013b) stipulates that a related method of self-co-assessment (wherein a teaching team reflects on its own practice) can be viewed as a multilayered and effective part of ongoing collaboration.

Geometry as a Unique Subject

Geometry is one of the major subjects in the curriculum of elementary and high schools, and is perceived as one of the most complex fields. Students frequently experience a sense of travelling to "an isolated island" where everything is structured in a "logical" or "unusual" way, without any relation to daily life (Patkin & Levenberg, 2012). Consequently, those engaged in geometry teaching refer to the various levels of thinking among students in the class, striving to overcome the students' difficulties in learning basic geometrical concepts.

At the first stages, geometry studies involve *visualization*. Pupils whose visual competence is insufficiently developed often encounter problems in this subject. Moreover, visual competence constitutes an important factor when examining learners already at the first stage, according to Van Hiele's levels of geometric thinking (Van Hiele, 1987). Developing visual competence in the course of teaching geometry aims to increase learners' mathematical power and to promote their ability to solve mathematical problems.

Walker et al. (2011) investigated whether or not the development of visualization skills in non-mathematical contexts may confer an advantage to an individual's geometrical reasoning. Their research findings clearly showed that the development of visual links has importance for, and a very great impact on, the level of comprehension of geometrical content.

During geometry lessons, the use of many types of visual displays, pictures, presentations, and videos that show geometry in the pupils' environment serve to constitute a bridge between the concrete and the abstract (Patkin & Levenberg, 2012).

In recent years, mathematics teacher educators have emphasized the importance of implementing a reform in mathematics teaching. Moreover, they have promoted the issue of professional development as part of learning throughout teachers' years of professional practice.

In order to strengthen teachers' mathematical and pedagogical knowledge, Israeli educational authorities decided at the beginning of the twenty-first century to develop professional programs that respond more directly to teachers' needs. The aim of the new in-service training program was to promote elementary school pupils' academic achievement in mathematics. The program was called

"Specialization in Mathematics." It was compulsory for all "non-professional" teachers, namely teachers who did not have a formal mathematics education background. The program aimed to enhance teachers' mathematics knowledge, as well as their acquaintance with the new elementary school curriculum. The didactic aspects were designed to present teachers with several models of teaching and learning, and the ability to adjust them to different age levels. The program also provided knowledge for implementing varied ways for assessing students' performance and emphasized teamwork skills as an important goal. According to the program's goals, teachers should learn to cooperate with their colleagues, design the work plan together, set goals, and systemically test and assess outcomes of learning processes.

Teacher In-Service Training Program

Mathematics Teacher In-Service Training Program Model

The model of "personal practical knowledge of the teacher" (Patkin & Millet, 1997) comprises a set of six components:

- **Subject matter knowledge:** understanding the structure of the field of knowledge, ideas, principles, and key concepts of the discipline
- **Student learner knowledge:** understanding learning and development among students, levels of difficulty, and adjusting the material to the students' differentiation needs
- **Background knowledge of the school environment:** understanding contexts, norms, and relationships within the school and among the community, parents, and authorities
- **Curricular knowledge:** knowledge of the existing curricula, learning materials, and alternative materials; exploring connections between content areas, different subjects, and different levels
- **Didactic knowledge:** knowledge of teaching practices; recognizing and using different teaching strategies, varied classroom management, and organizational approaches
- **Self-knowledge:** personal goals, values, awareness, beliefs, and opinions that affect curriculum planning and teaching

In this chapter we will mainly relate to two aspects of the model: knowledge of the subject matter (mathematics) and didactic knowledge.

As lecturers in the teacher in-service training program, we decided to dedicate several sessions to co-teaching involving two lecturers simultaneously present in the same lesson. This model entails a partnership that requires preparation, complete mutual trust between the two lecturers, as well as full collaboration and a desire to experience a different type of teaching. All these elements aim to achieve optimal teaching results and illustrate to the teachers attending the training program the nature of collaboration between teachers and the outcomes that can be attained by means of co-teaching.

Prior to the co-taught lectures, the job allocation was pre-defined by the teaching team. One of the lecturers engaged in the theoretical part, and the other dealt with the practical aspect of the mathematical activity. Yet, the roles were interchanged regularly throughout the course.

During the very first session of the teacher in-service training program, we presented the concept of self-assessment to the participants. Self-assessment is defined as an assessment whereby learners are involved in the judgment of their own learning in general and judgment of their learning outcomes in particular (Boud & Falchikov, 1989). From the procedural aspect, self-assessment is a way to enhance students' active participation in their own learning (Boud, 1995).

Co-Planning and Preparation for the Teacher In-Service Training Program

The topic for the planned training program was the sum of interior and exterior angles of polygons. While planning the program, we realized that we did not wish to teach this topic with the more traditional method for two main reasons. The first was due to the perceived differences among the participants regarding levels of mathematical knowledge. The second had to do with our desire to search out teaching and illustration methods that would allow us to adequately differentiate classroom experiences based on learner needs.

The idea that we discussed during the planning process was to use hands-on teaching aids like paper and scissors. In our current era, teachers are often expected to use technology at every possible opportunity. Hence, we believed that using tactile, visual aids like paper and scissors represented a refreshing change, both for the teacher participants during the program and later on for their own students when they themselves would present the topic in their respective classes. The paper-and-scissors approach constituted auxiliary tools for illustrating the concepts, but also allowed for scaffolding within the inductive process, leading up to mathematical generalization (Patkin & Levenberg, 2014).

We decided upon teaching the content, one stage at a time, in the following order. The first polygon whose sum of angles is discussed is the triangle. Elementary school teachers usually tell their pupils: "The sum of interior angles in a triangle is 180°." Using this phrase, we can deduce that the sum of angles[1] in a square is 360°, as a polygon with four sides consists, in fact, of two interior triangles. By using the adhesive paper[2] models, teachers were able to visually determine that, likewise, the sum of the interior angles of any convex quadrilateral is 360°, or that of a full circle (see Figure 8.2 and Figure 8.3).

In the second stage, during the transition to polygons whose number of sides is greater than four, it is recommended to present an inductive process, namely the inference from the particular to the general. In our case, this process implies generalization for finding the sum of the interior angles of polygons. The conclusion drawn at the end of this process is that the greater the number of the polygon sides, the greater the sum of its angles. This conclusion applies to all polygon types, both concave and convex.[3]

A similar process is performed when attempting to find the number of diagonals within polygons. The first polygon that is normally presented to learners is a quadrilateral, and it is easy to demonstrate that a convex quadrilateral has only two diagonals. Thereafter, using an inductive process, we achieve generalization for finding the number of diagonals in a polygon with n sides, the generalization being valid for any type of polygon, both convex and concave. These two processes highlight the fact that when the number of polygon sides is greater, the sum of the interior angles is greater, as is the number of diagonals within the polygon.

Following a very accurate planning of the activity related to the sum of interior angles in polygons, we found out that the sum of exterior angles was not always taught in every class. Teachers prefer engaging with this topic in the classes where pupils are more proficient in geometry. In such classes, giving an explanation, and perhaps a superficial example, will persuade the pupils with regard to the often surprising sum. Because we wanted to continue the inductive process, we further anticipated that even the participating teachers would be surprised by this mathematical fact.

Based on the two previous inductive processes, namely finding the sum of interior angles of polygons and finding the number of diagonals, a similar assumption was made with regard to finding the sum of exterior angles of a polygon (see Figure 8.4): that is, the greater the

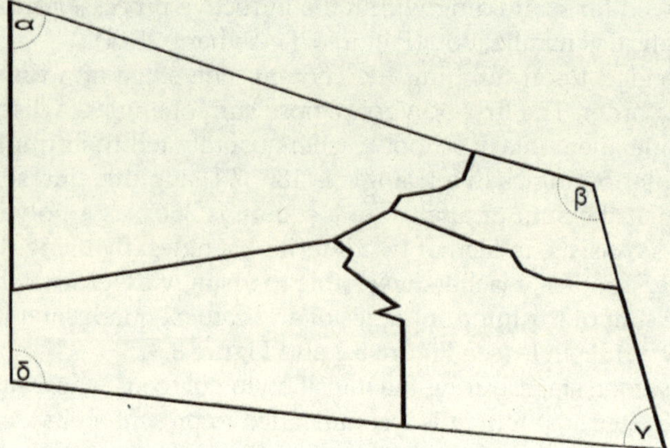

Figure 8.2. Quadrilateral divided into four random shapes using interior lines.

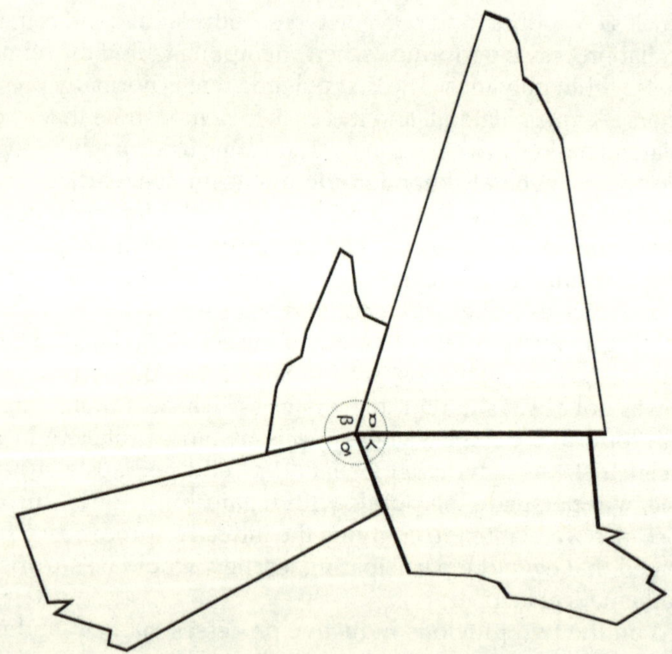

Figure 8.3. Four quadrilateral shapes re-arranged around a common vertex to illustrate 360°.

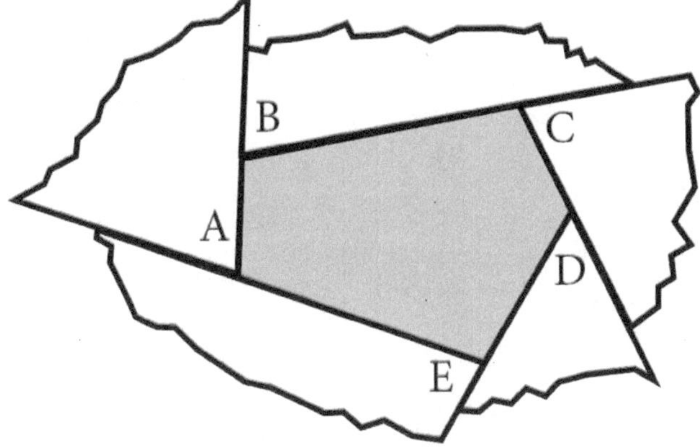

Figure 8.4. Pentagon shape with five sides showing extended lines and external angles.

number of the polygon sides, the greater the sum of exterior angles. However, this is not the case. By making appropriate drawings and paper cutting, learners can reach the surprising conclusion that there is actually no relationship between the number of sides and the sum of exterior angles of any convex polygon. Rather, the sum is actually a determined and unvarying size of 360°.

Using drawing and cutting as a simple and easily accessible illustration strategy can greatly contribute to the learning of new geometry concepts. Combining an active experience with an inductive reflection process, learners were able to make a generalization about the sum of angles of polygons.

Summary of Activities and Insights from the Co-Teaching Experience

The purpose of the paper-and-scissors activities was to illustrate, stage after stage in an inductive way, how to find a formula for calculating the sum of interior and exterior angles in convex polygons. The goal was to present a rich and in-depth inquiry assignment that integrates discovery, predictions, validation, proving processes, explanation, raising questions, and giving reasons. It is recommended that this type of approach be used while teaching other topics in geometry. Having experiences with inductive processes, combined with inquiry processes,

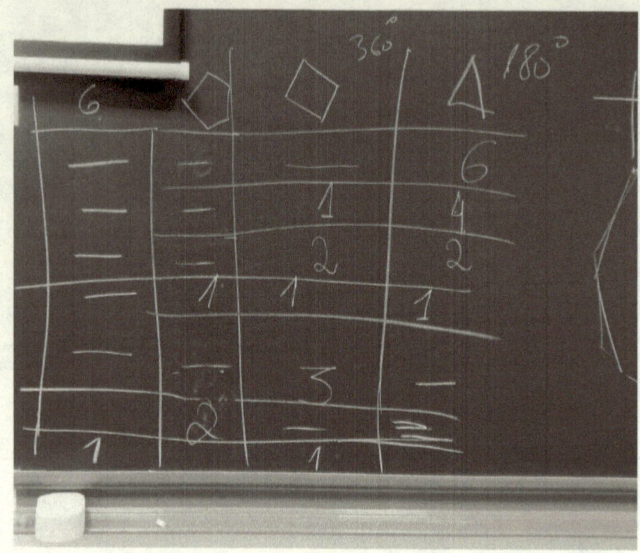

Figure 8.5. Chalkboard record of number of options for dividing an octagon into various polygons. Photo by Ilana Levenberg.

promotes the development of mathematical thinking. Combining illustration and calculation with numbers leads to generalization and constitutes an example for developing geometric thinking and nurturing creativity. Experiences of this kind directly and indirectly enhance mathematical insight and improve student understanding and achievement.

The co-teaching experience gave rise to both mathematical and didactical insights, and insights regarding co-teaching itself. Moreover, we presented another interesting inquiry activity, which had not been planned in advance of the beginning of the course but was put forward by a participant during one of the co-lectures. The notion of dividing a pentagon into a triangle and a quadrilateral, which was raised by a participant during the training program, lead to the related question of whether or not division into other polygons may also be possible. That is, how many triangles, or other polygons, could one potentially find? In a spontaneous manner, with full agreement between the two co-lecturers, we started a new, unplanned inquiry assignment. We were unable to say whether we would reach generalization, or how we would cope with this unknown situation.

We began by writing on the chalkboard all the options of different polygons (see Figure 8.5) that could comprise an octagon. One of us

Table 8.1. Options of dividing an octagon into various other polygons

No. of Triangles (180°)	No. of Quadrilaterals (360°)	No. of Pentagons (540°)	No. of Hexagons (720°)
6	–	–	–
4	1	–	–
2	2	–	–
1	1	1	–
–	3	–	–
–	–	2	–
–	1	–	1

conducted the discussion in class, while the other recorded the various options on the board, as shared and discussed by class participants.

This "back-and-forth" effect between the class and the two lecturers reinforced and enhanced the depth of the inquiry and of the mathematical discourse. It was a form of classroom management, from both didactic and mathematical points of view, which would have been difficult to facilitate with only one lecturer, in light of the large group of thirty teachers attending the program.

The sum of interior angles of an octagon is 1080°, and it can be divided into various combinations of other types of polygons for analysis purposes. Table 8.1 captures, in a more formalized manner, what was spontaneously shared and recorded on the board during the training program.

The teaching of geometry during the training program was the main and most important part. The co-teaching process exposed the learners not only to a variety of mathematical content items, but also to different teaching approaches. However, there still remained the assessment, which we had to perform during as well as at the end of the training program. We, as co-teachers, had to deliberate upon the assessment methods to be used, as well as concur with the participants on this point. We will discuss this collaborative process in the next section.

Methods for Assessing the Learners in the Training Program

Creating a Learning Diary as Part of the Training Program Assignments

We facilitated an initial discussion about assessment methods with the participants of the geometry teacher in-service training program. Following the discussion, we suggested that they maintain a learning diary, and the majority of the participants were in favour of doing so.

The learning diary was designed for the purpose of carefully monitoring the participants' learning processes and for developing the self-assessment of their own learning. The learning diary is not a collection of selected drafts, but rather a tool for documenting and developing the students' thinking in the form of writing. It aims to focus the learners' attention on their own learning methods, and also serves as a tool for reflecting and enhancing their awareness of everything associated with their learning (Klenowski, Askew, & Carnell, 2006). The learning diary was designed first and foremost to respond to the personal-academic needs of the participants themselves. The writing style used within the diary was entirely open to personal preference. We also jointly decided that the learning diaries would be made accessible to the lecturers for monitoring their own teaching processes, which would in turn allow the lecturers to adapt their methods based on participant feedback in a procedural way (Tidwell & Fitzgerald, 2004). Due to the participants' differing levels of mathematical competence, the option of reading the learning diaries at any time assisted us greatly in terms of planning the in-service training course and adapting the teaching focus and pace, as needed.

A Self-Assessment Indicator

The first suggestion for an indicator was based on the study done by Wolffensperger and Patkin (2013b), who implemented self-assessment of pre-service teachers during one of their courses. At the end of every training course, the pre-service teachers had to document in the diary their opinions regarding themselves and other participants. Moreover, they had to indicate those instructors whom they felt featured prominently in terms of content knowledge and teaching methods or, alternately, were ineffective regarding the presentation of the activities and the preparation of the learning materials.

We suggested using a modified indicator, based on the work of Wolffensperger and Patkin (2013b), which comprised criteria for navigating the course content and for performing both formative and summative self-assessments as a basis for deliberation (see Table 8.2). Discussing the indicator constituted part of the learning process regarding the participants' self-assessments. At this stage, we emphasized that the indicator stemmed from the learning objectives and the purpose of discussing it was to conduct a transparent negotiation and to jointly concur about the assessment criteria. The participants were

Table 8.2. The self-assessment indicator designed to guide the learning process and to assess outcomes

Performance Level	Process Dimension	Mathematics Teaching Dimension
Low level: Failure to achieve comprehension; performance on a satisfactory level and quality	– Failure to invest efforts in planning the work and performing it – Lack of involvement in learning – Failure to persevere with learning during the training program	**Mathematical knowledge:** – Failure to understand mathematical concepts and principles relating to the learned subject – Failure to understand the different aspects of the learned subject **Pedagogical knowledge:** – Acquaintance with a limited range of pedagogical competencies for teaching the learned subject – Failure to understand the need for putting a different emphasis on various pedagogical competencies during the different stages of teaching the subject – Failure to understand the adjustment of pedagogical competences to students with different needs **Curricular knowledge:** – Lack of acquaintance with the school curriculum in mathematics – Lack of acquaintance with the curriculum in mathematics for the specific age group – Failure to understand the "place" of the learned subject within the curriculum: its scope, importance, and its relation to other subjects – Failure to understand the spiral development of the learned subject within the curriculum
Intermediate level: Achieving comprehension; performance on a partially satisfactory level and some quality	– Investing partial or reasonable efforts in planning and executing the work – Only partial involvement in learning – Partial/reasonable perseverance while conducting and writing the research component	**Mathematical knowledge:** – Partial understanding of concepts and principles relating to the learned subject – Partial comprehension of the various aspects of the subject **Pedagogical knowledge:** – Acquaintance with a partial range of pedagogical competencies for teaching the learned subject – Partial understanding of the use of pedagogical competencies relevant to the learned subject – Partial understanding of the need for putting a different emphasis on various pedagogical competencies during the different stages of teaching the subject – Partial understanding of the adjustment of pedagogical competencies for students with different learning needs

(Continued)

Table 8.2. The self-assessment indicator designed to guide the learning process and to assess outcomes (Continued)

Performance Level	Process Dimension	Mathematics Teaching Dimension
		Curricular knowledge: – Partial knowledge of the school curriculum in mathematics – Partial knowledge of the curriculum for the specific age group – Partial understanding of the "place" of the learned subject in the curriculum: its scope, importance, and its relation to other subjects – Partial understanding of the spiral development of the learned subject in the curriculum
High level: Achieving comprehension; performance on a high level and with high quality	– Investing extensive efforts in planning and executing the work – Very active involvement in learning	**Mathematical knowledge:** – Full understanding of concepts and principles relating to the learned subject – Comprehension of all the various aspects of the subject **Pedagogical knowledge:** – Acquaintance with a wide range of pedagogical competencies for teaching the learned subject – Very good understanding of the use of pedagogical competencies relevant to the learned subject area – Understanding the need for putting a different emphasis on various pedagogical competencies during the different teaching stages – Understanding the adjustment of pedagogical competencies for students with different needs **Curricular knowledge:** – Full knowledge of the school curriculum in mathematics – Full knowledge of the curriculum for the specific age group – Full understanding of the "place" of the learned subject within the curriculum: its scope, importance, and its relation to other subjects – Full understanding of the spiral development of the learned subject within the general curriculum

Adapted from Yochi Wolffensperger and Dorit Patkin (2013b).

asked to familiarize themselves with, and critically evaluate, the indicator in order to suggest possible revisions. In the subsequent lesson, we discussed their written and spoken comments that had been made regarding the indicator.

Participants' initial comments regarding the self-assessment as part of the overall course assessment, and particularly to the self-assessment indicator tool, tended to support the findings from the related literature. Boud (1995) argued that self-assessment is a difficult and complex competency, and that therefore we cannot expect learners, even if they are in-service teachers, to master it overnight. In spite of the challenges inherent in self-assessment, we can conclude that most of our participants perceived this form of assessment as being beneficial to the learning process. This conclusion also complies with the literature in the field. Dochy et al. (1999), for example, reviewed sixty-three studies relating to self-assessment and found that learning generally improved in the following ways: increasing students' reflection on their performance; enhancing awareness of students' quality of work; promoting the quality of learning outcomes; increasing effectiveness of learning methods; assuming greater responsibility and promoting students' independence; increasing students' satisfaction; and improving the learning climate within a class.

To sum up this section dealing with assessment, we can say that the experience of involving the participants in self-assessment during the geometry course, alongside the co-assessment of the students' participation and assignments completed by the two co-lecturers, empowered the participants as learners and teachers. Another objective was improving the quality of our teaching while experiencing a form of self-assessment alongside the participants. Critical observation of this experience illustrated to us that while self-assessment within an in-service training program may not represent an obvious choice, it is nonetheless a meaningful form of assessment and therefore worthy of considerable teaching efforts.

Conclusions and Recommendations

When teaching in the twenty-first century, teachers are required to react quickly and to respond to a large number of learners within a relatively short period of time. Co-teaching with two lecturers allowed us to comply with this requirement as well as to be more flexible in relating to course participants and their learning needs within the program.

We paid special attention to the smaller working groups that were organized during activities, and this strategy facilitated comprehension of the thinking styles of a larger number of participants. The activities during the co-teaching sessions made it possible to open a different channel for enhancing and expanding the mathematical content and the didactic approaches. A single lecturer in a class may find it more difficult to develop a variety of suggestions or topics that emerge during the teaching process. As mentioned earlier, a single lecturer needs to make difficult decisions quickly, whereas in the case of two lecturers, this task is shared and thus often much easier. The inquiry activity that we presented in this chapter is but one example of many that took place. We can assume that it would not have been expanded in the same kind of way, in light of time constraints or lack of pre-planning, were only one lecturer involved in the overall process.

The presence of two lecturers in the class evokes a sense of confidence, and the participants know they have someone they can consult and trust when finding themselves in "a new field" or involved in an unexpected event. Co-teaching enabled us to experience the maximum benefits regarding both mathematical and empirical-didactic factors. We conclude that co-teaching involving two lecturers in the same lesson allows for higher levels of overall quality and professionalism, especially with regard to teacher education program subjects such as mathematics (and geometry more specifically), the teaching of which is often particularly challenging in terms of student competence and confidence.

ACKNOWLEDGMENTS

This chapter is dedicated to the memory of our dear friend and colleague, Dr Yochi Wolffensperger, who passed away in 2012. Yochi was a lecturer and researcher in the field of academic literacy, and was both unique and thorough in her work. Her research studies will no doubt serve to illuminate the paths of many students and researchers in this area. May her memory be blessed forever.

NOTES

1 Whenever the concept "sum of angles" is used in this chapter, it implies the sum of interior angles. In the case of the sum of exterior angles, this will be explicitly indicated.

2 Adhesive paper refers to a sheet that features a sticker, or some other form of adhesive, on one of the surfaces. Removing the sticker uncovers adhesive or glue, which makes it possible to attach the paper cuttings in the desirable location and sequence.

3 A concave polygon is a 2-D geometric shape that has one or more interior angles greater than 180°, with the resulting visual effect that some vertices point "inwards," towards the centre of the polygon. A convex polygon has all interior angles less than 180°, resulting in all vertices pointing "outwards," or away from the centre of the polygon.

REFERENCES

Bauwens, J., Hourcade, J.J., & Friend, M. (1989). Cooperative teaching: A model for general and special education integration. *Remedial and Special Education, 10*(2), 17–22. http://dx.doi.org/10.1177/074193258901000205

Boud, D.J. (1995). *Enhancing learning through self-assessment.* London, UK: Kogan Page.

Boud, D., & Falchikov, N. (1989). Quantitative studies of student self-assessment in higher education: A critical analysis of findings. *Higher Education, 18*(5), 529–49.

Cook, L., & Friend, M. (1995). Co-teaching: Guidelines for creating effective practices. *Focus on Exceptional Children, 28*(3), 1–6.

Danielson, C. (2001). New trends in teacher evaluation. *Educational Leadership, 58*(5), 12–15.

Dochy, F., Segers, M., & Sluijsmans, D. (1999). The use of self-, peer and co-assessment in higher education: A review. *Studies in Higher Education, 24*(3), 331–50. http://dx.doi.org/10.1080/03075079912331379935

Duchardt, B., Marlow, L., Inman, D., Christensen, P., & Reeves, M. (1999). Collaboration and co-teaching: General and special education faculty. *Clearing House: A Journal of Educational Strategies, Issues and Ideas, 72*(3), 186–90. http://dx.doi.org/10.1080/00098659909599625

Klenowski, V., Askew, S., & Carnell, E. (2006). Portfolios for learning, assessment and professional development in higher education. *Assessment & Evaluation in Higher Education, 31*(3), 267–86. http://dx.doi.org/10.1080/02602930500352816

Lake, V.E., Jones, I., & Dagli, U. (2004). Handle with care: Integrating caring content in mathematics and science methods classes. *Journal of Research in Childhood Education, 19*(1), 5–17. http://dx.doi.org/10.1080/02568540409595050

Leathwood, C. (2005). Assessment policy and practice in higher education: Purpose, standards and equity. *Assessment & Evaluation in Higher Education, 30*(3), 307–24. http://dx.doi.org/10.1080/02602930500063876

Mastropieri, M.A., Scruggs, T.E., Graetz, J., Norland, J., Gardizi, W., & McDuffie, K. (2005). Case studies in co-teaching in the content areas: Successes, failures and challenges. *Intervention in School and Clinic, 40*(5), 260–70. http://dx.doi.org/10.1177/10534512050400050201

Mok, M.M.C., Lung, C.L., Cheng, D.P.W., Cheung, R.H.P., & Ng, M.L. (2006). Self-assessment in higher education: Experience in using a metacognitive approach in five case studies. *Assessment & Evaluation in Higher Education, 31*(4), 415–33. http://dx.doi.org/10.1080/02602930600679100

Murawski, W.W., & Swanson, H.L. (2001). A meta-analysis of co-teaching research: Where are the data? *Remedial and Special Education, 22*(5), 258–67. http://dx.doi.org/10.1177/074193250102200501

Noddings, N. (1986). Fidelity in teaching, teacher education, and research for teaching. *Harvard Educational Review, 56*(4), 496–511. http://dx.doi.org/10.17763/haer.56.4.34738r7783h58050

Noddings, N. (2003). *Caring: A feminine approach to ethics and moral education.* Los Angeles, CA: University of California Press. (Original work published 1984)

Patkin, D., & Levenberg, I. (2012). Geometry from the world around us. *Learning and Teaching Mathematics, 13*, 14–18.

Patkin, D., & Levenberg, I. (2014). Investigating the sum of interior angles of convex polygons using paper and scissors. *Learning and Teaching Mathematics, 16*, 7–12.

Patkin, D., & Millet, S. (1997). Mathematics teachers' open-mindedness to changes in teaching means professionalization. *Dapim, 25*, 84–99. [Hebrew]

Reinbiller, N. (1996). Co-teaching: New variations on a not-so-new practice. *Teacher Education and Special Education, 19*(1), 34–48. http://dx.doi.org/10.1177/088840649601900104

Roth, W.M., Lawless, D., & Tobin, K. (2000). Towards a praxeology of teaching. *Canadian Journal of Education, 25*(1), 1–15. http://dx.doi.org/10.2307/1585864

Schon, D. (1987). *Educating the reflective practitioner: Towards a new design for teaching and learning in the profession*. San Francisco, CA: Jossey-Bass.

Shulman, L.S. (1986). Those who understand: Knowledge growth in teaching. *Educational Researcher, 15*(2), 4–14. http://dx.doi.org/10.3102/0013189X015002004

Shulman, L.S. (1987). Knowledge and teaching: Foundations of the new reform. *Harvard Educational Review, 57*(1), 1–23. http://dx.doi.org/10.17763/haer.57.1.j463w79r56455411

Stefani, L (1994). Peer, self and tutor assessment: Relative reliabilities. *Studies in Higher Education*, *19*(1), 69–79.

Taras, M. (2001). The use of tutor feedback and student self-assessment in summative assessment tasks: Towards transparency for students and tutors. *Assessment & Evaluation in Higher Education*, *26*(6), 605–14. http://dx.doi.org/10.1080/02602930120093922

Tidwell, D.L., & Fitzgerald, L.M. (2004). Self-study as teaching. In J.J. Loughran, M.L. Hamilton, V.K. LaBoskey, & T.L. Russell (Eds.), *International handbook of self-study of teaching and teacher education practices: Part one* (pp. 69–102). Dordrecht, The Netherlands: Springer. http://dx.doi.org/10.1007/978-1-4020-6545-3_3

Van Hiele, P.M. (1987). *Van-Hiele Levels: A method to facilitate the finding of levels of thinking in geometry by using the levels in arithmetic*. Paper presented at the Conference on Learning and Teaching Geometry: Issues for Research and Practice, Syracuse University, New York, NY.

Walker, C.M., Winner, E., Hetland, L., Simmons, S, & Goldsmith, L. (2011). Visual thinking: Art students have an advantage in geometric reasoning. *Creative Education*, *2*(1), 22–6. http://dx.doi.org/10.4236/ce.2011.21004

Wolffensperger, Y., & Patkin, D. (2013a). It takes two to develop professional knowledge of a student: A case study. *Teacher Education and Practice*, *26*(1), 143–60.

Wolffensperger, Y., & Patkin, D. (2013b). Self-assessment of self-assessment in a process of co-teaching. *Assessment & Evaluation in Higher Education*, *38*(1), 16–33. http://dx.doi.org/10.1080/02602938.2011.596925

9 Co-Teaching in Graduate Education

MUMBI KARIUKI AND DANIEL H. JARVIS

This chapter explores the phenomenon of co-teaching at the graduate education level within a university setting. We will highlight some of the lessons that we have learned while co-teaching two graduate level courses: Survey of Research Methods (compulsory master of education degree course; co-taught once over a twelve-week fall term); and Critical Conversations in Educational Research (compulsory doctor of philosophy in educational sustainability degree course; co-taught twice during two consecutive summer PhD residencies). A brief review of the literature pertaining to co-teaching will help set the stage for the ensuing reflections and discussion regarding post-secondary co-teaching.

Co-Teaching in Context: A Review of the Literature

Co-teaching is a common method of delivery for instruction in many teaching environments. It involves two or more teachers who agree to share responsibility for delivering instruction to a single group of learners (Cook, 2004; Scruggs, Mastropieri, & McDuffie, 2007; Villa, Thousand, & Nevin, 2004). Such instruction encompasses mutually agreed-upon content or objectives, as well as pooled resources and joint accountability. As Cook (2004) points out, "Although it is generally preferred that co-teaching be collaborative, it might or might not be. *Collaboration* generally refers to how individuals interact, not the activity they're doing" (p. 6). Co-teaching, therefore, is an activity that involves a range of collaborative practices based upon the teachers' instructional approaches, whether formally planned or inadvertent.

The practice of teachers collaborating to plan and deliver instruction is not a new phenomenon, and has been interchangeably referred to as team teaching, co-teaching, co-enrolment, collaborative teaching, and cooperative teaching (Luckner, 1999). Regardless of the nomenclature, there is consensus in the literature that the arrangement involves learning environments in which two or more educators or facilitators present instructional material to students during a learning experience, such as a course. Instructors in these cases would be aware of the joint responsibility at the outset of the co-teaching assignment, either by having been requested or required to participate in the teaching assignment, or by having elected to do so.

There are six main models or approaches to co-teaching that can be used collectively, separately, or in combination: teach-observe; teach-assist; parallel teach; station teach; alternative teach; and team teach (Cook, 2004; Vaughn, Schumm, & Arguelles, 1997).

As the name of the *teach-observe* approach suggests, one instructor teaches while the other observes. This approach is often adopted when it is important to collect some type of data for the purpose of improving practice, for example, if teachers want to provide feedback to one another or when a practicing teacher works with a mentor. In the latter case, the mentor could observe and provide feedback that the mentee could later act upon, or the mentee may simply observe the more experienced teacher in order to learn.

In the *teach-assist* approach, one of the teachers moves around the learning space and unobtrusively provides assistance when needed, as the other instructor teaches. *Parallel teaching* happens when the teachers divide the group of learners and teach the same material to their respective groups concurrently. In *station teaching*, each teacher presents different materials to groups of students as they move from station to station. *Alternate teaching* happens when some kind of differentiated instruction is desired; for example, one teacher may work with a large group while the other works with a smaller group to address the specific needs of both groups. *Team teaching* happens when both teachers teach the same content simultaneously, in what has been called a "tag-team" fashion (Vaughn et al., 1997). Team teaching has also been viewed as a "speak and add" approach, in which one teacher teaches while the other adds information at appropriate times, or as a "duet" approach, in which the two educators work seamlessly together to expand upon or enhance each other's ideas or sentences (Tobin, 2005).

Villa et al. (2004) provide a list of five specific elements that two or more co-teachers must agree to when undertaking to co-teach a course:

1. Coordinate their work to achieve at least one common, publicly agreed-upon goal;
2. Share a belief system that each of the co-teaching team members has unique and needed expertise;
3. Demonstrate parity by alternatively engaging in the dual roles of teacher and learner, expert and novice, giver and recipient of knowledge or skills;
4. Use a distributed functions theory of leadership in which the task and relationship functions of the traditional lone teacher are distributed among all co-teaching group members; and
5. Use a cooperative process that includes face-to-face interaction, positive interdependence, performance, as well as monitoring and processing of interpersonal skills, and individual accountability. (p. 3)

Other studies have looked at co-teaching specifically in higher education (Bacharach, Heck, & Dahlberg, 2008; Carpenter, Crawford, & Walden, 2007; Ferguson & Wilson, 2011; Gillespie & Israetel, 2008). Gillespie and Israetel's (2008) study was based on a model in which "instructors from diverse fields join to teach concepts which bridge two or more fields of study by merging each instructor's knowledge in their respective area of specialization" (p. 3). The study described how a psychologist taught one segment of a learning activity to twenty-three college students, while the same psychologist and a mathematician co-taught a second segment. Although results showed that students responded positively to the experience (for example, it helped maintain attention and made the class more interesting), data for the study were collected over only two class sessions, which may not have been sufficient for students to fully assess the impact of this type of co-teaching. Gillespie and Israetel recommend the use of broader samples for more conclusive results.

Co-teaching in higher education has also been used as a model for preservice teacher programs (Bacharach et al., 2008; Ferguson & Wilson, 2011; Wilson & Ferguson, 2012). Wilson and Ferguson's (2012) study reported on students' perceptions of having two instructors lead a co-taught course, and noted that "[c]omments on 'Who is in charge?' and 'Who do I contact for help?' were plentiful and occurred throughout the semester" (para. 7). In addition, the two instructors in the study reported having learned from one another but "struggled with identifying who had power and responsibility for the course as well as how to share that power" (Wilson & Ferguson, 2012, para. 8).

One of the most common applications of co-teaching is among children with exceptionalities (Arnold & Jackson, 1996; Bacharach et al., 2008, 2010; Cook & Friend, 1995; Tobin, 2005; Vaughn et al., 1997), and the aforementioned approaches to co-teaching are particularly helpful in such learning environments. However, co-teaching is a less commonly enacted and researched phenomenon at the post-secondary level. As Ferguson and Wilson (2011) have observed, "While it might be said that higher education faculty members are known to collaborate on research, they most often teach their courses singularly" (p. 53).

Design and Delivery of a Co-Teaching Learning Experience

Co-Planning the Learning Sessions

A new PhD program in educational sustainability was recently launched (2012) within the Schulich School of Education at Nipissing University, North Bay, Ontario, Canada. One of the stipulations of the program was that the PhD level courses would be co-taught. Subsequently, Jarvis and Kariuki formed one of two co-teaching teams for the first cohort of ten students. While the literature might have shed some light on practical applications of the approaches to co-teaching discussed earlier in this chapter, time constraints limited our ability to consult such sources, and we instead decided to primarily integrate and incorporate our respective time-tested, on-site (face-to-face, as opposed to online learning environments) teaching strategies during the course preparation process.

The preparation was very intense, and we met on a number of occasions in the months leading up to the course to discuss ideas, assignments, assessment, and other pertinent details. The discussion in our first meeting revolved around making a decision on the course readings: Should we use a textbook? Should we design a coursepack of readings? In the end, we agreed to select a suitable textbook to use as a primary teaching tool. We agreed to bring potential textbook samples to our next meeting, and we ultimately selected one of these after adequate deliberation. Our next step was to decide how to structure the doctoral research methods course. Not only was this course being designed for the first cohort of PhD students, but it also represented the first time that either of us had taught at the PhD level. We agreed that the easiest approach was for one of us to create a draft course outline as a starting point. The next several levels of discussion, which we undertook both in face-to-face meetings and via electronic communication, involved revising the initial outline with each of us making additions, deletions, and suggestions, as needed. Overall, our assessment of this stage of the course design process is that it took considerably longer than if either one of us had planned an individually taught course, due to the ongoing feedback and deliberations involved in our joint effort.

Co-Instruction

The next set of decisions involved assigning responsibility for the different segments of the classroom sessions. We created a detailed daily schedule and divided the various activities and sessions between us. We also planned to have instructor debriefing sessions at the end of each class session to discuss content that had been presented and to ensure appropriate continuity in subsequent sessions. To facilitate the presentation of information, we had divided the sessions in such a way as to allow one instructor to take the lead in any given lecture, discussion, or classroom exploration. During these sessions, the lead instructor often would defer to the co-instructor, either to incorporate summary comments from both instructors towards the end of a discussion or session, or to allow input from the other co-instructor that might enhance or shed some light on particular topics being discussed during the sessions. In addition, on certain occasions when one of the co-teaching partners sought additional information on a given topic, or may have inadvertently overlooked a key point or announcement, the other partner would provide the missing information, either by invitation from the other colleague or simply by way of a discrete interruption. In other words, co-teaching not only fostered enriched discussions but also (and frequently) allowed for better overall communication of expectations and reminders. Looking back, it is clear that we employed a combination of *teach-observe* and *team-teach* approaches, with most of the sessions using the latter method.

On one occasion, we co-facilitated private conference meetings with each doctoral student to brainstorm about their respective research ideas, which was quite conducive to the team-teaching approach (see Figure 9.1). We also took all our students, on two separate occasions,

Figure 9.1. Co-instructors Jarvis and Kariuki meet with a PhD student to discuss research ideas. Photo by Brendan O'Connor, Nipissing University Communications Department.

to a computer lab for hands-on data analysis practice. For the first lab session, an invited guest speaker did the majority of the teaching while the co-instructors assisted the students (mainly with navigating the software, where necessary). During the second lab session, one of the instructors did the teaching, and the second one was on hand to assist. These lab sessions were therefore instances of the *teach-assist* approach.

Co-Assessment

The next level of decision making involved assessment and determining who would be responsible for marking assignments. The course assignments included several individually written projects, some of which involved in-class presentation, as well as one major group planning and presentation project. We ended up dividing the individual written assignments (each co-teacher being given certain projects to mark in full), and then decided to mark the in-class presentations and the final projects together. Marking together meant that we both read and assigned a mark for each project and then met later to compare, discuss, and agree on the final mark for each student's assignment.

To communicate the feedback to the students we merged two ideas. One instructor suggested creating a candidate assessment file (CAF) for each student, an approach that he had often used for many master's level courses. This electronic file included each of the assignment descriptions, the corresponding marking rubrics, and marks with feedback comments for each assignment and was sent to each student several times throughout the course. The CAF was an excellent idea and the students loved it, especially because it meant having all their feedback comments in one file. In the process of using and building the CAF, the file itself needed to move back and forth between instructor(s) and students. To facilitate this process, the second instructor suggested creating a space on a learning management system (Blackboard, in this case), where the file would be housed. In the end, each student was assigned what we called a "feedback zone," accessible through their online Blackboard account. To accomplish this, we formed a "group" in Blackboard for each student, with both co-instructors and the student as the only members, and then shared with them their individual CAF document, through multiple iterations during the course, using the *File Exchange* option.

However, since we wanted to send the CAFs to the student in "portable document format" (.pdf) to ensure better access and to secure the files, it also became necessary to create a second (what we called instructor-only) zone to facilitate sharing the Word versions of each CAF with each other. When we finished assessing the first individually marked assignments for students, for example, we entered the details on their CAF files, saved and posted the Word versions of these files within the instructor-only zone, then saved .pdf versions of these same files and posted them on the students' feedback zones. The process worked seamlessly, and we therefore adopted it in the second round of co-teaching as well.

The Quirky Arithmetic of Co-Teaching

We are both well-accomplished teachers with many years of successful teaching experience. So, what happens when you take one experienced teacher and another experienced teacher and add them together? This leads to the first mathematical equation of interest: 1 + 1 = 1. In this particular co-teaching experience, the workload was configured on a 0.5 basis, meaning that each instructor received 0.5-workload credit, that is, remuneration for only half a course (even though both instructors were expected to be present in class 100 per cent of the time and for the full thirty-six hours of scheduled class time). In other words, the two teachers involved in the graduate course were only being reimbursed for half a regular course, yet were expected to treat it as a full, regular course in terms of their attendance and participation. Hence, 1 teacher + 1 teacher = 1 teacher (workload credit).

A second peculiar equation of interest would be the following: $0.5 + 0.5 \neq 1$. Using words instead of figures, what we mean to convey here is that one-half a course plus one-half a course is certainly not equal to one regular course in terms of teacher time/energy investment, but rather is equal to much more than one. The workload involved in planning, teaching, and assessing not only exceeds 0.5 of a course, but also exceeds the usual planning, teaching, and assessment requirements of an individually taught class. If we had to remove the ≠ and choose a number that represents our actual perception of the experience, we would likely arrive at something more like: $0.5 + 0.5 = 2$, meaning that teaching two such 0.5 courses would be the same (at least) as two professors each teaching one regular course.

Do the potential and varied benefits of co-teaching for instructors, and for graduate students, outweigh the reality implied in these somewhat quirky equations? This important question led to a desire to explore the perceptions of the students directly involved in the experience. The bulk of the remainder of this chapter will describe the results of this research-based investigation, but first we continue here with a brief account of our other two graduate co-teaching experiences.

Following our agreement to co-teach the PhD class in 2012, we decided to co-teach another graduate (master's level) course, Survey of Research Methods, the following fall semester. This decision was made mainly to address the workload issues. Each instructor has a normal full workload of five courses per year, but having taught a 0.5 course during the summer residency left the need to fill the remaining 4.5/5 course load. It therefore seemed reasonable to co-teach another course together.

Therefore, after completing the first co-taught course, we needed to repeat the process of planning and decision making for this second course. However, unlike the first instance, this time there was no requirement for both instructors to be in class 100 per cent of the time, which presented a new set of options with regard to teaching. Did we want to be there 100 per cent of the time, or should we aim for more of a 50/50 situation? By the time this class commenced, we had already completed the first co-taught course. For both of us, the realities of the

$0.5 + 0.5 \neq 1$ equation, in terms of required time/energy commitment, had certainly started to sink in, and so we agreed to more of a 50/50 type of arrangement. For the twelve on-site sessions, we scheduled ourselves to both be present in two sessions (first and last), and then to each take charge of five other sessions. We also agreed that one could choose to attend any of the other's five sessions, if available and interested in doing so (which did occur on a number of occasions). Ultimately, while the above plan seemed like a good idea in terms of shared responsibilities, it still demanded further brainstorming when it came to dividing up the marking of course assignments.

We adopted almost the same model used during the planning stages of our first co-taught course (meeting and discussing to agree on course outline contents and activities), except in this case we selected a textbook that one of us had used previously, and we also agreed to use many of the ideas (including assignments) that this same instructor had tried before in previous versions of the same course. In terms of the approaches described earlier, we used a combination of *teach-observe* and *team-teach* on the days that we both attended. Consequently, we asked ourselves two important questions: Would the fact that our students would be experiencing a constant switching from instructor to instructor matter to them? What were the students' major overall concerns in participating in such a course?

Another characteristic of the co-teaching events is that the students needed to complete separate course evaluations for each instructor. When we started teaching the first course, we had imagined that somehow they would be doing a combined course evaluation. However, since the course evaluation instrument has a section for instructor performance, it later occurred to us that a dual evaluation would make more sense. Again, here we had further questions: What will our students think about having to fill in multiple evaluations for the course and instructors? What factors will they take into account when filling out the evaluations?

We shared a third graduate co-teaching experience (similar to the first one, the required PhD educational research methods course) during the following summer residency session in July 2013. While the workload allotment was still 0.5 of a course, we were informed that each instructor was no longer required to attend 100 per cent of the sessions (although in our case, we still did both attend and participate in most classes). Our planning, delivery, and assessment were positively informed by our first two co-teaching experiences as described earlier. Moreover, it was during this third co-teaching experience that the idea for this book took shape. It was also during this time that we decided to survey the PhD students and their co-instructors to explore some of the questions we had raised. Having obtained approval from our university's research ethics board, we proceeded to conduct our study, including all the professors and students who had experienced the co-taught courses within the new PhD program to date as potential participants.

The Study

The main research questions guiding this study were (1) What are the perceptions of instructors regarding the strategies, challenges, and benefits of co-teaching a graduate level course?, and (2) What are the perceptions of students regarding the challenges and benefits of participating in a co-taught graduate level course? Consequently, we posed the following additional questions to the instructors:

1. What approaches did you and your co-instructor use to co-teach, and which ones did you find to be most successful?
2. What were your thoughts concerning co-teaching when you first started, and how did they change during the process?
3. What worked well, and what would you like to improve on if you have another opportunity to co-teach?
4. In what ways were you and your co-instructor similar/different, and how did this impact your decisions on how to conduct the course activities?
5. How did you conduct/divide the planning, grading, and response to student email/questions?

These specific questions and line of inquiry echoed those identified in a metasynthesis study by Scruggs et al. (2007) that explored how co-teaching was being implemented, the perceptions of teachers, the problems encountered, the perceived benefits, and factors needed for successful co-teaching. The majority of the thirty-two studies included in their metasynthesis were based on inclusive classrooms (classes which included special needs students) from both the elementary and secondary school levels. Our study, however, sought to answer similar questions as those already mentioned, but in relation to a graduate level teaching context. For the student participants, we posed the following questions:

1. How many times have you taken a co-taught class? [The purpose of this question was to find out whether this was a new or familiar phenomenon for each participant.]
2. In your most recent (graduate) co-taught course(s), what were the main advantages and disadvantages of the experience? [When asked this question, the students were reminded that it was important that the discussion should remain focused on the experience, rather than on the instructors.]
3. In what ways did having two instructors impact your experience and learning?
4. What could be done to further enrich a co-teaching experience?

At the time of the interview, each student would have experienced at least two co-taught PhD courses.

Data Collection and Analysis

At the point of recruitment, the participants were given the choice to do a face-to-face interview, a telephone- or Skype-based interview with the researcher, or to respond to the interview questions via email. The majority chose the third option, hence all responses were provided via email communication. One of the researchers recruited the participants and conducted the subsequent email communications with them. Upon receiving the questionnaire responses, we assigned an ID code and pseudonym to each, removed any identifying features, and saved the coded document. To facilitate analysis, we further organized the responses in tabular format with responses to each question appearing in the same column. Since the data file was relatively small, data analysis was conducted "by hand."

Due to the small sample population and the fact that there was uneven gender distribution among the participants, a decision was made to avoid (to the extent possible) the use of gender pronouns when reporting results for confidentiality purposes. For the same reason, we also decided to use gender neutral pseudonyms such as Lee, Morgan, and Sam. All the interview responses were received between 21 January and 24 February 2014. To maintain confidentiality, citations of participants' responses will feature these pseudonyms; since all responses were generated during the same time period, all are implied to be personal communications dated 2014.

Findings

Ten students (out of a possible twenty) responded to the questionnaires. Only four of the potential eight instructors offered to participate, and only two of these ultimately chose to complete the questionnaire. Because of the low participation rate among the instructors, we decided to include only the results from the students in this analysis.

When Advantage Meets Disadvantage

In terms of the advantages of being in a co-taught course, the main theme was that having two instructors gave the students an opportunity to be exposed to more than one theoretical and pedagogical perspective. As Lee explained:

> The main advantage of a co-taught course was the multiple perspectives and experiences that the instructors brought to the learning. In some situations the instructors had vastly different viewpoints on a particular topic. Usually their different perspectives on the topic would lead to rich discussions, based on critical analysis of that topic, and therefore deeper learning for the students … Learning in a co-instructed environment also meant that there was a wider breadth of knowledge that the "instructional team" brought to the course. If one instructor was not as familiar with one aspect of the course, then the other instructor had the knowledge in that area, and vice versa. Since it is impossible for an instructor to be an expert in all areas, having more than one instructor widened the field of expertise and experience. This advantage impacted the instruction, the assignments, and the resources accessed during the course.

The theme of advantages also included the idea that co-contribution of two instructors to the teaching space provided the students with, as Quinn stated, "access to the knowledge, experience, and expertise of two graduate professors," which often translated into a variety of teaching styles, and more dynamic and interest-sustaining classroom discussions.

However, advantages associated with the idea of multiple perspectives were ironically also tied to one of the major disadvantages that students clearly expressed. As Brice explained, this "main advantage is also a main disadvantage if the perspectives of the two instructors are in conflict with one another." Lee expressed a similar opinion, noting that "in some situations the different perspectives offered by the instructors led to discussions that were based on conflict and tension, not on critical examination; this left students feeling awkward and frustrated."

The notion of conflict was also described by Quinn and Morgan with terms such as "subtle disagreements," "tension," "a sense that the two professors did not have complete respect for each other's view," and "power imbalance." The following citations also indicate that although the instructors did not intend to openly show any disagreement, the students noticed otherwise. As Quinn observed:

> The one disadvantage that I noticed was the very subtle disagreements in the way a question was answered or handled. While the professors obviously tried hard to work together, one could sometimes tell when the answer that one professor provided was not in agreement with what the other professor thought.

Similarly, Morgan had noticed tension between instructors:

> They may think that differences are covered up in front of students, but it has been my experience that students can see through this very quickly. I have had classes where to us it was clear that the teaching team did not agree on points and had not reconciled these differences. This leads to tension.

In speaking about this advantage-turned-disadvantage, Brice said, "I felt somewhat underserviced when one person's opinion took precedence for no obvious logical reason other than a power imbalance." We therefore questioned what the solution might be for this conundrum in which a significant advantage to co-teaching can quickly turn to a major source of frustration for the students. An answer to our question can be gleaned from the perspectives of students such as Brice, who had expressed being "often preoccupied with the dynamics between the instructors and not focusing on ... learning." Brice further opined that "the co-teaching model has more disadvantages than advantages unless the instructors select who they want to co-teach with." The perception that the co-teaching model is successful or productive only to the extent that instructors voluntarily opt to work together was expressed strongly by several participants. Kim, for example, shared that "although it is important for two instructors of a particular course to present different perspectives, it is also important to select instructors who can work together effectively." Jaden essentially concurred: "The profs need to have mutually agreed that they want to teach together."

Coupled with this concept was also the suggestion that such awkwardness would be lessened if instructors disclosed their differing perspectives at the beginning of the course, instead of waiting until such differences inevitably became obvious to the students. Morgan suggested that we should "make the differences between instructors' approaches/views clearer," and further added, "It was helpful when these differences came out in class, but often we had to guess as instructors seem reluctant to express this." Ira made a similar suggestion:

> A clear breakdown of each instructor's responsibilities and how efforts were being collaborated would be helpful at the beginning of the course. For example, it was initially unclear how evaluations were going to be shared, and who (if anyone) was more knowledgeable in certain key areas. With a small class size and a lot of in-class interaction these unknowns became clearer, but it may have been easier to have it laid out in the course outline.

One other advantage, as alluded to earlier, was the benefit of having dual evaluators when it came to assessment. As Kim explained, "Grades are assigned by two instructors, and this method might allow for a more balanced approach to the evaluation process." Ira agreed, sharing that "feedback on assignments was more thorough and reflected a broader perspective." However, as in the case of the advantage of multiple perspectives described earlier, the matter of grading is also one where a potential advantage can create a negative outcome if not handled effectively. The students said it is important to identify clearly at the outset which co-instructor(s) will be responsible for grading assignments. Sam, for instance, believes that the courses should "designate each prof specific responsibilities within the course structure, for example making clear that either both profs will read/review/grade all assignments, or one will grade the first one and the other will grade the second, etc." Doing so would address Ira's concern that "it was initially unclear how evaluations were going to be shared, and who (if anyone) was more knowledgeable in certain key areas." Fran expressed a similar view on the matter of marking:

> It is my preference that the division of the course between the two instructors is outlined up front. Whether they are splitting each class and assessment in half – one teaching one week, a different one another. Who is assessing what? Commenting on what? ... So that roles and responsibilities are clear.

Evidently, assessment practices that are not transparent from the outset can potentially undermine the course in unnecessary ways. For example, the students are left guessing about specific course expectations, as Sam explained:

> It made the expectations of the course a little more challenging because now, as a student, you are trying to tailor your assignments to two different styles/personalities, et cetera; you're never really sure which way to spin things sometimes because you're not sure who is reading it.

If students know who they are "talking to" when completing an assignment, they feel better able to decipher the course expectations. Conversely, as Morgan observed, sometimes even the same assignments involved "differing expectations from instructors. One asks for something one way; the second, another." Consequently, as Lee noted, "different expectations regarding expectations for assignments and grading practices ... left some students confused and frustrated." Lee further articulated another frustration that arose from the marking practices:

> Assignment grading was also a source of frustration, as different instructors had wildly different grading practices. Some instructors focused on thorough descriptive feedback on assignments, others left only a few minor comments and a mark. It became clear that there were very different criteria that each instructor was using to grade the work in the class.

Lee's comment implies that even when students were aware of whom they were addressing in any given assignment (either because they had figured it out for themselves or had been told), the experience remained frustrating because, as Lee added, "[I]t was challenging to switch between the grading expectations of multiple instructors within the same course content."

The main theme here can be summarized by Sam's observation that sometimes students have "been conditioned to hand in assignments to suit the professors' style/interests and experience." This strategy can represent a major disadvantage in a co-taught environment because students do not know whom they are addressing; however, paradoxically, this can be viewed as a disadvantage even if they do know, because it then implies a perceived need to switch back and forth to satisfy different instructors' methods of grading.

Other Advantages

The co-teaching model provided students with an element of choice in terms of communicating with one or both co-instructors. As Ira noted, "[I]n two of the three courses, I was more comfortable approaching one of the two instructors with questions and/or concerns." Similarly, Lee expressed that another key advantage of the co-instructed courses was accessibility:

> Having more than one instructor means that a student had two different people to access after class time. Depending on area of expertise, or availability, we could choose to direct questions to either instructor, or both. Therefore we felt well supported for after class inquiries.

In addition to having a choice of whom to approach with questions according to instructors' expertise or availability, another benefit of co-taught courses was the use of both instructors' perspectives as resources that could doubly enhance the formulation of a student's own work, thereby resulting in a more enriched final product. As shared by Quinn:

> I enjoyed having two professors; it allowed me to seek answers to various questions from the professor who I felt had the most experience or the most knowledge. Also, to be perfectly honest, if I didn't like the answer I got from one professor, I could always approach the other! Also, everyone learns and teaches in a slightly different way so being able to have the opportunity to learn the same material from two points of view was helpful in the understanding – it made the knowledge more complete in some ways. I ended up with the first professor's understanding of the material,

> the second professor's understanding of the material, and then my own understanding, which was often some combination of the professors' and my own thoughts.

Overall, the graduate students in this study saw value in a co-taught environment. The underlying message seems to be: If done well, co-teaching potentially carries far-reaching benefits as described here; but if done poorly, then it can involve unnecessary confusion, frustration, and wasted opportunities as students spend precious time trying to sort through miscommunicated messages and course expectations.

Final Thoughts and Conclusions

Co-teaching in a graduate classroom brings together individuals who are relatively well set in their ways of doing things. Co-teachers have their preferred and often time-tested styles of teaching and assessment, but students also have their own preferred methods of learning, especially at the PhD level, as was highlighted, to various degrees, in the above-referenced co-teaching contexts. As Quinn advised, "At the graduate level, I also think it is important to recognize that the students are adults, sometimes well into their careers, with their own set ways of thinking."

In this chapter, we set out to share our experiences from having worked together and having engaged our students in these three co-taught graduate level courses. We are fortunate to have been able to enrol ten of our doctoral students from among the first two cohorts to participate in our research study, and to hear their voices as they reflected on their various co-taught course experiences in light of our questions. It is fitting, then, to summarize the important lessons that we have learned from the co-planning, co-implementation of lessons, and co-assessment aspects of our joint teaching endeavours.

We both agree that each of these three elements (planning, delivery, assessment) have required more personal investment within the co-teaching contexts than would normally be needed for comparable graduate courses that are taught by a single instructor. The challenge lies in the combination of several key factors: an increased amount of time and energy required at all stages of the process; the need for sensitivity regarding one's co-teacher in order to create and sustain a healthy, conflict-free learning environment; and the need to allow teaching partners to be themselves, and do what they like to do best while still meeting the needs of a diverse group of students.

Towards this end, we agree with and would echo the sentiments of participating students with regard to the nature of the co-teaching teams. The pairing of co-instructors represents a vital part of the process, and should therefore either be done on a strictly voluntary, self-pairing basis, or, at the very least, done by administrators in consultation with those involved. In our particular case, we were able to request these teaching assignments together as a team, rather than be assigned to these partnerships. Co-teaching that is effective must be based on a positive form of communication, trust, and respect between colleagues that exists prior to the session and is clearly manifested to the students throughout the session. This is not to say that the co-instructors do not, or should not, disagree on particular issues, theories, or teaching methods, but when they do, it must be clearly modelled with professionalism within and beyond the classroom.

One question that would help us to summarize our lessons learned from these experiences is the following: What would you like to improve on if you have another opportunity to co-teach? As described earlier, in our case, we were fortunate to have the chance to re-teach the same course a second time, with a set of ten new doctoral students. Based on student feedback, and on our own observations, we made significant improvements for the second iteration of this course. For example, we reduced the number of assignments and modified certain aspects of existing assignments (reducing the focus on quantitative methods, for which most of the students had little or no background; allowing for a large-group approach to the last assignment, which combined research methods around a particular topic). If we were to co-teach this PhD course a third time, we would draw not only from the first two versions, but also from the invaluable insights that were shared by the ten students within the research study.

We believe that co-teaching represents an incredibly empowering and productive potentiality for enriched teaching and learning. When planned and implemented with careful attention to the important elements described earlier, co-teaching appears to be able to offer an unparalleled opportunity for deeper knowledge acquisition and increased personal growth among graduate students and their co-instructors.

ACKNOWLEDGMENTS

The "Co-Teaching in Context: A Review of the Literature" section of this chapter represents an adaptation of M. Kariuki's previously published (2013) article, "Co-Teaching in Graduate Programs," which appeared in the *Review of Higher Education and Self-Learning*, *6*(18), 184–93 and is here reprinted by permission of the journal's editor.

REFERENCES

Arnold, J., & Jackson, I. (1996). The keys to successful co-teaching. *Thought & Action*, *12*(2), 91–8.

Bacharach, N., Heck, T.W., & Dahlberg, K. (2008). Co-teaching in higher education. *Journal of College Teaching and Learning*, *5*(3), 9–16.

Bacharach, N., Heck, T.W., & Dahlberg, K. (2010). Changing the face of student teaching through coteaching. *Action in Teacher Education*, *32*(1), 3–14. http://dx.doi.org/10.1080/01626620.2010.10463538

Carpenter, D.M., II, Crawford, L., & Walden, R. (2007). Testing the efficacy of team teaching. *Learning Environments Research*, *10*(1), 53–65. http://dx.doi.org/10.1007/s10984-007-9019-y

Cook, L. (2004, April). *Co-teaching: Principles, practices and pragmatics*. Paper presented at the New Mexico Public Education Department quarterly special meeting, Albuquerque, NM. Retrieved from http://www.ped.state.nm.us/seo/library/qrtrly.0404.coteaching.lcook.pdf

Cook, L., & Friend, M. (1995). Co-teaching: Guidelines for creating effective practices. *Focus on Exceptional Children*, *28*(3), 1–16.

Ferguson, J., & Wilson, J.C. (2011). The co-teaching professorship: Power and expertise in the co-taught higher education classroom. *Scholar-Practitioner Quarterly*, *5*(1), 52–68.

Gillespie, D., & Israetel, A. (2008, August). *Benefits of co-teaching in relation to student learning*. Paper presented at the annual meeting of the American Psychological Association, Boston, MA.

Luckner, J.L. (1999). An examination of two coteaching classrooms. *American Annals of the Deaf*, *144*(1), 24–34. http://dx.doi.org/10.1353/aad.2012.0180

Scruggs, T.A., Mastropieri, M.A., & McDuffie, K.A. (2007). Co-teaching in inclusive classrooms: A metasynthesis of qualitative research. *Exceptional Children*, *73*(4), 392–416. http://dx.doi.org/10.1177/001440290707300401

Tobin, R. (2005). Co-teaching in language arts: Supporting students with learning disabilities. *Canadian Journal of Education*, *28*(4), 784–801.

Vaughn, S., Schumm, S.J., & Arguelles, M.E. (1997). The ABCDEs of co-teaching. *Teaching Exceptional Children, 30*(2), 4–10. http://dx.doi.org/10.1177/004005999703000201

Villa, R.A., Thousand, J.S., & Nevin, A.I. (2004). *A guide to co-teaching: Practical tips for facilitating student learning*. Thousand Oaks, CA: Corwin Press.

Wilson, J.C., & Ferguson, J. (2012). *The experience of co-teaching in higher education: To be or not to be*. Retrieved from http://l09.cgpublisher.com/proposals/239/index_html

10 Coda: From Theory to Co-Practice in Higher Education

DANIEL H. JARVIS AND MUMBI KARIUKI

Within the preceding nine chapters, contributing co-author teams from Australia, Canada, Israel, and the United States have highlighted their respective co-teaching practices and reflective observations at the post-secondary level. Topics range from undergraduate projects/courses to graduate level co-teaching experiences at the master's and doctoral levels; from teaching pairs to small group co-teaching endeavours, some also involving an extended network of guest lecturers; from pre-service teacher education to in-service teacher training; and from co-taught single-subject courses to innovative cross-curricular, "dialogue course," and interdisciplinary experiments. Here in chapter ten, after having carefully read, discussed, and co-analysed the full manuscript, we seek to more fully compare, contrast, and summarize the work by returning to our original three categories that we asked the contributing co-author teams to discuss: (1) *co-planning* and the co-creation/development of co-teaching curriculum and experiences; (2) *co-facilitation*, or implementation, of the learning experiences; and (3) *co-assessment* considerations and practices for co-teaching. We will first look at the nature and purpose of co-teaching, then will take the bulk of this final chapter to explore the three overarching categories mentioned above, ending with a number of concluding thoughts by way of summary.

The Nature and Purpose of Co-Teaching

Much of co-teaching at any level involves a partnership or team approach, which results in, by way of description, a collection of active verbs with "co-" prefixes. Initially the process involves co-ideating, co-creating, co-developing, and co-constructing. These are followed by activities such as co-facilitating, co-implementing, and co-directing. The process also provides an opportunity for participants (be it the co-teachers themselves or the co-taught learners) to engage in co-thinking, co-learning, co-seeking, co-exploring, and co-producing. Finally, it includes the acts of co-assessing – an activity not only shared by the co-teachers themselves, but also commonly shared with students in self- or peer-assessment roles – and the co-reporting of student achievement.

The success of co-teaching practice appears to be dependent on several key factors, discussed by various co-author teams in their respective chapters, such as the need for co-teachers to possess a shared pedagogical vision (Steele and Ashworth); a shared inspiration and set of goals (Srigley and Winters); and a shared philosophy of education (Game and Metcalfe; Renshaw and Valiquette). Matlin and Carr (2014) emphasize the required and anticipated intersection of the two (or more) teaching philosophies that occur within the co-teaching context:

> As long as you are open and flexible and respect your co-teacher, you should be able to have a team teaching relationship that is productive for both parties. Through open discussion, you can come to a shared appreciation for one another's philosophy, which leads to "mutual understanding of the context." (p. 66)

Hatt and Graham point out, citing the work of Wenger, McDermott, and Snyder (2002), that what is needed is "a community of practice made up of individuals with a common interest and a desire to share, connect, and build on existing knowledge" (Chapter 4, p. 91). Maintaining a healthy and cordial professional relationship, both preceding and during the delivery of the co-taught course, is also essential for a successful co-teaching experience (all nine co-author teams attest to, and elaborate upon, this important point). Complete mutual trust (Patkin and Levenberg, Chapter 8) and collegial respect (La Haye and Naested, Chapter 6) are paramount in meeting the many challenges inherent to the co-teaching process.

Co-teaching should be motivated by a desire to model for students the nature of positive and productive collaboration, something that will no doubt be part of most future workplace destinations. As Wilson and Ferguson note, "We are preparing students to be active participants in a twenty-first century world that demands collaboration and effective communication" (Chapter 7, p. 176). More specifically, those working in teacher education explained how their "modelling of co-teaching to pre-service teachers may assist them should they one day be able or expected to co-teach within their own practice" (La Haye and Naested, Chapter 6, p. 160). By participating in co-teaching experiences, a new form of professional collaboration is also being modelled for fellow colleagues within the post-secondary institution (Steele and Ashworth, Chapter 5).

Prior to examining the specifics of co-planning, we must first acknowledge the process by which a co-teaching team comes to be established. How the co-teaching pair, or group, is formulated appears to be highly significant, having a potentially profound effect on the ultimate success of the experience (Kariuki and Jarvis, Chapter 9). In other words, are the participating members assigned to the course by administrators (randomly, or by design), are they self-selected for the role by virtue of a volunteering process, or is it perhaps some combination thereof (for example, an invitation to co-teach that could be accepted or rejected)? The number of co-teachers involved in a particular course is also a critical decision. While larger groups add a number of extra perspectives, having too many co-teachers involved can prove problematic in terms of decision making, consistent communication with students, and assessment (Hatt and Graham; Kariuki and Jarvis; Steele and Ashworth). In the case of the interdisciplinary experiences described by Renshaw and Valiquette, up to twelve instructors were involved in the various courses, but in these instances the majority of participating faculty members served as single-event guest lecturers from across the disciplines, with the two co-authors functioning as the actual course co-planners, co-directors, and co-assessors.

Another significant challenge in co-teaching is that of potential conflict between co-instructors, who are now being asked to work in close proximity over extended periods of time and often with little incentive or added remuneration. Wilson and Ferguson provide the related disclaimer: "Those seeking to engage in co-teaching should also be aware that there will be conflict" (Chapter 7, p. 173). Hatt and Graham concur, noting that "creating a community of practice is not an easy or seamless undertaking" and referring to the existence of a potential "darker side to the collaborative process" (Chapter 4, p. 102). Others used the words "apprehension" and "tension" in describing this aspect. The overarching lesson to be learned from the various chapters on this point is that there is a genuine and urgent need to proactively anticipate conflict and to prepare for how it might be effectively addressed and minimized. As Wilson and Ferguson explain, "The art of co-teaching is not in avoiding conflict, but in learning from the conflict and becoming stronger as a result of this process" (Chapter 7, p. 174). One of the ways to prepare for conflict, as suggested by this same co-author team, is "[k]nowing the foundational skills of collaboration and conflict resolution … such as active listening and interest-based negotiations, [which] becomes a valuable resource when engaging in co-teaching practice" (Chapter 7, p. 172). Hatt and Graham note the related need for "negotiation and reciprocity" (Chapter 4, p. 103), and Kariuki and Jarvis maintain, "This is not to say that the co-instructors do not, or should not, disagree on particular issues, theories, or teaching methods, but when they do, it must be clearly modelled with professionalism within and beyond the classroom" (Chapter 9, p. 219).

Closely related to the notion of conflict resolution is that of power struggles or power dynamics, specifically as perceived by students during the course. For example, Wilson and Ferguson explained that while both professors may imagine themselves as equally "important," students "might equate the name appearing on the course schedule, or the teacher who speaks the most in class, or even the one who stands at the front of the classroom most often as the one *in charge*" (Chapter 7, p. 171). The students surveyed by Kariuki and Jarvis also alluded to this idea of "power," highlighting perceived power dynamics that would sometimes occur between co-instructors as a source of discomfort for them. As noted by Crow and Smith (2003), successful co-teaching requires the wilful relinquishing of power and authority:

> The essence of coteaching must therefore be seen as a collaborative endeavour requiring careful planning, reflection, attention to the minutiae of the process and a commitment to a constructivist approach to learning. This will not happen if teachers are unwilling to relinquish their authority because the whole point of collaboration and indeed constructivist learning is the sharing of power and knowledge. (p. 54)

Co-teaching pairs or groups must proactively anticipate power issues, whether real or perceived, and attempt to manage the extent of these dynamics through careful planning and open dialogue with each other in advance of class sessions. Wilson and Ferguson suggest that co-teachers, when adopting the teach-assist model, should regularly alternate between the roles of teacher and assistant, since students have been known to perceive the "professor serving as the assistant to be less knowledgeable or engaged" (Chapter 7, p. 174) than his or her co-teaching colleague. Further, they note that co-teachers, to reduce the sense of power struggle, should identify exactly which learning objectives, class activities, or discussion questions that each will be responsible for during any given class session, and also attempt to learn each other's areas of relative strength so that these can be capitalized on within the structure of the course. These findings echo the work of Conderman and McCarty (2003), in which they found that reflection, confidence, and parity were essential characteristics of productive co-teaching:

> We found three conditions to be especially important for fostering our professional growth through coteaching ... frequent (if possible daily) time reserved for reflecting upon the day's events and planning for the following day ... confidence in the safety of the coteaching relationship ...[and] an environment that promoted a spirit of parity. (p. 4)

Co-teaching at any level of education requires adequate administrative support, and in higher education this reality perhaps becomes even more pronounced. La Haye and Naested maintain that "institutional support for the efforts of the co-teaching team members is often lacking, and university structures tend to prevent cross-disciplinary collaboration," further adding that "teaching innovations without support will not flourish, and will become short-term 'educational fads'" (Chapter 6, p. 160).

Wilson and Ferguson elaborate on the post-secondary level realities associated with workload issues:

> Most colleges and universities do not favour two professors in one classroom because of arguments such as, Who actually gets paid, and how much? (For example, is each professor only paid for 50 per cent of a regular course amount?) Sometimes in co-teaching arrangements, class size is also increased, making it appear even less worthwhile for instructors because of the associated stress. As a result, co-teaching is not often seen in higher education contexts, regardless of its benefits for classroom instruction, retention, and connection to a diverse range of students. (Chapter 7, p. 166)

Administrators must value co-teaching efforts by allowing for the creative manipulation of workload assignments where possible (Hatt and Graham); considering scheduling requests that permit co-taught courses to be offered in certain beneficial timeslots (Steele and Ashworth); and expressing their support for creative new course offerings and faculty collaboration (La Haye and Naested; Renshaw and Valiquette; Srigley and Winters).

Co-Planning in Higher Education

Effective planning is quite often a hallmark of any quality teaching and learning experience, and the specific realities of co-teaching serve to underscore this connection perhaps even more emphatically. Wilson and Ferguson claim that the most difficult part of co-teaching just might be the planning: "When done well, planning changes praxis for both the professors and the students in significant ways. However, when a co-taught class is under-planned or sporadically planned, the lessons and their subsequent utility for students and professors are often lost" (Chapter 7, p. 166). This theme was commonly echoed among the co-teachers in the various chapters. Some of the barriers to co-planning were the sheer amount of time required for planning such a course – particularly in the first instance – and the challenges relating to establishing regular co-planning meetings around often relatively divergent teaching, research, and committee service schedules at the university level. In addressing these challenges, Steele and Ashworth established a creative planning space:

> I'd say that more than half of our co-planning time was spent off-campus, often outdoors, whether we were sitting on your deck, or walking our dogs in the woods ... Perhaps by removing ourselves from the physical setting of the institution ... we were also removing ourselves from some of the perceived barriers to collaboration and integration, and awakening our creative selves. (Chapter 5, p. 125)

Co-taught courses were also perceived as simply taking much longer to co-design and co-deliver (Hatt and Graham; La Haye and Naested). In reflecting on just how much more time is involved, Kariuki and Jarvis estimated that it may take up to twice as long as a regular course. This estimate was confirmed by Wilson and Ferguson, who actually kept track of the time invested and found that it took over twice as long to prepare a co-taught class as compared to a solo-taught alternative (1.5 hours compared to 3.5 hours per class). According to all co-author teams, co-teachers need to be prepared to invest a considerably higher amount of time at every stage of the process (co-planning, co-teaching, and co-assessment) than they would if teaching alone. Moreover, in order for the time, effort, and energy to be deemed worthwhile sacrifices, the perceived worth of the goals that bring co-teachers together must surpass the "cost" implied by this demand (Hatt and Graham). In the words of La Haye and Naested, "It was our belief in the value of interdisciplinary teaching that convinced us to proceed, even while anticipating the time commitment involved" (Chapter 6, p. 139). Wilson and Ferguson went even farther, focusing on the increased time needed for negotiating teaching and learning strategies and activities:

> The amount of time it takes to work in collaboration, and through negotiation, is often considerably greater than that of teaching a course alone. When teaching solo, professors are able to design an activity and implement it as they see fit. In a co-taught classroom, where both professors come to the table with ideas and knowledge, it takes time to reconfigure what each activity will look like, who will implement it, and what support from the other co-teacher may be required. Such compromise of pedagogy and knowledge often does not come quickly or intuitively. (Chapter 7, p. 167)

La Haye and Naested found that roughly half of their weekly co-planning meeting focusing on the next week's session was devoted to reflection on the previous week's teaching, with the "remaining time being used to go over teaching strategies, synchronize the presentation, plan interjection strategies, and anticipate possible challenges" (Chapter 6, p. 153). Hatt and Graham noted: "Of necessity, we each put far more instructional hours and facilitation time into the course than was allotted" (Chapter 4, p. 96). However, by keeping their original vision and purpose foremost in mind, Hatt, Graham, and their team were able to persevere when co-planning, co-delivery, and co-assessment duties became increasingly onerous:

> But that didn't matter to any of us, because we were living the realization of a unique innovation in teaching and learning for our pre-service teachers and for us as instructors. We had taken an idea from imaginative inception through creative innovation to implementation, and so time, effort, and energy were worthwhile sacrifices. (Chapter 4, p. 96)

As indicated earlier, it is critical to proactively anticipate (and plan to minimize) issues that arise in the learning space, such as conflict and power struggles; one way of doing this is for co-teachers to clarify their roles and responsibilities among themselves and for their students. The creation and maintenance of a *collaborative schedule*, or shared planning document, for co-teachers was suggested as a useful tool in this regard. For some, these schedules would simply be a list of regular meeting dates and times for planning, but for most they would include further details regarding co-teaching roles and responsibilities throughout the course (Hatt and Graham; La Haye and Naested; Srigley and Winters), such as classroom facilitation, assignment grading, and replying to student emails. Wilson and Ferguson underscored the need for careful and specific pre-planning, while understanding that "[a]s time progresses, professors may decide that they do not need such a regimented schedule for their co-teaching, depending on their professional relationship, experience, and course knowledge" (Chapter 7, p. 169).

The commitment to, and importance of, regular debriefing sessions following co-teaching sessions was also highlighted in several chapters. For example, Kariuki and Jarvis reflected on this practice: "We also planned to have instructor debriefing sessions at the end of each class session to discuss content that had been presented and to ensure appropriate continuity in subsequent sessions" (Chapter 9, p. 206); as did Wilson and Ferguson, stating that "short debriefing sessions immediately following co-teaching experiences were helpful for recording shared memories of classroom activities, comments, and personal reflections" and allowed them to "revisit and refine plans for future lessons" (Chapter 7, pp. 168–9). Researchers Perry and Stewart (2005) similarly underscored the powerful connection between productive reflective practice and the co-teaching model: "Educators who engage in reflective practice often seek out colleagues to discuss their teaching … From this perspective, a successful team teaching partnership can be seen as the ultimate situation for reflective practitioners" (p. 572).

Co-Facilitation in Higher Education

Co-teachers need to bring certain qualities or characteristics to the co-table, as it were. One is a willingness to relinquish, surrender, or loosen one's grip and let go of some degree of control in the planning and delivery of the co-taught course offering. This is made possible by a "spirit of humility and openness to the possibility that together we can be more than the sum of our parts" (Renshaw and Valiquette, Chapter 2, p. 42). In addition, co-teachers must (1) actively seek to build a dialogic community; (2) cultivate being an "aware teacher"; (3) be able to relax in the presence of the "other," understanding that colleagues are not there to judge but to encourage; (4) model flexibility, "informed ignorance," and a confident vulnerability to students; (5) learn to tolerate the "unknowing and uncertainties of life"; (6) adjust to the role of unobtrusive observer/guardian; and (7) work to build on each other's strengths in order to maximize on shared resources. The teacher's primary responsibility is to "facilitate informed dialogue among and between teachers and students, retaining an awareness of the learning process itself" (Game and Metcalfe, Chapter 1, p. 16).

The aim should be to create a co-taught learning space in which (1) genuine collaboration is modelled by co-instructors; (2) participants feel safe and encouraged to take intellectual risks; (3) deep learning, which stems from unrestrained dialogue (Srigley and Winters), can occur; and (4) students regularly become teachers and vice versa, within a shared and deliberate pursuit of knowledge acquisition and creation (Game and Metcalfe; Renshaw and Valiquette; Hatt and Graham).

In a productive co-taught learning space, the nature of knowledge is emergent. The nurtured dialogic community gives rise to an environment that allows for a shared approach to knowledge creation leading to the existence of something new, which is not the personal property of any one individual. It is a potentially transformative space where "[a]ll those involved in the class are working at their creative edge, not simply repeating what they already know but finding words for the knowledge that is emerging for them" (Game and Metcalfe, Chapter 1, p. 29).

Specific teaching and learning strategies that were used with success within the co-taught courses were shared by the co-author teams. Though the teams represent several different disciplines and respective knowledge domains, they have suggested important strategies that can be applied in all courses, where applicable. One of these is the need for regular student participation or engagement in the weekly sessions using a number of different tools/methods. For Game and Metcalfe, the "student workbook" represents one of the most crucial components of their co-taught experiences:

> Workbooks are the course's lynchpin. Each week, before classes, students write about the readings and do an exercise that applies the readings to an everyday experience ... The workbook is a supportive, disciplined working space that teaches students how to stay with and draw out their thoughts and hunches ... The workbook produces a dialogic relation

> between students and their work, allowing them to teach themselves, to draw themselves out. (Chapter 1, pp. 20–1)

Likewise, for Renshaw and Valiquette, what they refer to as "student journals" served a similar critical purpose, helping their students to "foster dialogue outside of the face-to-face opportunities," and combine "the formal recounting of the disciplinary lectures with more creative entries for the interdisciplinary seminars" (Chapter 2, p. 56). Other forms of personal reflection tools were also used, such as "learning log/portfolios" (La Haye and Naested), "reflection papers" (Steele and Ashworth), and "student learning diaries" (Patkin and Levenberg).

The idea of reflective journals was also extended to the co-teachers themselves as a way of capturing what is transpiring in any given class, and with the goal of understanding and improving their shared practice. Wilson and Ferguson noted, "Both of us, over time, wrote in journals chronicling our thoughts and discussions regarding authority and power" (Chapter 7, p. 172). "Over the lifetime of this integration assignment, we have reflected individually and collaboratively in order to revise our assessment process and the rubric," stated Steele and Ashworth (Chapter 5, p. 129). La Haye and Naested likewise recalled, "[W]e both wrote weekly reflections on our experiences, which have informed our understanding of co-teaching" (Chapter 6, p. 138).

Srigley and Winters adopted a debate format for one particular class within their dialogue course, in which both instructors participated in a non-scripted open debate event, each one taking a side in arguing for or against the divine nature of the first century religious leader Jesus Christ, who had claimed to be God (John 8:58–9, 10:30), to forgive sins (Luke 7:36–50), to give eternal life (John 4:10–15), and to ultimately judge the world (Mt. 25:31–46). Students found the debate to be highly effective.

Student engagement and participation was also heightened by the use of multiple venues for class sessions. Hatt and Graham used large theatre-style classrooms for presentations, a local elementary school for literacy and numeracy explorations involving young children and their parents/guardians, a technology-enhanced classroom, a visual arts education studio space, and a local art museum for a planned gallery walk. Likewise, Steele and Ashworth had students meet in the science and art rooms, as well as in outdoor venues, as part of their integrated projects. Kariuki and Jarvis booked computer labs for research software explorations and also arranged for a library tour as part of their graduate courses.

Co-Assessment in Higher Education

In education, we often speak of three main forms of assessment: diagnostic, formative, and summative. Student reflective journaling, in its various forms and names as described earlier, provided an excellent tool for all three types of assessment to happen regularly within co-taught courses. In this regard, La Haye and Naested elaborated on their use of learning log/portfolios in which students documented "each learning experience, the created artefact, and their reflections (as student and teacher) on the experience" (Chapter 6, p. 156). These portfolios required students to reflect on learning from both disciplines involved in the learning experience (mathematics/visual arts), and the document was submitted three times during the course for instructor reading, assessment, and feedback.

In terms of formative assessment, Steele and Ashworth highlighted the informative window into student impressions that their reflective student journals provided to them as co-instructors: "Regardless of whether they are individual or group reflections, they help us to understand not only how learners experience integration, but also how they experience a collaborative assignment" (Chapter 5, p. 129). Similarly, Patkin and Levenberg suggested that their students keep a written "learning diary," which was "designed for the purpose of carefully monitoring the participants' learning processes" and for developing a regular "self-assessment of their own learning" (Chapter 8, p. 194). Renshaw and Valiquette explained how their student journals not only allowed them, as co-instructors, to better gauge student comprehension of the disciplinary material, but were also used on an ongoing basis to further enrich seminar discussions:

> Details from the journals are collated and used during the seminars to help facilitate the sharing of ideas among all participants ... Students who don't feel comfortable speaking in class can rest assured that the best of their ideas can still help to shape interdisciplinary discussions by way of the journals. In this sense, the journals extend into course assessment the students' role as co-creators of knowledge. (Chapter 2, p. 56)

Another interesting innovation of this co-teaching team was to have their large group of participating guest lecturers each submit a number of questions from their respective presentations, which were then incorporated by Renshaw and Valiquette into the final examination.

Formative assessment of the course assignments and pacing, as well as of each other's role and effectiveness as co-instructors, was noted in several chapters. For example, Steele and Ashworth reported using their own reflections on their integrated project assignment to help modify related assessment practices: "One of our first revisions was adding specific questions for [teacher candidates] to use as prompts for their group reflections," adding that "more recent discussion has been around moving from group reflections to individual ones in order to 'hear' the voices within the groups" (Chapter 5, p. 129).

In terms of summative assessment, Srigley and Winters made particular reference to the final essay in their co-taught course, which was assessed (numerically and with comments) by both instructors, thereby providing an extra layer of feedback for the improvement of learning. "Each student also received back two sets of final comments, as well as two marked-up copies of the graded essay. This richness in evaluative feedback was one of the great advantages of the course for students" (Chapter 3, p. 72).

Clear communication of assessment practices both before and during the course, if there are modifications made en route, was described as being critically important by all co-author teams. According to La Haye and Naested, this included "making expectations clear for all assignments, ensuring a common grading scheme is implemented, and alternating the assessor on assignments (so that there is only one instructor marking each assignment)" (Chapter 6, p. 157). Similarly, Wilson and Ferguson noted, "Letting students know who is in charge of grading or if both professors will be grading will drastically improve both the experience of the students and co-teachers within the co-taught classroom" (Chapter 7, p. 170).

While co-assessment can be challenging enough to organize with two co-teachers, it can become even more difficult with a larger co-teaching group. Steele and Ashworth noted having such difficulty in group assessment meetings in which there seemed to be "too many cooks," all with different perspectives on how assignments should be marked. They reported that these individual preconceptions "got in the way of smooth assessment and evaluation sessions," ultimately took "far too much time to complete and added much frustration to an otherwise positive experience" (Chapter 5, p. 114–15).

Concluding Thoughts

As we noted in the introduction, this collection was born out of a realization that "while substantial formal and anecdotal research has been reported by teachers at the elementary and secondary levels, far less material exists at the post-secondary and graduate study levels" (Introduction, p. 4). Indeed, researchers such as Kluth and Straut (2003) have specifically called for work in this area:

> We must also explore the role of colleges and universities in cultivating collaborative models. We need to better understand how to develop curriculum, instruction, and assessment approaches that will serve as models for students as they enter the teaching profession. We must also get creative in tackling administrative and institutional barriers. (p. 238)

This led to a desire to "more thoroughly investigate the practice of co-teaching in higher education and to document some of the very creative co-teaching practices that we knew were happening here in Canada and internationally" (Introduction, p. 5). Having conducted and documented this investigation, it is fitting, as we conclude, to offer a brief comparison of co-teaching as it has evolved and is generally practiced in the two areas: elementary/secondary levels (K–12) and post-secondary or graduate levels (higher education).

One underlying theme in K–12 co-teaching literature, which also marks one key contrast with co-teaching in higher education, is the need or rationale for entering into the practice of co-teaching. In K–12 circles, co-teaching often arises out of the necessity for addressing diverse learning needs within a group of students (Bauwens, Hourcade, & Friend, 1989; Cook & Friend, 1995; Dieker & Murawski, 2003; Mastropieri, Scruggs, Graetz, Norland, et al., 2005; Murawski & Swanson, 2001; Platt, Walker-Knight, Lee, & Hewitt, 2001). As Richard Villa, one of the leading voices in the study of effective co-teaching in K–12, states:

> With inclusion on the rise, teachers are sharing classrooms more than ever and becoming an effective co-teaching partner is a teaching essential. With the onset of a new school year right around the corner, meanwhile, it's imperative to begin devising and building positive *co-teaching strategies.* A co-teaching team typically includes a general and a special educator who teach the general education curriculum to all students as well as implement Individual Education Programs (IEPs) for students with disabilities. Both educators on the co-teaching team are responsible for differentiating the instructional planning and delivery, assessment of student achievement, and classroom management. (Villa, n.d., para. 1–2)

As such, while it is fair to say that co-teaching in the majority of K–12 environments revolves around the need to create co-teaching teams for the express goal of facilitating differentiation of instruction (Dieker & Murawski, 2003; Mastropieri et al., 2005; Santamaria & Thousand, 2004), post-secondary co-teaching is born out of a different set of needs and goals. For example, even though some gains have been made in these areas of late, the concepts of inclusion, differentiation of learning, IEPs, accommodations, or the need to decrease the student-teacher ratio are far less prominent in the typical university classroom. Second, while the creation of an enriched learning environment or experience for the students is an intended outcome, it has also been implied by a number of the co-author teams in this collection that an equally important driving force for co-teaching in higher education is the concept of *change*: for example, changing the role of the instructors, changing the structure of classroom experiences, changing the types of assignments and related assessments, and even changing the goals regarding professional learning among teaching faculty. This change affects all learners and co-teachers.

If we were to suggest the differences in terms of emerging definitions, co-teaching in K–12 settings might be described in the following way:

> *A teaching arrangement wherein two or more individuals come together to creatively capitalize on their co-planning time, mutual presence, available resources, and different areas of expertise and backgrounds in order to design a teaching and learning environment that facilitates the differentiation of instruction with the main goal of addressing diverse student learning needs.*

Co-teaching in higher education could likewise be described in a similar way:

> *A teaching arrangement wherein two or more individuals come together to creatively capitalize on their co-planning time, mutual presence, available resources, and different areas of expertise and backgrounds in order to design a teaching and learning environment that challenges the traditional forms of post-secondary course delivery with the main goal of facilitating unique and powerful learning opportunities for both students and the co-instructors themselves.*

Implied in these definitions is the idea that, from an institutional perspective, co-teaching in K–12 is often a much desired and sought-after practice which meets an existing need in student learning

(Villa, Thousand, Nevin, & Liston, 2005; Walther-Thomas, 1997). In contrast, however, and as has been brought out by several co-author teams in this collection, co-teaching in higher education tends to be characterized as an unfamiliar, less desirable (at least initially), and often problematic institutional occurrence, one that is much more difficult to rationalize and initiate, and even harder to sustain over time without institutional support.

Finally, as previously mentioned, literature on K–12 notes different types of co-teaching, a list of which would include parallel teaching, alternate teaching, station teaching, and supportive teaching. Villa introduces the idea that for effective co-teaching, different approaches can be employed in a progressive manner:

> Many beginning co-teachers start with supportive teaching and parallel teaching because these approaches involve less structured coordination among the co-teaching team members. As co-teaching skills and relationships strengthen, co-teachers then venture into the complementary teaching and team teaching approaches that require more time, coordination, and knowledge of and trust in one another's skills. (Villa, n.d., para. 5)

It is worth noting that the most common approach employed by the co-teaching partners in this collection was team teaching, wherein the co-teachers worked alongside one another and shared the planning, teaching, and assessment responsibilities. It is our conclusion that while post-secondary co-teaching teams might benefit from such a progressive style, the logistical challenges unique to higher education environments, such as workload allocation and end-of-term course evaluations completed by students, might be seen to have the potential to work against any arrangement in which one teacher seems to be performing a different role.

In summary, this collection contributes to the field of co-teaching by bringing to the forefront important ways in which co-teaching at the post-secondary level is creatively practiced, highlighting the positive learning outcomes and benefits that are a product of this pedagogical approach and discussing the related challenges encountered by those involved, many of which are unique to higher education environments.

A number of clear overall benefits of the co-teaching model are presented throughout the text. Successful co-teaching partnerships need to be primarily based on the beliefs shared by the co-teachers that people working in groups generate more ideas than they would individually (La Haye and Naested); that together they bring something of value, which is bigger than the sum of the individual parts (Game and Metcalfe; Renshaw and Valiquette); and that there is potential for learning to be exponentially increased (Hatt and Graham; Jarvis and Kariuki; Srigley and Winters) by this kind of collaboration.

Some of the highlighted benefits include (1) unlocking teacher creativity and promoting calculated risk-taking; (2) creating an opportunity to model collaboration to students, as well as to fellow colleagues; (3) increasing levels of synergy in the classroom; (4) allowing for multiple learning and teaching styles; (5) encouraging personal growth for students and instructors; (6) presenting multiple perspectives on issues being discussed; and (7) reigniting passion for, and engagement in, learning. Wilson and Ferguson summarized their post-secondary co-teaching experiences as follows:

> Working with a colleague who also possesses expert knowledge in one's own field serves to change one's perception of self and position in positive ways. The co-teacher represents a knowledgeable other, full of expertise and accumulated experiences, with whom one can dare to implement new instructional paradigms in ever-deepening ways. Co-teaching at the university level also provides the opportunity to minimize the stereotypically stressful, judgmental, and competitive nature of post-secondary teaching. (Chapter 7, p. 178)

As many professors in the co-author teams in this collection recounted, they started their co-teaching experience by simply initiating the process, most without any prior exposure to this form of pedagogy. Therefore, we present this collection as a resource for both beginning and experienced co-teachers, as well as for different stakeholders who are intrinsically involved in the decision-making processes surrounding the creation and maintenance of co-teaching experiences. In reading this text, the reader will have become more aware of the potential *challenges* associated with co-teaching at the post-secondary level, which, if not addressed early in the process, can easily become central and counterproductive, thereby taking away from the richness of the co-teaching experience for both the co-teachers and learners and, by extension, for the institution. Further, the reader will have become acquainted with some of the potential *benefits* of successfully implemented co-teaching efforts, as well as with a set of teaching and learning strategies that can be explored in future co-planning, co-facilitation, and co-assessment initiatives.

We trust that this rich collection of practice-based perspectives will serve to provide new insights and to stimulate further discussions and future research relating to co-teaching in higher education – from theory to promising co-practices – with a shared view of positively transforming student, and teacher, learning experiences.

REFERENCES

Bauwens, J., Hourcade, J.J., & Friend, M. (1989). Cooperative teaching: A model for general and special education integration. *Remedial and Special Education, 10*(2), 17–22. http://dx.doi.org/10.1177/074193258901000205

Conderman, G., & McCarty, B. (2003, Winter). Shared insights from university co-teaching. *Academic Exchange Quarterly, 7*(4), 1–7.

Cook, L., & Friend, M. (1995). Co-teaching: Guidelines for creating effective practices. *Focus on Exceptional Children, 28*(3), 1–6.

Crow, J., & Smith, L. (2003). Using co-teaching as a means of facilitating interprofessional collaboration in health and social care. *Journal of Interprofessional Care, 17*(1), 45–55. http://dx.doi.org/10.1080/1356182021000044139

Dieker, L.A., & Murawski, W.W. (2003). Co-teaching at the secondary level: Unique issues, current trends, and suggestions for success. *High School Journal, 86*(4), 1–13. http://dx.doi.org/10.1353/hsj.2003.0007

Kluth, P., & Straut, D. (2003). Do as we say and as we do: Teaching and modeling collaborative practice in the University classroom. *Journal of Teacher Education, 54*(3), 228–40. http://dx.doi.org/10.1177/0022487103054003005

Mastropieri, M.A., Scruggs, T.E., Graetz, J., Norland, J., Gardizi, W., & McDuffie, K. (2005). Case studies in co-teaching in the content areas: Successes, failures and challenges. *Intervention in School and Clinic, 40*(5), 260–70. http://dx.doi.org/10.1177/10534512050400050201

Matlin, T.R., & Carr, A. (2014). Just the two of us: Those who co-teach, co-learn. *Collaborative Librarianship, 6*(2), 61–72.

Murawski, W.W., & Swanson, H.L. (2001). A meta-analysis of co-teaching research: Where are the data? *Remedial and Special Education, 22*(5), 258–67. http://dx.doi.org/10.1177/074193250102200501

Perry, B., & Stewart, T. (2005). Insights into effective partnership in interdisciplinary team teaching. *System, 33*(4), 563–73. http://dx.doi.org/10.1016/j.system.2005.01.006

Platt, J., Walker-Knight, D., Lee, T., & Hewitt, R. (2001). *Shaping future teacher education practices through collaboration and co-teaching.* Paper presented at the annual meeting of the American Association for Colleges of Teacher Education, Dallas, TX.

Santamaria, L., & Thousand, J. (2004). Collaboration, co-teaching, and differentiated instruction: A process-oriented approach to whole schooling. *International Journal of Whole Schooling, 1*(1), 13–27.

Villa, R. (n.d.). Effective co-teaching strategies. Retrieved from http://www.teachhub.com/effective-co-teaching-strategies

Villa, R., Thousand, J., Nevin, A., & Liston, A. (2005). Successful inclusive practices in middle and secondary schools. *American Secondary Education, 33*(3), 33–50.

Walther-Thomas, C.S. (1997). Co-teaching experiences: The benefits and problems that teachers and principals report over time. *Journal of Learning Disabilities, 30*(4), 395–407. http://dx.doi.org/10.1177/002221949703000406

Wenger, E., McDermott, R.A., & Snyder, W. (2002). *Cultivating communities of practice: A guide to managing knowledge.* Brighton, MA: Harvard Business Review Press.

Index